D0261433

LEFT BACK IN TIME
The Autobiography of
Len Ashurst

LEFT BACK IN TIME

The Autobiography of

Len Ashurst

Know The Score Books Limited
118 Alcester Road
Studley
Warwickshire
B80 7NT
01527 454482
info@knowthescorebooks.com
www.knowthescorebooks.com

A CIP catalogue record is available for this book from the British Library

ISBN: 978 1 84818 512 8

Printed and bound by TJ International Ltd, Padstow, Cornwall

Contents

KNOW THE SCORE BOOKS SPORTS PUBLICATIONS

CULT HEROES	*Author*	*ISBN*
CARLISLE UNITED	Paul Harrison	978-1-905449-09-7
CELTIC	David Potter	978-1-905449-08-8
CHELSEA	Leo Moynihan	1-905449-00-3
MANCHESTER CITY	David Clayton	978-1-905449-05-7
NEWCASTLE	Dylan Younger	1-905449-03-8
NOTTINGHAM FOREST	David McVay	978-1-905449-06-4
RANGERS	Paul Smith	978-1-905449-07-1
SOUTHAMPTON	Jeremy Wilson	1-905449-01-1
WEST BROM	Simon Wright	1-905449-02-X

MATCH OF MY LIFE	*Editor*	*ISBN*
DERBY COUNTY	Nick Johnson	978-1-905449-68-2
ENGLAND WORLD CUP	Massarella & Moynihan	1-905449-52-6
EUROPEAN CUP FINALS	Ben Lyttleton	1-905449-57-7
FA CUP FINALS 1953-1969	David Saffer	978-1-905449-53-8
FULHAM	Michael Heatley	1-905449-51-8
IPSWICH TOWN	Mel Henderson	978-1-84818-001-7
LEEDS	David Saffer	1-905449-54-2
LIVERPOOL	Leo Moynihan	1-905449-50-X
MANCHESTER UNITED	Ivan Ponting	978-1-905449-59-0
SHEFFIELD UNITED	Nick Johnson	1-905449-62-3
STOKE CITY	Simon Lowe	978-1-905449-55-2
SUNDERLAND	Rob Mason	1-905449-60-7
WOLVES	Simon Lowe	1-905449-56-9

PLAYER BY PLAYER	*Author*	*ISBN*
MANCHESTER UNITED	Ivan Ponting	978-1-84818-500-1
TOTTENHAM HOTSPUR	Ivan Ponting	978-1-84818-501-8

GENERAL FOOTBALL	*Author*	*ISBN*
BEHIND THE BACK PAGE	Christopher Davies	978-1-84818-506-7
BOOK OF FOOTBALL OBITUARIES	Ivan Ponting	978-1-905449-82-2
FORGIVE US OUR PRESS PASSES	Football Writers' Association	978-1-84818-507-4
JUST ONE OF SEVEN	Denis Smith	978-1-84818-504-3
MAN & BABE	Wilf McGuinness	978-1-84818-503-6
NORTHERN AND PROUD	Paul Harrison	978-1-84818-505-0
OUTCASTS: The Lands That FIFA Forgot	Steve Menary	978-1-905449-31-6
PALLY	Gary Pallister	978-1-84818-500-5
PARISH TO PLANET	Eric Midwinter	978-1-905449-30-9
TACKLES LIKE A FERRET	Paul Parker	1-905449-46-1
THE DOOG	Harrison & Gordos	978-1-84818-502-9

| THE RIVALS GAME | Douglas Beattie | 978-1-905449-79-8 |

RUGBY LEAGUE	Author	*ISBN*
MOML LEEDS RHINOS	Caplan & Saffer	978-1-905449-69-9
MOML WIGAN WARRIORS	David Kuzio	978-1-905449-66-8

CRICKET	Author	*ISBN*
ASHES TO DUST	Graham Cookson	978-1-905449-19-4
CRASH! BANG! WALLOP!	Martyn Hindley	978-1-905449-88-0
GROVEL!	David Tossell	978-1-905449-43-9
MOML: THE ASHES	Pilger & Wightman	1-905449-63-1
MY TURN TO SPIN	Shaun Udal	978-1-905449-42-2
WASTED?	Paul Smith	978-1-905449-45-3

FORTHCOMING PUBLICATIONS IN 2009

CULT HEROES	Editor	*ISBN*
ARSENAL	Luke Nicoli	978-1-84818-105-2

MATCH OF MY LIFE	Editor	*ISBN*
BRIGHTON	Paul Camillin	978-1-84818-000-0

PLAYER BY PLAYER	Author	*ISBN*
EVERTON	Ivan Ponting	978-1-84818-305-6
LIVERPOOL	Ivan Ponting	978-1-84818-306-3
REPUBLIC OF IRELAND	Christopher Davies	978-1-84818-307-0

GREATEST GAMES	Author	*ISBN*
ENGLAND	Ivan Ponting	978-1-84818-207-3
SCOTLAND	David Potter	978-1-84818-200-4
SUNDERLAND	Rob Mason	978-1-84818-204-2
WEST BROM	Simon Wright	978-1-84818-206-6

GENERAL FOOTBALL	Author	*ISBN*
A SMASHING LITTLE FOOTBALL FIRM	Nicky Allt	978-1-84818-402-2
NEVER HAD IT SO GOOD	Tim Quelch	978-1-84818-600-2
NO SMOKE, NO FIRE	Dave Jones	978-1-84818-513-5
PLEASE MAY I HAVE MY FOOTBALL BACK?	Eric Alexander	978-1-84818-508-1
WARK ON	John Wark	978-1-84818-511-1

CRICKET	Author	*ISBN*
THE BEST OF ENEMIES	Kidd & McGuinness	978-1-84818-703-1
THE BODYLINE HYPOCRISY	Michael Arnold	978-1-84818-702-3
KP: CRICKET GENIUS?	Wayne Veysey	978-1-84818-701-6

Foreword

It is with great pleasure that I write this introduction to Len's book, which I know he has written himself – a great feat!

LEN HAS been involved with the game in various capacities over 55 years. Starting with Liverpool Schoolboys in 1953 and continuing to this day in his role as a Match Delegate for the Premier League.

Len's playing career was dominated by his time at Sunderland, joining the club in 1957. He made his debut a year later against my beloved Ipswich Town and went on to make 458 first team appearances at left full-back, a lesson in loyalty for many of our present day players and a club record for an outfield player which stands to this day.

Eventually Len went on to manage Sunderland and I have vivid memories of him leading his team out of the Wembley tunnel for the Milk Cup final of 1985. Over a twenty five year period he also managed Hartlepool, Gillingham, Sheffield Wednesday, Newport County and Cardiff City, as well as coaching abroad as far afield as the Middle East and Malaysia. His strength was in his ability to survive and succeed with no money for transfers. Utilising players to their full potential required all of his management and motivational experience, achieving his objectives through these qualities and his deep-rooted love for the game.

Len is a bright intelligent man with quality organisational abilities, which he brought to his input into the establishment of the FA Premier League Academies in 1998. It is a legacy which will remain in the game for many years.

I wish Len every success with this book and I am sure it will prove extremely interesting to the genuine football observer as well as those who like a good story.

Bobby Robson

Sir Bobby Robson

Acknowledgements

Special thanks to Russell Foster and Tavistock Leisure for their support and sponsorship and Rob Mason for working closely with me from the first drafts to the final publication.

A very special 'Thank You' to Sir Bobby Robson for his contribution in introducing my book.

In writing my Autobiography I am indebted to the following for their guidance and advice:

Albert and Robin Ashurst, Arthur Davidson QC, Sir Tom Cowie, John Morton, Chris Lightbown, Richard Shepherd, Tom Vasey, Alan Stephenson, Chris Hutchinson, Malcolm Bramley, John Simmons, Alan Hill, Peter Shreeves, Trevor Braithwait, Roger Malone, Colin Biott , George Taylor, Jimmy Shoulder, Ted Evans, Brian Tinmouth of the Edward Thompson Group, Donald Mills, John Relish, Ken Vallis, Richard and Jayne Walden, Dan Johnson of the Press Office at the Premier League

Also thanks to everyone at Know The Score Books, especially Simon Lowe and Graham Hales. And to my friends and colleagues for their encouragement, including Sid!

Introduction

THESE INDELIBLE nine words:

"Lenny, you should have been a Liverpool player, laddie." This was the comment that was uttered to me by Liverpool manager, the great Bill Shankly, as we met under that famous trademark logo at the end of the players' tunnel at Anfield, which simply says 'This is Anfield'. As he walked away I stared after him, humbled by his words.

He had searched me out on my return to the club as a twenty-one year-old opposition player, even though it was now two years since Liverpool Football Club had released me. The previous manager Phil Taylor had told me I was not good enough to be offered a professional contract. Here I was now, in January 1959, returning with my new club Sunderland to play in front of those I had once stood alongside, those same Liverpool supporters that included Mum, Dad and family, all of them born into the red of Anfield.

The game, which Sunderland lost 3-1, paled into insignificance on this special occasion, as my family celebrated the win and the two points gained, but also one of their own coming home to bring great pride and pleasure to them all.

As a Liverpool-born lad, Sunderland supporters will, I am sure, understand the pride those remarks uttered by the great man meant to me at that time. I told only my father – it brought tears to his eyes! As a professional footballer and a proud Sunderland player, those nine words that Shankly spoke to me so many years ago meant an incredible amount to me. I lived off them throughout my fifteen-year playing career. To be a Liverpool player then and ever since you had to be made of a certain something. Many have been found to come up short. Under Shankly it pretty much meant you were a winner, the best – and he had said he felt I could have achieved that under him. What if I had been given that rare opportunity to see if I had what it took to wear that all-red jersey in front of The Kop? Would things have been different? I was never to have the opportunity to know what that certain something was, so I was never to become a hero in my own land.

* * * * *

Would you ever think that during your lifetime, you would be interrogated by the Iraqi police? Come face to face in Palestine with Yasser Arafat, the former Palestinian leader, as well as Tariq Aziz, who at the time was the acceptable face of Saddam Hussein's vile Iraqi regime? I didn't. And yet these things happened to me – in fact I experienced all that in the space of just ten days in the summer of 1994 whilst working as a coach in the Middle East. I was also nearly killed by a flying boulder which took the head off our coach driver in Baghdad. As Arafat and Aziz never spoke to me, the significance of the eye to eye contact I had with both of them was minimal compared to the fleeting moment I spent in the company of Bill Shankly at Anfield.

During over 50 years of privilege in professional football I have touched all sides of the game as a player, Football League manager and my experiences when coaching abroad, then latterly as a Premier League administrator. I would like to use the opportunity of this book to give you an unabridged insight into my experiences along the way, also to express an opinion or two on the professional game whose fabric, in my opinion, has been scarred nearly beyond redemption by greed, celebrity, personal ego and poor leadership by the guardians of the game: the Football Association.

The final ignominy for me, as well as many of my well known contemporaries, the caring professional people connected with the game both past and present, has been the torrent of, in the main, highly paid overseas players of poor-to-average ability, who have been creaming off the bottomless barrel of 'Sky' money to the detriment of many ambitious talented youngsters from our own island, who have thus been denied the opportunity to fulfil their promise.

If managed properly from the outset, the millions of pounds that has disappeared into greedy agents' pockets and bulging overseas bank accounts, could have been ploughed back into the grassroots of football from Penzance to the North East of England. Drive or walk around your local community and try to spot a group of youngsters knocking a ball around on the green bit, the chances are you will be disappointed. We know the reasons being put forward, they are boundless. It could and should have been very different. Disgracefully only lip service has been paid to the problem by the people who could make the difference.

We now have the possibility of staging the World Cup once again in 2018. Imagine the financial waste that will involve. If only a fraction of that money could be channelled in such a way that no school or junior team in any sport would have to go cap in hand for practically inaccessible funds, or to pay exorbitant fees for a local sporting facility (if they can find one which is not a sixties relic with a flat roof). Will this change across all sports when the costly £9 billion Olympic Games come to London in 2012 and so fulfill Sebastian Coe's dream of providing a legacy for our sporting youth? We hope so. In fact it has to.

Sadly, in today's climate of 'The more expensive, the better' there is no trusted structure in place for grassroots football to flourish. It has been eroded and destroyed because of poor leadership. Consequently at school and junior team level disenchantment has never been higher.

There is an old adage, 'Never say never.' However I will. England's football team will never win the World Cup again. Some of the reasons I have already touched upon – there are plenty more.

Len Ashurst

1 The Pretenders and the Pretentious

IN ALL the years I have been involved in professional football I have never witnessed such a remarkable incident as occurred in the spring of 2005 when Kieron Dyer and Lee Bowyer, both players wearing the black and white stripes of Newcastle United, fought each other on the field of play during a 3-0 home defeat by a useful Aston Villa side.

From my position in the stands it seemed to me that the pair had an undercurrent of dislike crackling between them throughout the match as neither seemed to want to pass the ball to the other: strange when you consider they were supposed to be working together to win this game for their club.

I, along with thousands of spectators, was utterly flabbergasted by this incident. It took my breath away and around 50,000 home fans howled their anger at the pair of them. It wasn't just Bowyer and Dyer who invoked the supporters' ire. The man in the middle also got the bird. Two reasonable penalty claims had been turned down earlier in the game, in which Villa were now cruising, by referee Barry Knight. This had caused anger and frustration amongst both the home fans and the Newcastle camp in the technical area and the players on the pitch, culminating in the 82nd minute bust up. As the two players were sent off after trading punches and almost tearing each other's shirts off their backs, a number of home supporters tried to get at them from the stands, only to be thwarted by the diligence of the stewards around the players' tunnel.

I was the official Match Delegate appointed by the Premier League for this game and below is the report I had to submit to the authorities about the incredible goings on.

Significant Incident Report Form

Newcastle United v Aston Villa (0-3)
2nd April 2005. KO: 3pm
Match Official: Barry Knight

Serious Incident involving Kieron Dyer and Lee Bowyer of Newcastle United

In the 82nd minute of the match, with their side just having conceded a third goal and already having had one man sent off, two Newcastle players who had previously had words with each other, Kieron Dyer and Lee Bowyer, got embroiled in a fight between themselves. No Aston Villa players were involved.

There had been a tetchiness between these two players throughout the match, culminating in Dyer standing just over the half-way line and 15 yards from the touch line with his back to the play, which was continuing in the Aston Villa penalty box, his arms outstretched looking at Bowyer, only 10 yards away. I am speculating that Bowyer had made a comment to Dyer. Bowyer moved towards him and attempted to headbutt Dyer, who grabbed hold of Bowyer's head to protect himself. Bowyer then proceeded to throw punches as other players, including some from Villa, stepped in to separate them. Dyer did not start the fracas, but, needing to protect himself, raised his arms in self-defence and I would generally exonerate him from blame.

Match Official Barry Knight, who was concentrating on the flow of the game, was alerted to the incident by the Fourth Official alongside the technical area. After consulting his colleague he red carded both players and sent them from the field of play.

Len Ashurst (Premier League Match Delegate)

*For privacy and confidentiality reasons this is a shortened and paraphrased report sent to the Premier League.

Judging the 'Elite' Group

During 2004, in the final twelve months of my work at the Premier League looking after the members' Academies, I was offered the opportunity to become part of a new scheme designed to help improve the standard of referees in this country by becoming a Premier League Match Delegate. My brief was to assess the Match Officials' (referees to most of us) performances at Premier League games, conclude a de-brief with the officials twenty-five minutes after the match, also provide an overview of the behaviour of both sets of players and managerial staff, include comments from the two managers themselves, the crowd, police and any other germane factors in a match day scenario and then send a written report within three days to the Premier League.

A pilot scheme had been running for some twelve months, which in principle had been accepted by the Premier League, League Managers' Association and the Match Officials chief and former referee Philip Don. It was hoped that Match Delegates would also act as calming influences before and after games and neutral eyes close to the action and behind the scenes.

The incredible incident which the report above refers to came towards the end of that second season of the scheme. Thankfully it was pretty unique, although in December 2008 Ricardo Fuller of Stoke City managed to get himself into similar trouble for slapping his captain, Andy Griffin, after the Potters conceded an equalising goal at Upton Park. The point is that the Match Delegate's role is to act during these major incidents to try to smooth the waters between the aggrieved parties, whether they be managers, officials, stewards or supporters. Our reports are submitted to the Premier League, who then take suitable disciplinary action.

I have been fortunate enough to spend five years or so working in this role and I hope that I have contributed to quelling disputes and improving our officals, our game and its image both domestically and around the world.

To give you an example, of the hundred plus games I have covered as Match Delegate for the Premier League I have chosen to highlight the report of one other infamous game which I covered. This was between Manchester United and Arsenal at Old Trafford in October 2004. Arsène Wenger's Gunners arrived in Manchester attempting to achieve a 50 match record-breaking unbeaten run in the Premier League, having won the league title the previous season by going the whole campaign without losing – a quite incredible feat.

Premier League Match Delegate Report

Manchester United v Arsenal Result 2-0
Sunday 24th October 2004 Kick Off: 4.05pm
Match Official: Mr Mike Riley
5 cautions in the match

Many clichés were used by the media and fans alike in the build up to this match, so piling the pressure on all contestants and particularly the match officials for the day. Pressure was applied to Mike Riley from the outset and throughout the match certain players from both teams seemed to think they had license to 'bait' the official, which in turn drew in other players to intimidate in numbers, something I have not witnessed to this extent in any other game I have watched.

Considering how highly charged this match was Mike Riley sensibly applied patience early on and got through the first 35 minutes without issuing a caution, allowing the players to get on with it, use up their adrenalin and in the process gave the players second chances. Throughout the match he thought hard before making his decisions and was generally correct. The five cautions he administered were justified as all the players booked had been warned beforehand. In fact GARY NEVILLE could have gone into the book in the 24th minute for a late challenge on REYES, while VIEIRA was also shown leniency in spite of persistent offending.

Once again I have to question the role of an Assistant Referee in not making a decision. The Assistant in question, Dave Babski, was on top of the incident when COLE was cynically 'studded' by RUUD VAN NISTELROOY, subsequent events on this incident proved my point.

Disappointing at times in my opinion was WAYNE ROONEY'S youthful petulance towards the official, culminating in the 63rd minute when he gesticulated at Mike Riley, then, when Mike pulled play back from a free kick, ROONEY kicked the ball back in the official's direction. This was not picked up on television or dealt with by Mike, who apparently had not seen it happen. ASHLEY COLE was another young player who also showed a lack of respect to the match official in staying at distance from Mike Riley when being cautioned.

Only once in the match did Mike Riley not use advantage to good effect, this was in the 80th minute when he pulled LJUNGBERG back when through on a break. To compound matters he allowed Arsenal to take the kick from a more advantageous position.

Finally, on constructive issues, in Mike Riley's previous report I had indicated his tendency to make some decisions from too far away from play and once again this was highlighted for me on a number of occasions (55th and 57th minute), generally occurring when his assistant on the diagonal was closer to the play than Mike. Is this a trait in Mike Riley's game that needs to be changed? We discussed some of these issues in our de-brief after the match.

The turning point in the match was the penalty decision in the 65th minute in favour of Manchester United, with which at the time I concurred, although later video evidence threw doubts in the mind. In addition the coming together of FERDINAND and LJUNGBERG in the first half, when the Arsenal player looked clean through on goal was a huge decision made in FERDINAND'S favour. I agreed, thinking that LJUNGBERG had pushed the ball too far ahead of himself and would not have reached the ball.

Overall Mike Riley came through this game with a lot of credit in view of its high profile nature and the way this match was played. He was calm in his approach, used early patience, was more than tolerant throughout and allowed the game to flow as and when he could. There was so much going on between players that it was impossible to get all decisions correct. He nearly did and certainly was not conned by the play acting of certain players in both teams.

Managers' Comments

Pat Rice (Assistant Manager, Arsenal)

Pat thought Mike Riley's performance was disgraceful and was alarmed at what Manchester United were allowed to get away with, in view of the history between the two clubs and the intimidation which had occured in last year's FA Cup semi-final at Villa Park. He felt the appointment of this official in the first place was disgraceful; especially considering his penalty record involving Manchester United. Rice was also disgusted that the treatment and intimidation of REYES was allowed to happen, as he finally had to leave the field injured.

Sir Alex Ferguson (Manager, Manchester United)

Responding to the allegations on the treatment of REYES by his team, Sir Alex commented on the number of fouls, eight in all, committed on RONALDO by three different Arsenal players. He was unhappy at Mike Riley allowing PATRICK VIEIRA to 'run the game'. He had no complaints at the yellow cards shown to his players, but could not understand why Arsenal keeper LEHMANN, who ran to get involved in the 'fracas' after Manchester United's second goal, was not disciplined. Overall he thought Mike Riley had done well.

Len Ashurst (Match Delegate)

*For privacy and confidentiality reasons this is a shortened and paraphrased report sent to the Premier League.

The volatile nature of this game, which contained five cautions, along with the ensuing bitterness of both sets of players and their respective managers towards each other, made for compulsive viewing. I am sure a billion other people around the globe would have concurred with my view. But it left a nasty taste in the mouth and consequently I filed a 'Significant Incident Report' to Keith Hackett at the Premier League on the treatment Mike Riley received from numerous players from both teams.

Significant Incident Report Form

Manchester United v Arsenal (2-0)
Sunday 24th October 2004
At Old Trafford

Attention of Keith Hackett (PGMOL Manager)

Dear Keith,

I would like to express my deep concern about the trend amongst Premiership Footballers from most teams to make it their aim during the course of a game to consistently 'bait' Match Officials and in the process draw in other players who surround the official in trying to sway his decision making one way or another on a decision made.

Having been a Match Delegate for the past eighteen months, as far as I was concerned this huge issue all came to a head on Sunday at Old Trafford in the above match, where Mike Riley the Match Official was invariably surrounded by players from both teams, an intimidating vogue which is becoming more prevalent.

In view of the global image of the Premiership and the modern professional supposedly being a role model for our youngsters, a dangerous trend is fermenting which could lead to all sorts of problems in the future, not least in inciting crowd trouble at our football stadiums. My concern is for the best image of our game to be preserved for the future. With this and the above in mind, I am writing to you hoping this issue can be addressed as soon as possible within the Premier League or with the Football Association.

Kind Regards
Len Ashurst (Match Delegate)

*For privacy and confidentiality reasons this is a shortened and paraphrased report sent to the Premier League.

This Manchester United versus Arsenal game was the day that the 'cup of soup incident' occurred involving Sir Alex Ferguson. I was breezing down to see Mike Riley in his dressing room and thought after a 2-0 win that it could be a good moment, if I got the opportunity, to ask Sir Alex for his comments on the game instead of having to call him on Monday morning. I soon had that thought scuppered as he came storming past me from the opposite direction. Under normal circumstances I would have stopped him, not this time though as his clothing was splattered with what looked like carrot soup. Steam was coming out of his ears. He was past me and gone in a flash.

These two clubs and subsequently others wouldn't thank me for bringing this 'baiting' of referees to the table, not least because of the consequences that ensued – heavy financial penalties for guilty clubs. However I stand by what I thought at that time, which was that the game's image was running downhill faster than water. Many of our well-respected sports journalists also thought that the time had come for the FA to get tough. To their credit, in response the FA put legislation in place that held Premier League clubs responsible for their players' behaviour on the field of play and it was decided that any group of players surrounding Match Officials in a 'threatening manner' would lead to their club being disciplined and fined up to a maximum of £250,000.

Chelsea were hit with a record fine of £40,000 in January 2008 for their behaviour at Derby County the previous November, when Michael Essien was sent off for pushing Kenny Miller in the face. On that occasion his colleagues surrounded referee Andre Marriner in intimidating fashion. Chelsea admitted and accepted the charge.

Of course it is not always entirely the fault of the players. Newcastle United versus Wigan Athletic on 1 September 2007 provided a prime example of how match officials' errors can create issues which quickly escalate out of control. Referee Steve Bennett sent off Kevin Kilbane of Wigan for a second yellow card. In my opinion, and in that of many others, it was not a cautionable offence and indeed Bennett's decision caused a lot of dissent and something of a melée amongst the players. As a result the FA fined the club £20,000 for 'failure to control their players'. Wigan pleaded guilty, but also submitted mitigating circumstances. It was to no avail. Of course respect must be shown to officials at all times, but they must also understand their part in keeping matters fully under control on the pitch.

A very good example of how a big error on the part of the officials can cause untold problems both during and after the game came in season 2006/07 when West Ham visited Blackburn Rovers on Saturday 17

March, a game which West Ham won 2-1. Remember those three points became crucial on the final day of the season as Sheffield United were relegated by a narrow margin, with the London club surviving thanks mainly to a huge contribution over several months by Carlos Tevez, the little Argentine forward. Of course the controversy surrounding the status of his ownership rumbles on even as I write in January 2009, still being the subject of a joint Premier League and FA enquiry. The South Yorkshire club, who felt they were unfairly relegated to the Championship at the end of the season, were awarded compensation by an FA-appointed arbitration panel.

You may also recall that the winning goal in this particular game was subsequently shown by television pictures not to have actually crossed Rovers' goal line and so therefore should not have stood. That would have had a major impact on the relegation battle that season as had West Ham only drawn they would have been ten points behind Sheffield United with just eight games to play. We will, of course, never know. Just as we can never quantify what Tevez's individual contribution actually was in any legal sense.

Needless to say the controversy which reigned around the major incidents in this match led to huge shows of dissent from players and those in the technical areas. The pressure and intimidation applied to all four officials was enormous. I was shocked to witness it.

Below is a clip from my Match Delegate report on the game at that time, which shows the effect the whole situation had on the men at the centre of the controversy.

> Match Officials' performances are judged on getting the BIG decisions correct. Unfortunately assistant referee Jim Devine's mistake, shown repeatedly on television when indicating incorrectly that the ball had crossed the line for West Ham's second goal, changed the outcome of this game. This certainly did not help referee Howard Webb's cause and Jim's body language when I entered the dressing for the post-match debrief, indicated that he knew he had made a huge mistake.
>
> I also got the feeling that Howard may well have been having second thoughts over his decision to award a 'soft' penalty to the away team, as well as the second yellow for handball on 90 minutes to Blackburn's DAVID BENTLEY as it would appear that he had been pushed in the back by an opponent.
>
> On entering the Officials' dressing room 20 minutes after the game had finished there was a deathly silence hanging in the air.

All four men were still in their match official yellow jerseys. It was obvious from their body language that they knew the football world outside was that night a hostile place because of some of their decisions. They had obviously discussed long and hard the incidents during the game and all knew that there was no escape.

My presence was an obvious embarrassment to all of them. I knew the score, as well they did, and I told them so. I was in and out within minutes and presumably my quick exit told them a story! It was the shortest post-match debrief that I have ever conducted, with the exception of once telling Mark Halsey that I wouldn't be having a debrief with him: "You have had a good game and you seem to do your own thing anyway," I remarked.

In spite of this overall poor match by Howard Webb I continue to be a great admirer of his professional skills.

Over twenty-one Premier League games that I observed in that first 2004/05 season, I believe that I developed a very clear picture as to who were the capable Match Officials from the Elite Group. In addition, I also knew that the majority of the sixteen exclusive Match Delegates who were assessing the officials could not be bettered. With the exception of three all were either former managers, like myself, who had ten to fifteen years of management experience behind them, or were former coaches and ex-players, some of whom were employed on a full-time basis by the Professional Footballers' Association. I had been both manager and player, so felt myself well qualified to impose my opinions on those Match Officials who wanted to listen, learn and so become more proficient in their work.

Three of the Match Delegates who were appointed had been extremely capable administrators in the professional game, but had never 'trodden the boards' on the green grass. This was a surprise to most and was probably also a surprise to the officials in the elite group. Although dedicated to the job, diligent and hard-working, the fact that these three gentlemen had not been involved as managers, coaches or professional footballers at the highest level means their views possibly do not carry the same weight. Those three delegates are David Dent, ex-secretary of the Football League and former secretary at Carlisle United FC, Graham Mackrell, who held a prominent executive position at West Ham United, and Mark Blackbourne, the former Chief Executive of Sunderland Football Club under Bob Murray's chairmanship. I believe the Premier League have made a mistake in appointing these men and I stress again, this is nothing to do with their ability, but their credibility in the eyes of officials. I feel it undermines what is in all other ways an excellent scheme.

Disappointingly despite the agreement reached through their League Managers' Association that they would do so, over half of Premier League managers do not respond to commenting after a game, leaving it instead to their assistants or first team coach. Fully co-operative and supportive of the scheme are the likes of: Sir Alex Ferguson, David Moyes, Sam Allardyce, Sunderland manager Ricky Sbragia and Gareth Southgate. Former Sunderland boss Roy Keane was also a big supporter.

In addition to the Match Delegate, a former referee is also in attendance at the game as an Assessor to ensure that the Match Official applies the laws of the game during the course of the ninety minutes. These officials will have been top referees in their time such as George Courtney, David Elleray, Rob Hart, Roy Pearson, David Laws, who is the chief executive at Newcastle airport, and the recently retired Dermot Gallagher. They have all officiated at the highest level in football. They also have a separate de-brief with the Match Officials after the final whistle. Referees and their assistants can have plum appointments removed from them or be allocated games much further down the league pyramid for failure to perform. Contrary to popular belief – particularly where the gentlemen of the press are concerned – there is no escape for the man in charge of Premier League games in this billion pound industry. A referee may be at the top of his profession one week, but officiating at Cheltenham or Accrington the next. All managers are well aware of this. Whether they choose to acknowledge it in post-match conferences is of course an entirely different matter!

Keith Hackett's appointment to replace Philip Don as the country's most senior referee, brought change and a much-needed pragmatic and realistic approach to a process that seemed to be going around in circles, becoming unproductive and repetitive. An assertive approach adopted by Hackett to put in their place some of the highly paid and highly opinionated senior Match Officials was badly needed at the time. It is apparently said the likes of Graham Poll and Jeff Winter had become particularly aggravating with their attitude. Some of the other Match Officials who had observed the behaviour of these two referees became protective of their position and so a small clique of officials grew up that started to think they were bigger than the game itself.

Every summer at Staverton Park Country Club, officials from the Premier League plus the hundreds of others who officiate at a lower level gather for an annual conference. Working groups of a dozen or so come together for an overall assessment of the salient points that are worth bringing to the table. During one of the breaks in the proceedings in summer 2008's gathering I met up with former Premier League referee Dermot Gallagher, who was near to his wits end at the goings on at his first conference as a Match Assessor. His finely put comment to me was that he was ready to 'pin my penis to a burning building,' after watching what had gone on in what I could only describe as 'The Hall of Chaos'.

Arrogant, puffed up, dismissive and abject are some of the adjectives levelled by the press, public and electronically-guided television pundits at the elite group of match officials. These accusations are easily vented towards referees who can't defend themselves. That is wrong. However at times they are defenceless because some of them contribute to their own downfall as their desire and intent is to grab centre stage. Fortunately in recent times we have rid ourselves of a number of the personnel with that scourge.

It's not all sour grapes and red cards, though. Match Officials develop a thick skin as they have to take so much flack from within the game, from the media, both spoken and written, and from paying spectators. Sometimes they even have the bottle to dish it out to the club staff in the technical areas. One example came when Sam Allardyce was in charge of Bolton. Sam invariably watched the first half of a game sitting in the directors' box and then came down to the technical area for the second half. On this particular occasion, during a Bolton versus Arsenal match, his side had a penalty claim. As Sam turned to the fourth official to appeal the response he got was a real put down, "Sam it can't be a penalty as I can't see any of your monkeys jumping out of the dugout." Allardyce wasn't best pleased. But if you give it out you have to be able to take it!

A former player of mine at Hartlepool, Neil Warnock, is another famously excitable manager. When in charge of Sheffield United, in a game against Reading early in the 2006/07 season, a match the Blades lost 1-2, post-match Warnock generated an air of disbelief in the officials' dressing room. I had just come out of the room after completing my debrief when Warnock asked me if it was clear for him to enter? I could tell something was in the air so I hung around. I wasn't disappointed, although not in the way I was expecting. As he exited just a minute or so later with a broad grin on his face, despite his team's defeat, Neil's words to me were, "Len they are in shock, they thought I was going to give them a bollocking." Andre Marriner had been in charge of the game that day and Warnock had, in fact, gone in to compliment all the officials on a good game.

After he departed, I returned to the officials' dressing room to discover a surreal atmosphere generated by Warnock's brief visit. His attitude had come as a complete surprise to all of them. In fact Marriner was flabbergasted that Warnock had been so complimentary. Andre is a personable sort, but on duty often portrays in his face a man who expects the worst. In the past he has lacked confidence in his ability. He has to start being a bastard at times. If he does he should become a very proficient referee. His recent performances indicate this!

Another nice touch to the humorous side of officiating at the top came when Mark Halsey took charge of a game between Sunderland and Liverpool at the Stadium of Light. Fernando Torres the Liverpool centre-forward went down in the Sunderland penalty area and Xabi Alonso made a futile appeal for Liverpool to be awarded a penalty. "Who do you think I am, Rob Styles?" came the quip from referee Mark Halsey. This was just a week after the Styles debacle at Anfield when he gave a penalty to Chelsea when the Liverpool right-back Finnan was deemed to have fouled an opponent in the penalty box. This sort of exchange between player and official, albeit a little cruel on Rob Styles' reputation, is crucial at times. It is important to a referee's credibility that he is accepted for who he is and why he has been given the responsibility. In the heat of the game a professional footballer accepts a comment like this as it is meant – that is if Alonso the Spaniard understood it. Of course it entirely depends who it comes from. There are not too many men in the middle that could deliver a punch line as good as that one.

Rob Styles himself is now more readily approachable, although still liable to the odd mistake, such as the penalty awarded to Manchester United in their win over Bolton Wanderers on 27 September 2008 for Jlloyd Samuel's perfectly good tackle on Cristiano Ronaldo. But do remember that referees do incur penalties themselves when they make major ricks like that. Styles had suffered badly for his mistake in that major televised Liverpool versus Chelsea clash, being pilloried by the media. What surprised me was the reaction towards him from inside his own camp. He was apparently treated shabbily by the P.G.M.O. Instead of keeping that one in house, dirty linen was washed in public.

Mark Halsey was one who showed his disquiet at the public scrubbing down that Styles received, considering him to have been treated shabbily – in fact he intimated that being dragged into the street and stoned could not have been a worse fate. Mike Dean and Chris Foy, two very capable Merseyside officials, also felt that Styles had been put through the mill. However it is said that within the Match Officials' close knit group there was a certain amount of quiet satisfaction about the situation that Styles had found himself in. There was a feeling amongst some of his professional colleagues that it might well sober him up. Thereafter maybe he could show some feeling towards those who had gone before him and empathise with those who will have similar experiences over the coming seasons, as surely they will.

No sooner had the ink dried on the pages of the national newspapers' crucifixion of Styles did the opportunity arise for them to go to town on Mark Clattenburg, who was one of a clutch of extremely promising, young, up and coming match officials. The game was Everton v Liverpool at Goodison Park and Clattenburg made a number of major mistakes during a fiery Merseyside derby. Late on he was no more than twelve yards away from an incident in the Liverpool penalty box when Carragher pulled down Lescott from behind. In my opinion he turned a poor day's work into a disastrous one when ignoring the penalty appeals of most of the players in blue and their manager David Moyes, who was going ballistic on the touchline. This incident brought another of our officials out of the clouds and down to earth with a bump. None of the elite group can afford an ego as it will catch up with them in the end.

Interestingly, as punishment, Clattenburg was missing for the following weekend's batch of Premier League games. It is my belief that just as players can go through a bad patch and need to be taken out of the action for a while, so should a referee who repeatedly gives under par performances. It gives officials time to reflect on the whole of their game. Surely that has to benefit in the long run the match official who wants to improve.

However referees should not be castigated, tarred and feathered and thrown to the lions for individual errors. One mistake, albeit a mental aberration which turns a game, is simply human error. Of course that is unacceptable and suitable punishment should be duly meted out to the perpetrator. But it must be those who display a persistent pattern of such behaviour that are weeded out – and there are very few of them in my opinion. Incompetent I can categorically say Match Officials are not! When technology takes over, as surely it eventually will for goal line incidents, decision-making for referees and their assistants running the line will become less punitive.

Incidentally the sprightly Clattenburg is not short on confidence. I learned this when Sheffield United played Manchester City at Bramall Lane on Boxing Day 2006. Telephoning him the day before to tell him that I would be arriving just before kick-off as I had to travel down from Scotland to cover the game, Mark's words to me were, "I shouldn't worry, Len, if you don't arrive in time to see the match, I will have had a good game anyway." Tongue in cheek I am sure, but said with an air of supreme confidence garnered with the brashness of youth. I liked this and I believed at that time he had the ability to go far.

I wrote:

> 'This up and coming Match Official has a bright future, but only if he keeps his feet on the ground and is made aware and remembers the pitfalls that will confront him in the future.'

Those few lines from my match report reminded this young man of the boundless happenings in the game that can put you on an enormous high, but then drop you to the depths of despair. Clattenburg didn't have long to wait for his inevitable howler as he was brought down to earth with a bump ten months later in that Merseyside derby. Off the field controversy then robbed him of a large slice of Premier League and European appointments. Only time will tell if he ever returns.

Graham Poll has not always endeared himself to people in the professional game as he adopted a stringent and outwardly pious approach to his officiating. Poll famously came unstuck in the 2006 World Cup when he failed to send off Josip Simunic of Croatia during a group F match until he gave him a third yellow card. He found difficulty in recovering from this debacle and after one more mixed season officiating at the Premier League, making some mistakes he was not accustomed to making, he retired from the game at the age of 43 years. It was a self-inflicted wound.

Poll was reputedly England's best when he was sent to the World Cup to represent the country and the Premier League. He didn't perform well under the pressure and was put on an early plane to London. Yet in his mind his reputation was still intact and even after his decision, 'to retire from competitive international refereeing to spend more time with his family,' he then proceeded to officiate shortly after in a Euro 2008 qualifier between Poland and Macedonia. Not surprisingly his downfall evoked little sympathy back home amongst his peers and especially the colourful Jeff Winter, who was reportedly quoted as saying: "It could not have happened to a nicer bloke, but it won't change his ego."

To Graham Poll's credit he correctly sent off Bernado Corradi of Manchester City when giving the striker a second yellow card for 'simulation' (diving) in the big local derby at Old Trafford during season 2006/07. In my eyes this sickness that still pervades football can only be described as cheating. And yes it is, generally, committed by overseas players! Along with Corradi, amongst other perpetrators of this sin are El Hadj Diouf and Cristiano Ronaldo.

Occasionally, to their shame, some home-based players have been enticed into the diving domain. For me they sour the whole ethos of the game and cheat their fellow professionals with whom they share the same playing field.

That said, the king of them all for simulation in recent years has been Chelsea's Didier Drogba. Drogba is a wonderful centre-forward whose power, speed and presence are dramatic. This was lost to all outside of Stamford Bridge as he ran out of control, siezing every opportunity to try to con a match official. Drogba's loose comment uttered immediately after the heat of one game: "Sometimes I dive, sometimes I stay up. I don't care about this," hardly endeared him to the public. He quickly retracted this statement, but too late. We had seen his true colours. This charade lasted for a full season or so and was brought to a conclusion when other professionals alongside him in his own dressing room made him take charge of his actions. His then Chelsea manager Jose Mourinho refused to condemn the tall French striker in public, but, clever man that Mourinho is, I would imagine he was probably the prime mover in guiding some senior players to rid the dressing room of this blight in Drogba's game. I do have to point out, however, that as I write Didier Drogba has never been cautioned for 'simulation'. Perhaps that shows just how good he is at it.

We all know that being a referee is an utterly thankless task. That much hasn't changed. Back when I was playing and managing, when referees were amateurs who had to work for a living and received measly match fees and expenses in return for being amongst the most unpopular men on the planet, chants, screams and howls would rain down from the stands dissenting at every decision. That aside, pretty much everything else about the period from the 1960s to the 1980s is in sharp contrast to today's game. Now match officials' changing rooms are stocked with energy foods and drinks. I remember during the late seventies, when managing in the old Third and Fourth Division, going into the referees dressing room before an away game with my team sheet or to check on a technical issue with the referee and seeing bowls of fruit wrapped up in cellophane for them, a similarly-wrapped plate of sandwiches and lots of beers for consumption after the game or on Saturday evening at home. A bottle of whiskey for the match referee was often sitting there so they could help themselves. The bottle, I can report, usually went unopened and would be taken home. I can also report that I certainly never saw one left behind after the referee had departed the ground. This practise changed as suspicious guys like me considered this a sweetener from the home club, so I complained to the Football League. It was not something

I adopted at any of the clubs I took charge of. In any case it was banned soon afterwards by the Football League.

In the 1970s and 1980s the referee struck an insignificant figure, always bedecked in black and generally patrolling the centre of the pitch, with no red or yellow cards to flourish and no instant replays to worry over as he arrived home to watch *Match of the Day's* edited highlights on BBC Television. He would toddle off to work on the Monday morning to walk the gantry of his workmate's opinions and then await the call for the next Saturday's game from the authorities. In between he would indulge in the good life with very little training and arrive at the following week's match ready to perform within himself. Today that referee would not survive as the game is many times quicker than it was then. Pro-Zone tells us so. I suggest that next time you watch a Premier League game on television forget the ball as it is punted up field and watch Howard Webb or Martin Atkinson sprinting past some of the players on the pitch, it will tell you how quick they are about the field. There is only one referee and each team has eleven players to cover the pitch. The referee is one of the fittest men out there, and he doesn't get rest while the ball is down at the other end.

Unlike during my time as a player and manager, for some years now, rightly, elite officials have held a full-time position in a high profile, enjoyable career, buoyed by an attractive salary, plus additional bonuses. Indeed the Premier League men in black, yellow or sometimes green earn in the region of £70,000 to £90,000 per year, with FIFA officials, who also cover internationals and European club games, reaching six figures. The package is made up of a basic salary between £35,000/£45,000, topped up with a substantial payment for officiating each match. In addition they are accommodated in top class hotels and ferried around the country in the comfort of private limousines, as well as being kitted out with the best that the giants in the sports industry can supply.

It's not a bad life, but that status has brought with it added pressures. We all know that in dressing rooms the length and breadth of the country Match Officials are looked down upon as people the players have to grudgingly accept and tolerate, but not necessarily respect. 'Respect' became a key word in the game in 2008 following several high profile incidents, highlighted when Ashley Cole very pointedly turned his back on referee Mike Riley whilst the official was issuing him a caution when Chelsea played Tottenham Hotspur at White Hart Lane in March of that year.

Various similar high profile incidents provoked the 'Respect' campaign from the FA which demanded respect be shown by players and managers towards officials. Everyone signed up to it before the season began, but inevitably in the heat of battle behaviour soon continued as if nothing had changed. I confidently predict that as the 2008/09 season winds up to its conclusion it will be thrown even further out of the window as matters of silverware, promotion and relegation become the only things which matter.

Respect will be attributed at all times from the winner. When it comes to losing in professional football human nature rarely allows goodwill to rise to the surface. To understand what I am saying, listen to managers' comments immediately after a game when standing in front of the camera. Although occasionally justified, they often subject the culprit of the day to grossly exaggerated criticism and accusation, without first examining themselves or their own players as to why they have lost points and why the behaviour of some of their players has been shameful towards both opposition and the Match Official.

To climb to the top of the refereeing ladder in today's game, you will have gone through hell and high water. Starting with parks football and working your way through the ranks, taking searching examinations and undergoing stringent assessment procedures and suffering the abuse, not to mention the almost inevitable physical threats along the way. I believe you need to have a certain type of arrogance and certainly a toughness about you to attain the heights required. Keeping control of twenty two highly trained athletes who are earning up to and possibly above £100,00 a week, as well as the management teams in the technical area, both utterly dedicated to doing anything to win, takes a certain sort of man.

Despite the scheme having been in place for five years or more now, I still feel there are improvements which we can help implement. For example, I believe that as Premier League match officials are now full time, they should be asked to stand in front of the media after a game for an explanation on how they came to make some of the controversial decisions that are always a hot topic during post-match discussions between supporters, media and the professionals within the game. At the moment this is optional and at their discretion. I believe they would reap a greater acceptance and credibility for their reputation from their critics if they were up front and told how they or their assistant had seen an incident. It would be to their credit if they were to be shown as being correct on the majority of incidents that are disputed, which I believe they would be.

To their shame the authorities at the moment say no to the officials being put under scrutiny. One reason, I think, for this is that the media would try to dwell on the negative aspects of the game deliberately to make hay out of the controversial incidents in a match. I say to hell with the media. It is the supporters who deserve this. Maybe at the moment the P.G.M.O. are not keen. However as time moves on it is my opinion that this could quite well be a normal feature at the conclusion of a game.

I feel improvements can also be made in the disciplinary system. As I write the FA disciplinary procedure does not allow for an appeal against a second yellow card issued to a player which results in dismissal. An automatic one match ban ensues. On numerous occasions I have witnessed players and their clubs in my opinion being unfairly penalized for an innocuous second yellow card, leading to them losing that player for their next match. This is wrong. The clubs should be allowed an immediate appeal procedure. I believe this should be reviewed and put in place immediately.

I also believe that we have gone too far down the road to making our once great game a non-contact sport. Some of our match officials have seemingly been indoctrinated by UEFA directives to such an extent that we have a whistle for most challenges involving physical contact, especially around a goalkeeper. We now have 20 outfield players who are tip-toeing through ninety minutes of football, which is regularly interrupted for minimal contact between frustrated footballers. Generally speaking shoulder-to-shoulder contact and sliding tackles are shadows of the past, but to me they are important elements within our game, and ones in which supporters revel. Losing them entirely would be disastrous.

While you can never legislate for the human element in the equation where referees are concerned, equally neither can you legislate for the fact that they also have two very active working partners during the match in their Assistant Referees (Linesman). These officials are not full time. They have to make a living from an occupation outside of the game. I have known some of them go straight to work after officiating in the Premier League and they often work odd hours to make up the time lost travelling to and from the matches. Mistakes will be made by them which can wreck a competent professional performance of the man in the middle. Surely it is time to recognise the need to pay these gentlemen commensurately in order to relieve stress and so hopefully they could achieve better performances?

What we can categorically say is that in this country Match Officials and their Assistants are straight – unlike referees who used to officiate in the now defunct East Germany. Corruption prevailed, with two or three of the top teams in the East German League being government-sponsored football clubs with the referees on the payroll. One of these clubs invariably ended up as champions. Of course there have also been other scandals involving match officials in countries such as Belgium, France and, most notably, Italy, where Juventus were stripped of two league titles won whilst under the managership of England coach Fabio Capello, due to their General Director Luciano Moggi manipulating the appointment of referees to his club's games, for which he was sentenced to 18 months in jail in January 2009. British referees are human, not cheats.

After a lifetime in football, being one of the Premier League Match Delegates team has allowed me to stay in touch with the game in a role which involves a lot of meeting and talking to people. This I find highly enjoyable and has the added bonus of throwing up a number of funny and lovely stories. One of the senior Match Delegates is the highly respected former manager Peter Shreeves. Peter is a humorous cockney who told me a story from when he was in charge of the Tottenham Hotspur youth team when they were playing Manchester United's youngsters at White Hart Lane in the latter stages of the FA Youth Cup. Peter had noticed that sitting on the end of the bench was an inconspicuous individual, let us call him Mr Porter, who he had seen within the confines of the club on previous occasions appearing to be busy. Peter, though, had never been sure what he was doing.

The Liverpool born Tommy Cavanagh, a gregarious character in charge of a rampant Manchester Youth team, was sounding the bugle charge every time there was a concerted attack from his team. The guy sitting on the end of the bench had seemingly had enough of this and started to mimic Tommy, who could verbally mix it with the best. Tommy let fly with some choice expletives including the withering line, "Shreevsy there are enough f****** idiots in the crowd behind me, without you sitting one next to me." This condemned Mr Porter to silence.

Peter Shreeves had always thought that this guy was one of the electricians employed by the club and was seated there in case there was a power failure or an electrical fault. But the incident led him to inquire within the club of the status of this mercurial figure. He found, to his astonishment, that none of the staff knew of him, and neither did manager Keith Burkinshaw know anything of the mysterious Mr Porter.

So when next seen at the end of the bench, the gentleman was asked who he was and how he came to be sitting amongst the football staff on the touch line. Mr Porter explained that he was a porter from the local hospital and had been invited down over a year ago to watch a game by one of the departed medical staff as a return favour in assisting a player to have medical treatment at the hospital. He then had cleverly melted into the everyday fabric of the club, eventually honing to perfection the activity of looking busy on a Saturday afternoon at the first team game at the side of the pitch. If he had not made himself conspicuous with his ill-timed mimicking of Tommy Cavanagh, he could well have still been masquerading as the electrician and sitting there today. This little story is a cameo that could have been repeated at dozens of clubs up and down the old Football League. Most clubs had a Mr Porter around the place, although maybe without as much brass neck as the Spurs fan had!

At the Stadium of Light on Boxing Day 2007 I stood back against the wall of the corridor leading down to the away team dressing room and watched the Manchester United team arrive for their game against Sunderland. I let my mind wander and started counting the noughts on the end of the players' reported weekly salaries as they strolled nonchalantly towards their dressing room, which incidentally is painted out in a dingy mustard and blue, supposedly to give the home team a psychological advantage. These United players had a natural swagger about them and why not as they certainly fancied their chances on the day. I lost count as the likes of Ronaldo (£122,400), Rooney (£116,663) and Giggs (£83,194) took the amount very quickly to over £1,000,000 a week well before the last of the squad had passed me by.

Watching the millions of pounds-worth of talent go by, I was enjoying the privilege of being appointed as the Match Delegate for this huge game, vital to both teams even at this half way stage of the season. I was working for the princely sum of £150 plus out of pocket expenses. It is not for the money that my colleagues and I have filled this Match Delegate role, it is because we still enjoy the special atmosphere of a Premier League Football Club, as well as meeting acquaintances old and new from around the football circuit.

Most importantly, although a touch disillusioned, I am still passionate about the game that I have watched and grown up with. My job has enabled me to have a small influence on the improvement and future careers of some of our elite group of Match Officials. With my input from the experience I have acquired throughout my professional life, I am pleased to say that their reaction and response to me has been a positive one. Who else but ex-players, coaches or managers could they have turned to for the necessary improvement in their game?

Soon the time will surely be upon me when my enjoyment becomes a chore and the magic disappears. Then there will be a host of applicants for this most prestigious of positions when I decide to quit or if I am asked to resign.

2 **Fazakerley**

I GREW up in an era of strong, stable social respect and responsibility, particularly towards our parents, but also, importantly in my opinion, to neighbours and authority. This gave me a sense of balance and judgement, as well as respect for others which has stood me in good stead throughout my professional football life. As to who gave me those life qualities and virtues there is no doubt, it was my devoted mother and father, Elsie and Joseph.

I was born in 1939 in Fazakerley, a tram ride from the heart of Liverpool and the infamous Scotland Road district, which, over the years had bred many a professional footballer, three of whom were to work alongside me on the Liverpool groundstaff a decade later.

In 1938 my father had somehow managed to relocate to Fazakerley from his terraced back-to-back house in Liverpool to become the owner of a semi-detached, three-bedroomed property. This was close to the small country village of Kirkby, which had approximately 250 residents at that time, mainly farming and country people. Kirkby later became a thriving town in its own right with a population of around 38,000 people, mostly relocated from Liverpool's inner city. How my father came to buy his own house came to light many years later when he told my brother Albert that he had been a bookie's runner and the money had come from laying the bets himself, instead of handing the betting slips over to the bookie he was collecting for. Betting shops were things of the future in those days.

There was no deprivation in my young life, or those of my three brothers. After all we had a three-bedroom house wrapped around us with a privy upstairs, as well as one outside attached to the property. We even had spacious back garden.

World War Two broke out in the year I was born. Towards the end of the war, at four or five years of age, I can recall hiding under the stairs as the German bombers took their toll on the port and the City of Liverpool.

Dad did not go to the front line during the war, but was a firefighter on the Liverpool docks, so invariably he would be out at night on duty. My mum told me later that she saw very little of him at this time. Although this was difficult for Mum, my father survived, unlike one of his two brothers who perished in Malaysia during the war, along with thousands of our soldiers.

After the war was over, I can recall the numerous street parties in and around Fazakerley. It was a joyous time. People who had bonded during the war years were able to let their hair down and celebrate not only in the winning of the war, but also the homecoming of our soldiers from the battlefield.

Around the time of my seventh birthday, life seemed to come alive for me as I embarked upon a huge learning curve. My eldest brother Albert was a very fine sportsman, though my elder brother David was not the least bit interested in sport. He was a nature 'nut', which was a good thing for all three of his brothers, Robin, my younger brother, included, as we were taught another side to life as David took us, along with our dogs Trigger the labrador and Pablo a mongrel, into the local countryside, exploring and learning about outdoor life throughout those long sunshine months of our boyhood days.

We were chased by farmers for trespassing, fell into ditches and bogs still cushioning the precious Rook's eggs we had climbed trees to retrieve, sat in glorious corn fields eating jam butties and peanut butter, swigging Dandelion & Burdock, and fished and swam in the local streams and ponds as well as the Leeds/Liverpool canal, which ran alongside Aintree Racecourse.

We had dozens of things to engross us as mother sent us out of the house so she could get some peace from the bedlam of four boys. There always seemed to be blue skies and hot summer sunshine as well as mates peeling the sunburnt skin off your back! Little did we know that this was the passing of our paradise!

I was obsessed with cricket and football throughout those early years and one particular Christmas, though Santa was a doubt in my mind at seven years of age, the magic stocking and pillow case was still placed at the foot of the bed. My wish was for a pair of real football boots. I awoke around five a.m. with the street light in the cul-de-sac where we lived seeming to shine brighter in to my room this Christmas morning. There, silhouetted against the window, was, I thought, a football. Also glistening in the light were some shiny polished toes. They had to be football boots? I couldn't restrain myself, thirty minutes later I was out in the snow wearing boots that were pinching my heels and toes, with a leather football I could hardly see let alone move across the foot of snow that had fallen during the night as I waited for the approaching dawn.

What sticks in my memory from that time are football pitches coated with snow and that laced, leather football, a dirty orange brown in colour as it was kicked around the field. Real leather boots had polished toe caps made of steel, with leather-capped studs protruding. They were nowhere near the multi-coloured moccasins that are worn today.

I was on my way down life's path! School football became the be all and end all for me as my Barlow's Lane Junior School, a mile and a half from home, took on the might of the Catholic schools closer to the heart of Liverpool. Although younger than the rest of the boys I was chosen as a centre-half and I never played anywhere else again until my last year at school.

For the next half decade I was a slave to both cricket and football at school as well as the local youth club within the local Fazakerley Cottage Homes, which was founded by Eamon Rudolph in the early 1800s. All our waking hours we were to be seen along with dozens of others playing sport on the numerous patches of ground surrounding our home. Anything you could find was used for goal posts and cricket stumps. The ground would be a mud heap in the winter and a dust bowl during the summer months, but who cared? We were free and our parents knew we were close to home and more importantly safe.

The highlight of the year for all the local boys was to be allowed, just the once, inside the gates of Fazakerley RAF Camp on Boxing Day morning for the annual soccer match between fathers and their sons. It was played on a proper football pitch with goal posts that had nets attached to them. The game usually ended up in a fight between father and son as they were so competitive. Sadly nowadays, a match such as this might not happen as in today's climate health and safety would prevail.

Aintree Racecourse, the home of the Grand National steeplechase, was close at hand. We always joined the throngs on 'Jump Sunday' to walk the Grand National course, which would be run the following Saturday. To be so close to the fences such as Beecher's Brook was inspiring. I remember the Canal Turn and The Chair were awesome.

Our favourite area for ball games was a small patch of ground near to the local tram terminus. We would be there most evenings after school when dad would come walking past on his way home from work. He would always stop for a while in spite of the late hour, watch one of his sons tuck a goal away at soccer or hit a four onto the road in cricket, wave goodbye and walk on home for his meal at around 8pm. That was all the watching support he could give us at that time. It was all we wanted, a few minutes and a wave of the hand. His work as a fitter meant he spent all week, including Sundays, repairing railway wagons on the Liverpool docks.

Friday, after school, was a good day to be on our terminus 'pitch' as our Nana, after spending the afternoon with our Mum, was making her way to catch the number 19 tram on her way home to Cavendish Road in Walton. She always brought to the house a homemade meat pie for Mum and Dad and an apple pie for the boys. It was a special treat for us and something to look forward to after school.

Grandad is a distant figure in the memory. He kept chickens in the back yard of his back-to-back terrace house. In those days everybody supplemented the food table with fresh eggs. When a hen stopped laying its neck would be rung and it would become meat for the table. Our parents spared us the pain of attending the funerals of Gran and Grandad. They seemed to be there one week and then gone for ever!

That same tram that Dad and Nana travelled on also brought out to the country in the summer holidays the 'Townies' from the heart of Liverpool. They attended the Catholic schools in the tough areas of the City, Saint Francis Xavier, All Souls, Saint Anthony's and Saint Gabriel's. There was always the challenge to play each other at whatever sport was in season, and they were tough games. More often than not they ended in dispute, acrimony and a punch up with one of the gobby Scousers, who invariably had a snotty nose, wiped away with the back of his hand or the sleeve of a filthy shirt. They always had plenty to say for themselves.

At Barlow's Lane Junior School I failed the eleven plus examination. Not being placed in the Grammar School a mile up the road did not have much significance to me, more to Mum and Dad. They saw it as family pride, a reflection on the Ashurst name when I had failed to gain entry. Albert, my eldest brother was the only one in the family to succeed academically and moved on to Technical College to become an electrician.

Barlow's Lane was a gem of a school with sports-mad teachers only too willing to give their time to the boys who were just as keen. I was one of many who benefited from their generosity in the time they gave up. I vividly remember our geography teacher Arthur Corrin, a huge, dark-haired man with a raucous, infectious laugh. He was a fast bowler in the local Merseyside and District Cricket League and his enthusiasm and love of the game could not help but rub off on his boys. He was also prone to using the cane quite liberally, wielding it as if he was chopping wood. My schoolmates and I tended not to be back for seconds.

I was encouraged by my parents to take an early morning paper round, being paid 2/6p a week, (12½ pence in today's money). I then walked a mile to school. In the school morning break, which lasted fifteen minutes, and our lunch hour we ran around after anything that would roll. It was generally a tennis ball pinched in the summer from the Adlam Park tennis courts and stockpiled for this very thing. With a chalked goal on the school wall at one end and the same on the toilet wall at the bottom of the yard, we played out our fantasies. I was always Billy Liddell, a Scottish international in the days when it meant something special to be capped. He was my hero from Anfield, who was the star of Liverpool's forward line at the time.

After school ended at 4pm, unless we were held back for disciplinary punishment, we walked home, finished another paper round, then played outside until dark. If it wasn't paper rounds to earn some pocket money it was tidying gardens and brushing paths or washing down bicycles. Cycling was the popular mode of transport for those fortunate enough to be able to afford one. We did not possess one. We probably walked and ran over 30 miles per week as youngsters, which I am convinced set us up in later life for a powerful cardio vascular system and helped to make us physically strong for our sporting life.

I was surprised to be made Head Boy for my final year at Junior school. It happened at a morning assembly with the first year admissions at the front of the large hall and the last year scholars at the rear. It was a week into our new term. The bell sounded to summon us for assembly when prayers were said and a hymn was sung. Once assembled Mr Copestake the Headteacher made his important announcements for the day: normally a warning against truanting or improper dress code. My ears pricked when he mentioned a football breaking a school window yesterday, then I gave a sigh of relief as he refrained from following this one through.

He continued: "And now to a more pleasant subject, It has been agreed by the staff and myself that the head boy for this year will be . . ." not my mates Wally Hampson or George Quirk, nor scouser Smithy, it was to be Leonard Ashurst. A spurt of urine, I am certain, entered my underpants. I made my way forward to be congratulated by the Mr Copestake. My Head Boy plaque, faded and scratched, hangs on my office wall today.

School sport was thriving. Whatever sport you wanted it was available. What a sad contrast in today's schools. Despite my general sporting prowess I was actually a non-swimmer, something which led to a harrowing incident at the school swimming gala at Walton Queens Drive Baths. We had a house system in our school and Croxteth House, Walton and Sefton, along with my house Knowsley, fought it out to see who could become the swimming champions of the year. The teaching staff, aware that I was not a swimmer still entered me for the neat dive. I was literally in at the deep end. As I waited for my turn I remember being told by the master, "After your dive look for the bamboo pole as you come up." As I walked the plank I was terrified in case the bamboo pole held by the master to which I could cling was not in sight as I surfaced for the first time. After my dive I emerged from the deep at the 8 foot end of the swimming bath searching desperately for the pole, splashing desperately to keep my head above the surface, water streaming from my red, burning eyes. Thankfully there it was hovering above my head. I was third of three contestants, gaining a valuable point for my house. That kind of thing was normal practice in those days, but what, I wonder, would the Health and Safety people have to say about that sort of occurrence today?

School sport, along with the Youth Club, meant life was a dream. There was, for some, the inherent distraction of the admirers in the school yard; the Paulines, Normas, Eleanors, Mavises and Anitas. But if there was a football to be kicked around, or a cricket ball to be hit, then I was oblivious to those temptations!

As adolescents growing up, we began to go to watch both Liverpool and occasionally Everton, especially if a star player was in the opposition team. If we couldn't attend the big game we would watch the reserve teams of either club, who also played on a Saturday. We would then come out early from either ground and slip across the mile of Stanley Park, where both grounds are still currently situated, and arrive at the big match that was being played in time to gain access when the gates were opened ten minutes before the final whistle.

At Anfield we would always make for the main stand and, after the crowds had dissipated, collect up a dozen discarded pop bottles and glasses and in return get paid a twelve-sided threepenny piece, which would help to pay for next week's match.

In those days, supporters with flat caps were draped with long, knitted woollen scarves in their team's colours and some of them had wooden rattles. On the way to the ground you passed kiosks selling unshelled peanuts and another where a heavily-built women would be dispensing plastic cups of Bovril and being serenaded by opposition supporters who might be singing, "Show us your drawers and the money's yours!"

A match to look forward to in the early fifties was Everton versus Blackpool as playing in that match would be a certain famous England international who had great significance for me later on in my career as a professional footballer. I remember when this footballing legend first came to my attention. Our sports master, a Welsh man called Idris Jones, had just finished an after-school coaching session with us when he told us to make sure that we go to the match on Saturday as Stanley Matthews would be playing for Blackpool against Everton at Goodison Park. "It could be the last time he will be seen on Merseyside as he is about to retire," Mr Jones informed us.

Little did Idris know then, that one of his own prodigies from his school team would actually play against the great man on 23 December 1961. I have sometimes wondered if Idris was still alive at that time. I would have liked to have shared his joy with a hand shake and a 'Thank You' at the achievement of one of his own climbing the football ladder to actually play against the great Stanley Matthews.

The Youth Club my younger brother Robin and I attended was in a warm, well-decorated hall inside the Fazakerley Cottage Homes. The youngsters were a mix of orphaned boys and some girls who had a poor deal in life, ending up here to be cared for and rehabilitated. The Master in charge was short, stocky and bald-headed and was the man I remember being the prime mover in all the social activities at the youth club. My recollection is of an all male membership, taking part in male sports, but when I look back at some of what happened, it all seems rather strange now in view of what has emerged over the years with the growing awareness of sexual wrong doings. This Master was a 'stroker' and a 'toucher.' I know that now. However, he also encouraged us with kindness and was strict when it came to discipline, taking off his leather belt and using it when necessary. We would not complain, otherwise he would drop us from the football team and tell our parents we had broken the rules. My brother Robin fell victim to the Master's regime. Robin had a small job delivering the *Liverpool Echo* and one day he departed a match early to earn his pocket money, he was never chosen again.

After playing for the school team on a Saturday morning, I was often crying off injured for the afternoon game in the Liverpool Boys League as on occasions I was not up to the rigours of a second game in a day, Growth spurts were unrecognised in those days. Because of that I also fell foul of Master. He told my brother Robin that I was too soft! Len Ashurst 'too soft' – little did he know!

If Dad was not working he would make the effort to watch us play, or would occasionally be at Anfield to watch the Reds. He took pleasure and pride later on in life as all three of his sports-mad boys made good.

My early teenage years at the Secondary Modern School were joyous. They are years that I never want to forget, etched as they are in the memory for a dozen reasons, unlike the sad and distinctly unhappy experiences of Alan Bennett in *Untold Stories*. In that book Bennett openly admits he would rather forget and abandon those premature years, in particular because of that feeling of being 'shut out.' That I never was!

One memorable day in the Ashurst household, during a half term school holiday, I was lying on the floor in the lounge reading a comic when Albert and David, who would be in their early teens at the time, started fighting in the upstairs bedroom. They rolled off the bed on to the floor of the bedroom, bringing down the ceiling in the lounge below on top of me. Father was out at work at the time and mother was in the kitchen cooking, where else would mothers be in those days? It was generally all work and not a lot of happiness for parents. I remember all the plaster coming crashing down around my ears, and then mother came rushing in to see what had happened. She took one look at me and broke into laughter as I muttered, "It wasn't me, mum." Apparently I had the appearance of the Abominable Snowman, having been showered with lime dust.

We both looked up at the non-existent ceiling, which seconds before had been lime-coated white plaster. Only the wooden laths remained. Mum rushed upstairs to warn both of my brothers of the consequences with those tell all words, "Wait 'till your father comes home." That exposed ceiling remained in that state for a number of years. When friends and neighbours walked into the lounge their eyes immediately shot up to a gaping hole. It was part of the Ashurst welcome that has never changed through the decades.

The downed ceiling never stopped mum and dad having the odd party. It would be early in the evening when uncle Syd arrived with his wife Tilley, who was mum's best friend from their schooldays. My brothers and I were ritually chased up the stairs to bed by Syd, a portly man of great humour, who was an absolute double for the band leader of the time Billy Cotton. Wielding his leather belt which he had stripped from his trousers, we always made sure we were a step or two ahead of him. All of us looked forward to this regular charade, he probably did too!

Vera Lynn songs were still in vogue in the early fifties and during the evening aunty Tilley, who seemingly had a fine voice (she had every chance as she had a huge chest) gave most of those songs an airing. Multiple renderings of Vera's popular songs of the time punctuated the air as the clock ticked towards midnight. Then finally, and inevitably, if you were not awake by now you certainly would be by the finale. It went something like:

'Goodnight Irene, goodnight Irene
I will see you in my dreams . . .'

Liverpool v Wolves
2 February 1952 FA Cup 4th round Attendance 61,905

This attendance is a record for a football match at Anfield. I was there, standing in the Boy's Pen at my favourite spot in The Kop end of the ground. I had queued for hours before the gates opened so we could assure ourselves of our favourite spot. The Liverpool programme kept us focussed on the match ahead as we salivated at the thought of those illustrious names in red and white taking the field, whilst listening to sporadic announcements on the crackling tannoy system. No canned music then to have to withstand, only the building hubbub of excitement amongst the bumper crowd as the clock ticked closer to the 3pm kick off.

It was a bright Winter's day with the huge Spion Kop casting a shadow over one end of the pitch. What an experience for a young twelve year-old to smell the atmosphere with Liverpool's bright red jerseys contrasting vividly with the old gold of Wolverhampton Wanderers. As a youngster I never foresaw that sometime in the near future I would feature with both these famous clubs, first as a boy and then later on in my senior professional career.

The Wolves team, which would go on to dominate much of the 1950s' silverware, was led by the England International captain and centre-half Billy Wright. It was a thrilling game as the Reds went 2-0 up early on, mainly due to a pre-match tactical switch made by Don Welsh, the Liverpool manager. He chose to play my hero, the ebullient Billy Liddell, at centre-forward straight up against Billy Wright, rather than on the wing. Cyril Done and Bob Paisley were the Liverpool goalscorers, with winger Jimmy Mullen replying for the visitors later on.

There was always a downside to watching a match from the Boys' Pen. Liverpool followers will remember that the great Kop ran around the back of the Boys' Pen, with this area of the Kop accommodating additional adult spectators. As the afternoon wore on those spectators used the back wall of the Kop as their toilet! What started as a trickle during the first half then became a virtual torrent of urine during and after half-time. A sit down on the terrace in the interval was out of the question. This was an accepted part of the famous Kop end, which held 28,000 all-standing, fervent fans at that time. Anfield was not yet the cathedral of football that it was to become in later decades, after the great Bill Shankly became their manager in 1959, revolutionising the club from top to toe.

Cricket was high on our agenda during the summer months and I was encouraged by father and led by Albert, who was County standard, although he was never given the opportunity to test his ability at that level. A star of the Liverpool Competition, fielding at cover point he once, in the first over of an innings of a charity match, ran out Rohan Kanhai, the famous West Indian batsman. Albert questioning the 'Not out' decision of the umpire was told emphatically: "Albert, the spectators don't want to see you field, they want to see Kanhai get some runs." Albert also batted at number five for Ormskirk Cricket Club in Lancashire and scored numerous centuries in Flintoff style. Our dad was often a proud man!

The visit of the Australians to Manchester in the summer of 1953 was something we sports nuts could not miss. At Old Trafford you paid at the gate, so it was up with the larks to catch a train to arrive an hour before play began to join a never-ending queue stretching around the ground. It was worth the wait to see those greats of the time: Cyril Washbrook and Jack Ikin for Lancashire, with Lindsey Hassett and Bill Morris for Australia the respective openers for either side. The celebrated opening bowlers were Statham for Lancashire and Lindwall for the 'The Baggy Greens.'

Good fortune blessed me at the start of the 1953/54 season, fortunately not for the last time in my life. I was selected for a trial with Liverpool Schoolboys as a centre-half. When I arrived at Penny Lane (yes the place which would later inspire the famous Beatles track) it transpired that they were missing a left-back and being a natural left footer they put me in the team and I never looked back. I was a regular first choice for all the games in a hugely successful season, a shrewd decision by Tom Parry, who was the manager of the team. Tom was a big genial man with a left foot akin to Puskas's. His assistant was Tom Saunders, who later became Chief Scout for Liverpool.

Liverpool Schoolboys cleaned up that season, winning all but one of the trophies that we competed for. The campaign culminated with an 8-1 win over two legs against Southampton Boys in the prestigious English Schools Trophy. I still have the treasured medal. Looking on amongst the crowd of 17,205 for the second leg at Anfield were all my family, including mum, who had until that point never seen me play. She was always too nervous to go to a match in case I was injured or made a mistake. In fact she hardly saw me in action that night as she closed her eyes and covered her face with her hands every time the ball went near me. Derek Temple destroyed Southampton on the night then signed for Everton when he left school. Temple went on to play and score for Everton in the 1966 Cup Final as the Toffees won 3-2 against Alan Brown's Sheffield Wednesday.

I signed for Liverpool Football Club in the summer of 1954, aged 15, and was also capped at cricket for South Lancashire Schoolboys versus

North Lancashire at Old Trafford. I scored 23 not out opening the innings, and a full county cap followed for Lancashire against Durham Schoolboys at Rochdale. It was all happening for me. Dad and friends made the trip to see me open the batting for the Red Rose County. We won the toss and batted first. Dad had just settled in to his seat in the ground after a long train and bus journey in time to see me luckily survive two appeals in the opening over. I middled the third ball into the covers and then was out next ball for a 'blob'. Two minutes at the crease, then for me it was back to the pavilion. Dad, along with his pals, headed for the nearest pub. I think that was the day my sights shifted firmly onto football.

I joined Liverpool as a privileged ground staff lad – there were no apprentice schemes in those days. I was taken on alongside three lads, all from the Scotland Road area of Liverpool, and all a little older and physically more mature than myself. They used that maturity against me at a later time, it wasn't pleasant! I was now having to learn quickly in a new world and finding that life was always a challenge! It was actually a double signing by Liverpool as when the club signed me they also got brother Albert as an amateur. He was playing local football in goal for Burscough at that time and it would appear that my father, knowing how keen the club were to get my signature, convinced them that if they wanted me they also had to sign Albert, who in all honesty was playing at his level were he was.

Albert was and still is a real character. He often acted the fool as a goalkeeper to try to distract the opposition – he was the Bruce Grobbelaar of his day! When the opposing team had been awarded a penalty he would hang on the crossbar as the penalty taker was about to take the kick then drop down onto the goalline and spring into action as the kick was taken. Or he would do the 'rubber leg wobble' that Grobbelaar so cleverly used in the 1984 European Cup final when playing for Liverpool.

Signing for the Reds meant me brushing out and washing down the home and away dressing room floors at Anfield, sweeping the terraces and, of course, cleaning and polishing the first team players' boots. Yes the boots with the toe caps. I have often wondered where the time was to actually practice and play football. Those boots had to be shining otherwise you would have the trainer Albert Shelly on to you, as well as that boisterous manager of the time Don Welsh, a real 'nutter.' Keen on golf, he used to keep all the young ground staff busy during the lunch hour as he belted golf balls into the Kop. We had to first dodge them as they ricocheted dangerously around our heads and then chase around collecting them to return to our manager.

The thrill for me was that I had been allocated the boots of my hero Billy Liddell, the 'Prince of Anfield', to clean. If you think Dalglish, Callaghan, Rush or Aldridge, all Liverpool heroes later in time, then you will get a picture of the quality of the man as a footballer. He was later compared with all those greats and became an ambassador for the club, the City itself and the professional game. Those four giants of Liverpool who played their game in the 70s and 80s would, I am sure, concur.

Liddell was to visit me a month later in Alderhay Hospital. I had been carrying an injury during the cup run with the Liverpool Schoolboys team and was to have a minor operation on my right knee, which had occasionally flared up during matches. Whilst recuperating, a nurse came to tell me that I had a visitor and the door to the ward opened to reveal the great man! Liddell was so busy at that time with his many interests providing him with a thousand things to do – being a lay preacher and a local magistrate in addition to being a Scottish International footballer with a family at home in a suburb of Liverpool – yet he found time to visit me. Outstanding.

Billy Liddell's visit to see me as a young boy gave me a yard stick for life that I have always tried to live up to. Because of that experience, throughout my professional career I have never said 'no' to similar requests. Even to this day I am involved with two North East charitable organisations, as well as attending many a presentation for good causes. It may mean giving of your time, yet it means so much to the recipients.

During this period after signing for Liverpool and my meteoric rise to local fame, I was to be spared the ritual of the weekend footy match in the tough local Liverpool and District League. Players of all shapes and sizes would be dragging on a Senior Service or a Players Craven A fag before a game, having already sunk two or three pints of beer at the local pub beforehand. Many a budding footballer was ruined by both this puerile attitude and the tough environment that the game was played in. A few managed to rise above the mayhem in the years after me and survive to go on to bigger things in the Football League, amongst them were Jimmy Case and Brian Hall, both of whom became Liverpool players and that tough, old-fashioned centre-forward Peter Withe, a European Cup winner with Aston Villa in 1982.

These games were played with a 'No Prisoners Taken' approach. You learned how to look after yourself quickly or you got hurt. When the game was over, it was a return to the pub from where you came. Then you drank till late, getting rat-arsed, and finally on for the obligatory hot chicken curry to finish off the day.

Two other famous footballers emerged from the area where I lived to make a telling impression on the English game. The three of us, good friends to this day, grew up within shouting distance from each other, although not contemporaneously, without realising it until very much later in life. The other players? Colin Harvey of Everton and Steve Coppell of Manchester United, 5 years and 15 years my junior respectively. Both had distinguished careers as players and managers, winning plenty of silverware between them.

Back then the ball was leather, with a lace you threaded after tucking in the teat of the bladder. The goal posts and cross bar were square, painted with white lime, with nets hanging on tent poles. The pitches were hard and dusty or were knee deep in mud, squelching over those highly polished boots. If you could see the pitch markings amidst the mire, they would be marked out with a white lime, which would irritate your skin once in contact. This stuff was lethal in an open wound!

The fat referees who lived off dripping butties and pop, had no substitutes or fourth officials to worry about or yellow cards to flourish. It was different, especially as you could barge a goalkeeper into the net and apply grievous bodily harm to an opponent with a tackle into the groin and suffer little punishment!

I was at Anfield along with more senior groundstaff players Connie Philips, who drifted out of the game, Bobby Campbell, later manager of Chelsea, and Jimmy Melia, who would take Brighton and Hove Albion to the 1983 FA Cup final. All three were Catholics and they took the piss out of a certain protestant newcomer named Ashurst. This sort of teasing between Protestants and Catholics was regrettably commonplace in Liverpool at that time. It was almost part of the city's culture. Sometimes the trio tied me down and tarred me or blacked my privates with the black polish used for cleaning the players' boots. There was, from time to time, a teasing prank from senior lad Jimmy Melia, who was an excellent but selfish inside-forward in his own right. Jimmy was a footballing, likable Scallywag. I am told he amassed properties in the South of England later in life, although the numerous interest rate rises into double figures in the 1980s damaged his finances.

All three would at times annoy me after training by locking me out of the dressing room after I'd taken a bath. With my clothes inside, I was pretty helpless, which meant me having to wander around the corridors of Anfield clothed in whatever I could find to wrap around my waist, trying to find the groundsman who had the spare key to the dressing rooms. It got to the stage that I would dress without washing, take the bus home and have a bath in the comfort of the family house. They invariably took the piss out of me for having paper thin legs as well as being slight of build. My 'zits' didn't help either.

My father got wind of this sort of behaviour and told me to look after myself, so the following morning it was Connie Philips I chose to sink my right fist into at the first sign of piss-taking – and that was the end of the nonsense. I had put down my marker and they had accepted it. Len Ashurst was not soft.

It was at this time that my father made a decision that I would be better off having another string to my bow in case football did not work out and placed me as an apprentice compositor in the printing trade. This meant that after only a few months amongst the elite at Anfield I was on a five year learning curve at a small print works named Elliott and Yeoman behind the Adelphi Hotel in the heart of Liverpool.

Working full time in the print trade and training two evenings a week at Melwood didn't hinder my progress at Anfield as I moved up the team structure from the 'C' team through to the 'A' team and in the process was chosen to represent my country in the England Youth team for their first international of the 1956/57 season. It was at Brighton and Hove Albion's Goldstone Ground that September, and we drew 2-2 against Switzerland. One of my team-mates was the affable John Barnwell, who forged a decent football career for himself as manager of Wolves and until 2008 was the Chief Executive of The League Managers' Association.

Six England youth caps followed for me and one of those international matches was at Roker Park, Sunderland in November 1956 against Hungary. Winters started early in those day, especially in the North East of England. It was the coldest October night that I had ever experienced when playing football. Both teams lined up for the national anthems to be played over a public address system that was also affected by the cold weather. I remember it particularly struggled through a Hungarian anthem which seemed to go on for ever. You really don't need a long national anthem to wait through before a game of football on a brusque north east evening! There was a great response towards the match from the north east football public as the official attendance was put at 15,999. Little did I realise at the time that this game would be the first of many that I would be playing at Roker Park in the years to come.

The match was played at the time of the upheaval of the Hungarian uprising as the government, led by Imre Nagy sought to sever links with the Soviets, and a 2-1 victory for England did not help the mood of the visitors, who sought shelter in England for a number of weeks as the political situation was resolved back home.

The spring of 1957 took us to Oberhausen in Germany for a match against the German youth team. This was a preparation game for the Youth International Tournament at Easter in Barcelona. This was the opportunity to use my limited grasp of German. In the early 1950s I had been taught German at Barlow's Lane Junior School and although I'd had the option to continue at Fazakerley Secondary School when moving up at eleven years of age I had declined.

I often wondered why the curriculum included German, given the close proximity of the Second World War. Maybe it was thought that if Germany ever went to war again we would have all the answers as their panzer divisions piled in to Britain and rampaged north up country to Fazakerley.

Both of my elder brothers were posted on National Service to separate towns about fifty miles from Oberhausen. Without me or either of them knowing about each other being present they both attended the game. Albert, a keen photographer at that time took many pictures on the day, one of which I still have. It was of the England team, containing me, walking out onto the pitch for the start of the game. On later and closer examination this photograph amazingly showed my other brother, David, cheering the England team a mere ten yards away from me completely unnoticed by Albert taking the photograph.

I had to graft for my success and, when I had achieved it, I had to graft and graft again to keep it. There was no clearer example of this and the treacherousness of the professional game than when, after the high of gaining seven youth international caps, I was discarded by my club. I had played in all of the England Youth team's last three games of the season, which were in the Barcelona International Youth Tournament against Greece, Austria and Holland. My family were overjoyed to have me home after representing England and doubly so on learning that I had been chosen for Liverpool reserves to play Bolton Wanderers at Anfield the next evening. In spite of picking up a dickey tummy in Spain, plus the arduous travel as well as three games in four days, I played in the match but not surprisingly, with my body at a low ebb, made a mess of my reserve team debut. I was called into the manager's office afterwards and to my utter disbelief was told by Phil Taylor that I would not be offered a professional contract. I had been discarded by my beloved Liverpool. I was devastated. At such an early age, and in such cruel circumstances, I had been tossed onto soccer's scrapheap by my team. I was looking for another football club.

The bad news spread through the neighbourhood. Mum went into her shell and would not answer the door. Any well-wishers were rebuffed.

Dad was mortified. It was as if he had lost a son. He also had to face his mates down at the pub! The house was in mourning as my three brothers took plenty of stick amongst their pals. Robin, being the youngest, had to endure the scathing remarks of the school playground.

But my torpor was to last just a single day as early the next evening the local scout for Wolverhampton Wanderers called. Before I knew it he was sitting in our lounge painting a vivid picture of the Midlands club, who were one of the biggest in the land in the 1950s. My father was duly impressed and I signed amateur forms for them there and then. Dad had decided that I should not wait for another offer: 'A bird in the hand' so to speak. I have since speculated as to what my decision would have been if the blue of Everton had knocked on the door that evening instead of the old gold of Wolves. Ours was a house steeped in the red of Liverpool – now that would have been a conundrum.

3 Cranes, Parrots and The Bomber

PROVIDENCE played me an improbable Ace as a chance meeting in the Midlands changed my life. I was standing in the foyer of the Molineux ground, home of Wolverhampton Wanderers Football Club, waiting to depart to play in a third team game for Wolves against the local Bilston Rovers. Fate contributes to everybody's life story for good or for worse and in my case my story was effectively written on 31 August 1957 at approximately 1.45pm. It was then I met George Curtis. George had been the England youth team coach the previous season under whom I had gained my seven International Youth caps. He was now the first team coach at Sunderland, handling some huge international stars of the time.

As the Sunderland team entered the foyer of the club to play their first team game against Wolves George was not aware that I had signed for the Wanderers a few weeks before, so he enquired in surprise as to why I was standing there? I told him of Liverpool's decision to release me and within seconds he had given me his telephone number and told me to call him on Monday morning. His parting words were, "You will be a Sunderland player by then." I cannot remember the score at Bilston. I do remember it was a 0-5 defeat on that day for Sunderland, one of many heavy losses around that turbulent time in the club's history.

Having made that definitive phone call the following Monday morning, which sealed my destiny, there were two hurdles to overcome before my move to the north east could be completed. Firstly the club had to make arrangements to have my apprentice credentials transferred to a printing company on Wearside. And secondly I had to obtain my release from the amateur forms that I had signed for Wolves only a few weeks before.

Stan Cullis was the legendary manager of Wolves, known for his quick temper and cutting wit. But, although a formidable figure in many ways, he duly agreed to release me after I had intimated that I would not be travelling to the Midlands club again and instead wanted to play for a local club near Liverpool called Prescot Cables. This was a ploy to gain my release. If he had known the true story he would never have agreed to let me go. I played my one game for Prescot Cables and then a seven day notice was submitted by Sunderland to the local Lancashire League club. A week later I was on my way to the north east. Through all this subterfuge I understood very early in my soccer career that collusion was a bedmate of football, especially at the club I was about to join.

Opening the train door as it pulled in to a grubby Sunderland station, I was met by Sunderland's manager Alan Brown. He was wrapped up against the cold in what seemed like a dark navy blue overcoat with gloves and scarf. An upright military-type figure, he stood out amongst the waiting public. I was to learn in time that he never delegated and his presence at the station was typical of his desire to make sure everything for the club was done properly. In fact he would not or could not trust anyone else. I remember I stepped down from the train with the station clock showing exactly 7pm.

It was 27 December 1957 and I was 18 years of age. This had been the day I said "farewell" to my mother, father and three brothers and departed our family home in Fazakerley. Gripping an old brown leather case, which had belonged to my Grandad and contained all my belongings, I embarked on what proved to be a no return train journey from Liverpool Lime Street Station. It was a journey that was to eventually fulfil everything I could have wished for from life.

The journey north took an age as we passed through many of the industrial towns of Lancashire and Yorkshire and then on to the bleak County of Durham. Nearing the stop at Durham City I remember popping my head out of the carriage window, but only for a second or two as the bitter cold pierced my eyes and ears.

As Mr Brown and I drove away from the railway station, I crossed the Wearmouth Bridge for the first time in my life. You couldn't help but notice through the dark the dozens of huge cranes on both sides of the River Wear standing steadfast and lit up by the thousands of electric blubs shining through the night. It had been thirteen months previously when I had played for England Youth at Roker Park against the Hungarian national team. That evening as a member of an England team our transport had brought us in from the north of this great shipbuilding town, which at the height of its powers had employed nearly 20,000 people.

On crossing the bridge I had a flashback of nine years or so to my junior schooldays at Barlow's Lane, as I suddenly thought of my English teacher Mr Corrin. One day during his lesson he had read out a verse from a poem by Ralph Hodgson. He then asked everyone in the class to pick out a line or a verse and draw in coloured crayon of how you would see it as a picture. The poem went something like this!

'Cranes and gaudy parrots go up and down the burning sky.'

Fifteen minutes later, after one of the class monitors had collected all the papers in, Arthur Corrin let out a huge and prolonged belly laugh, which on resting his gaze on me from his elevated position in front of the class told me that he had seen something amusing in my drawing of what I thought the line depicted. I was not wrong. To my embarrassment I had drawn a huge dark steel crane rising above the greenery of the forest trees, in which I had crayoned in the bright yellow, greens and blues of a host of parrots roosting amongst the leafy green! "Not those kind of cranes, Ashurst . . ." he guffawed. That must have been a conversation stopper in the staff room that particular day. You can understand why I failed my eleven plus!

Alan Brown's car stopped outside the wooden double doors of Roker Park. Clutching my granpa's case, I alighted from the vehicle into a freezing cold, biting wind, not dissimilar to the chill I had felt when standing on the Roker Park pitch side respecting the Hungarian national anthem. I followed my new Boss in through the door and up those stairs.

Alan Brown had the contract drawn up and ready for me to sign, which I did on the dotted line of a faded blue document that I did not read or ask for it to be read to me. I accepted emphatically what terms and conditions had been written in to the agreement. It was, as we all now know, a charter highly biased towards the football club as the employer, with the player having very few rights. That was not my concern at all at that point. I became a professional footballer that day.

My contract confirmed that I had signed as a part-time professional footballer with one of the most famous clubs in the country. A signing on fee of £10 was to be paid on top of my first week's salary of £11. I was not yet aware that I had joined a club in decline after a golden period in the fifties when huge gates watched a galaxy of individual stars but crucially not a team. That had been a period of a lost opportunity for Sunderland Football Club.

I was then driven by Alan Brown to a terraced house in Zion Terrace in the city, where I was to meet a widow by the name of Mrs Edie Spain, who would become my landlady. She was to be my surrogate mother for the next three years as I competed with sixty or so other full and part-time professionals at the football club to catch the eye of manager.

Although I was Edie's first lodger, she immediately made me feel at home with her friendly nature and her wonderful cooking. In that fifties and early sixties era there was no drug or sex education from parents or school and many young people were taken to the brink and beyond by experimenting with drugs. As to sexual activity, you were left to work things out for yourself and use your imagination until nature, as well as trial and error, took over. Although embarrassing at times, there was no shame in being a virgin in those days. There were a number in the players' dressing room. It was only in the middle sixties and early seventies that it became fashionable to have free and open sex.

Without question most dressing rooms were definitely heterosexual. There was never the suggestion that any of my team-mates or for that matter any opposition players at that time were gay. In fact I am only aware of Justin Fashanu, who played for Norwich City and Nottingham Forest in the 1970s and 80s, as a footballer who came out. What pressures he must have been under, especially with such a red-blooded brother also making a name for himself in the game and the media at the time. It must have been intolerable to take the inferences so easily foisted upon an unprotected target at that time from team-mates, opposing players and his own and opposition supporters alike. It obviously took its toll as Fashanu tragically took his own life.

Make an effort to read Alan Bennett's 'Untold Stories'. It is a cracking read containing the following extract from Joe Orton's biography *Prick Up Your Ears*.

(Orton on seeing a youth coming)
Orton: Look at the package on this. He's lovely
Halliwell: *(frantically)* Where? Where?
Orton: Here. *(The youth looks back.)* We're on.
Halliwell: How? What did he do? I didn't see anything.
Orton: What do you want a telegram? Come on. *(They follow.)* He's built like a brick shithouse.
Halliwell: He's probably a policeman.
Orton: I know. Isn't it wonderful?
Halliwell: We don't want it to make us late for the Proms.
Orton: Listen, sweetheart, which do you prefer, him or Sir Malcolm Sargent?

This is a wonderful montage from the other side of life. If we replace the youth with a pretty girl with a nice figure, the storyline coming from inside a football environment would be the same! Most certainly over the years none of my colleagues and team-mates in our dressing room were of Orton's persuasion, as they laid many a female who ventured across their path.

9. In consideration of the observance by the said player of the terms, provisions and conditions of this Agreement, the said *George Crow* on behalf of the Club hereby agrees that the said Club shall pay to the said Player the sum of £ *11 0 - 0* per week from *24 Dec 1957* to *3 May 1958* and £ *10 - 0 - 0* per week from *4 May 1958* to *30 June 1958*.

10. This Agreement (subject to the Rules of The Football Association) shall cease and determine on *30 June 1958* unless the same shall have been previously determined in accordance with the provisions hereinbefore set forth.

Match Bonuses according To Rule

Fill in any other provisions required

(1) It is hereby agreed by the player that if he shall at any time be absent from his duties by reason of sickness or injury he shall, during such absence, be entitled to receive only the difference between his full weekly wages, and the amount he receives as benefit under the National Insurance Act, 1946, or The National Insurance (Industrial Injuries) Act, 1946, and for the purpose of this Clause his wages shall be deemed to accrue from day to day.

(2) If at any time during the period of this Agreement the wages herein agreed to be paid shall be in excess of the wages permitted to be paid by the Club to the player in accordance with the Regulations of the Football League, the wages to be paid to the player shall be the amount the Club is entitled to pay by League Regulations in force from time to time, and this Agreement shall be read and construed as if it were varied accordingly.

As Witness the hands of the said parties the day and year first aforesaid

Signed by the said George Crow and Leonard Ashurst

In the presence of
(Signature) *Alan Brown*
(Occupation) *Manager*
(Address) *Meadowlands, Whitburn Road, Cleadon, Nr Sunderland*

Leonard Ashurst
(Player)

Geo. Crow
(Secretary)

My first professional contract witnessed by Alan Brown the manager and signed on 27 December 1957 by the secretary of the club George Crow.

The day after signing my professional contract for the club I experienced the football passion and fervour of the North East soccer fans when I played in front of 10,000 spectators for the reserves against South Shields at Simonside.

Sunderland Reserve Team
Ronnie Routledge
Allan Graham, Len Ashurst
Graham Reed, Tommy Robson, Fred Chilton
Clive Bircham, Alan Spence, Charlie Fleming, Harry Godbold, John Hannigan

It was an unremarkable induction into the ways of the north east, but I was to learn much more when I attended my first game at Roker Park a week later on 4 January 1958. It was an FA Cup third round match between Sunderland and Everton. The attendance was 35,000 and a spattering of snow sprinkled the surface, which heightened my expectation of the red and white colours of Sunderland and Everton's blue jerseys against that white backdrop. A vivid memory of this day was the noise generated from all sides of the stadium. I was becoming acquainted with the famous Roker Roar, which was to envelope me and the team on many occasions in the future. Sunderland centre-half Charlie Hurley was given a torrid time by Everton's Merseyside titan Dave Hickson, whose mop of blonde hair bobbed seemingly all over the pitch. The late Billy Elliott also stood out for his ferocious tackling for the home side. Was that what you had to do to win a place in the team, I wondered? The lesson on that day struck home.

My apprentice indentures were duly transferred from the Liverpool printers Elliott and Yeoman to a small Wearside Printing company in Borough Road, Sunderland. I was to see out the time to attain my compositor qualifications over the following two years, during which I experienced two huge and significant happenings. The first landmark was my first team debut for Sunderland, the other was in avoiding National Service by three months as the government of the day brought to an end compulsory National Service just as I was about to complete my printing indentures. It was a relief not to have to experience service life as it would have played havoc with my football career over that two year span.

I don't remember much of the rest of that season, aside from picking up our weekly wages in small brown envelope from the assistant secretary's office window at the top of the stairs at Roker Park, but I must have felt I'd done OK as I recall there was a buzz about journeying home to Fazakerley during the month of May 1958 for my first close season break. After having been away from home for five months, in my pocket was the treasured first contract, along with some money for mother and father. Walking through the front gate and seeing the beaming faces of my parents told me a story that a thousand words could not describe. There were no smart cars on the road in those days or on our front drive. There was the concrete front garden bird table made by Dad and, as the only ornament, a jolly-looking gnome that was Mum's pride and joy.

Stepping inside our house made me feel as if I had never been away. Those familiar, treasured items that make a home were still in place: in the hall a cut glass flower vase, which we still have, the picture on the wall, an ornament on the sideboard and, in the lounge, a cuckoo clock brought back from abroad by one of my brothers, home on leave from the forces. Standing in the corner was the radio gramophone that had provided the music for those mighty sing songs from yesteryear. It had been bought from new when I had won £300 forecasting ten results on the fixed odds pools a few years before. The familiarity was comforting, but also told me that I was making a new life for myself elsewhere, although I would always be welcome here.

WHILE MY 1958 had thus far gone well, history shows that it was not a good time for Sunderland Football Club. They were relegated at the end of the 1957/58 season, losing their top flight status for the first time in their long, illustrious history. Alan Brown gave the senior players eight matches at the start of season 1958/59 and then lost patience with most of them as they lost five games and conceded twenty seven goals, including successive defeats 0-5 at Swansea, a game for which I was chosen by Alan Brown for my first taste of first team football, albeit as non-playing twelfth man, and 0-6 at Sheffield Wednesday.

Ipswich Town at Roker Park on 20 September 1958 was the ninth game in that long, hard season and this was the moment when the manager swept away the old and brought in the new. He gave debuts to three teenage boys, the late Jimmy McNab, Cecil Irwin and 19 year-old Len Ashurst. It is incredible to think that is now over fifty years ago!

Alan Brown had instructed all the professional staff to report to the dressing room an hour before the kick off and yet I had no inkling as to what was to happen. I was one amongst at least four dozen other players packed in to that home dressing room before the game. George Curtis, the first team coach, addressed the entire dressing room, firstly informing us that the manager was away on business. George was a really nice guy with a dash of panache about him. A smart and snazzy dresser, also prone to a theatrical disposition, who was in his element as he licked the end of his fingers and pulled an envelope from his inside jacket pocket. He took his time opening it, delaying announcing the team for what seemed an age, so adding to the drama of the moment.

"The team to play Ipswich Town today will be read out," he announced. "Those not chosen please leave the dressing room and report for training on Monday morning." Another delay ensued and then, lifting his eyes from his piece of paper, he pronounced, "The team will be Bollands, Irwin, Ashurst . . ." I didn't hear any of the other players' names being read out as I was enveloped in the joy of an immediate adrenalin rush followed by a wave of anticipation. What I vividly remember was a host of disappointed players walking out of the dressing room, leaving the eleven fortunate ones to prepare for the match in an hour's time. Amongst those who departed the room, some of whom would never again return, was Billy Elliott, that same player who had caught my eye playing against Everton only nine months before. I had taken the place of this former England International and Alan Brown had started his purge of a great club, which through poor management and misguided judgement had lost not only its First Division League status, but its reputation and its soul. There the dream ends, however. My debut ended in a 0-2 defeat.

The major event of significance for me and a host of Sunderland supporters from Brown's swathing changes to the team was the emergence of Charlie Hurley as a footballing centre-half. Particularly in the match at Swansea, despite the result, Chas showed all his abilities and skill as a new breed of defender who could use the ball and was comfortable with it at his feet emerging from the fading and obsolete 'Stopper' era.

I held my place in the team for all but one of the remaining 33 games of that 1958/59 season and then into the following campaign. Amongst those games was a momentous homecoming to Anfield on 3 January 1959 for my first visit there as an opposition player. Losing the game 1-3 was a bitter-sweet occasion as amongst the near 37,000 crowd was not only my family, but also Phil Taylor, the very manager who had released me 18 months before and to whom I wanted so desperately to prove my point. He would last only another 10 months in the job before being sacked. I say no more.

This period at Sunderland saw a clear out over a couple of seasons of many of the old brigade of players as Brown rid the club of ageing if talented players as well as those who would not accept the prevailing discipline. Included in the culling was the singing winger Colin Grainger, an England international and a talented vocalist who had appeared on the stage with the famous Ted Heath band at the Sunderland Empire. Taking their places were fine young players that were to become synonymous with the early sixties history of Sunderland Football Club: Nelson, Irwin, Ashurst, Harvey, McNab, Lawther, Sharkey, Herd, McPheat, Dillon.

By now I had completed my apprenticeship in the printing trade and had signed full-time professional forms for the club in the autumn of 1960.

Holding the team together for two full seasons as it adjusted to the massive change in image and personnel was the ever reliable and solid captain Stan Anderson, a great leader and a man who I have a lot of respect for. Alongside him at centre-half was the imperious Charlie Hurley, who would later be voted as Sunderland's player of the century by the fans. Think of the best in character as well as standing in people, add stimulating professional prowess and then you are talking about these two men. Very few contemporaries compared to either of these football giants in my opinion.

Stan had led the team in 1960/61 on a run of twenty games with only one defeat. In addition a pulsating FA Cup run saw the team emerge into a young, exciting unit. After success against Arsenal 2-1 and Liverpool 2-0, a Charlie Hurley header gave us a 1-0 win in the fifth round at Norwich City. The draw threw up a home tie in the sixth round against the mighty Tottenham Hotspur, who were at the time the runaway leaders of the First Division. It was made an all ticket game, with thousands camping overnight to buy a ticket for this huge match. Sunderland fans had at least now grown to believe that we had a great chance of beating Tottenham. And so did we, especially with that famous Roker Roar behind the team. 61,326 people saw us take the game to Spurs after Cliff Jones had given them the lead. When Willie McPheat scored the equaliser on 51 minutes, the game was stopped as some of the crowd joyously invaded the pitch.

Danny Blanchflower, the Spurs captain, regrouped his team and they survived the battering that they received over the last 40 minutes or so from a rampant home team, who had seven players less than twenty three years of age. They earned a 1-1 draw and the replay at White Hart Lane on the following Wednesday night showed why this imperious Spurs side would go on to win the first double of the twentieth century by winning the league title and the FA Cup by the end of that season. The game was won handsomely by Tottenham 5-1.

Alighting from the train on our return to Sunderland the following evening, we discovered hundreds of supporters thronging the railway station wanting to express their appreciation for a great cup run. That was touching and more emotion was to follow as in the excited homecoming a couple of supporters had shouted to me that I was an

England player. At the time I considered it over-exuberance by animated Sunderland fans, however, as I reached the top step of the stairs and walked out of the station into the daylight, there on the newspaper stand was a placard saying, 'Len Ashurst chosen for England'. This was the same location in which I had met Alan Brown less than three years previously. My consistent displays in the team had now earned me an England under-23 call up against Germany, coincidentally at White Hart Lane on 15 March 1961. We won the game 4-1.

I had become engaged to Valerie, a local girl I had met and fallen in love with in 1960 and on 13 May 1961 we were married at St. Cuthbert's Church in her home village of East Rainton. It proved to be good timing in more ways than one as English football was about to undergo a sea-change that would enable young married couples such as ourselves to have a much better standard of living.

4 Double Your Money

ENGLISH FOOTBALL reached a watershed in January 1961 when the maximum wage was lifted. The financial floodgates opened after threatened strike action by the players, led by Fulham striker Jimmy Hill, then Chairman of the Professional Footballers Association, achieved the long-stated goal of having the ceiling on our earning capacity lifted.

At the time I was the PFA representative in the Sunderland dressing room and, after having attended numerous meetings at the PFA headquarters in Manchester, where secretary Cliff Lloyd, a wonderfully pleasant gentleman, eventually authorised all club representatives to go back to their clubs and ask their members to decide on what would be a historic decision, I had the onerous, unpaid task of putting the case for strike action to my playing colleagues.

As a PFA meeting concluded in Manchester on a Monday afternoon in that winter, Geoff Twentyman, the Liverpool representative, told me he had no need to return to his club and put the proposition to a vote. He already knew what the answer would be. At the time Liverpool were top of the old Second Division and their players had long decided if changes did not come soon that they would be taking unilateral action of their own within the club. More interestingly Geoff revealed that they had the backing of their shrewd but colourful manager Bill Shankly, who saw the unfairness of the existing system, but also had the foresight to know that if the players' wages rocketed then the managers' salaries had to increase accordingly.

Pressure had been mounting on the Football Association and the game's authorities for some time. They knew that illegal payments had become prevalent in the game and that had led to shame being heaped upon Sunderland Football Club in the fifties when payments of illegal bonuses to players were uncovered, culminating in them being heavily fined and certain directors being banned for life. The incident caused ignominy at the club and began the downward spiral which led to relegation in 1958.

As well as the imposition of a ceiling on our earnings, there was a good deal of disquiet about being tethered to clubs indefinitely due to the terms of our contracts.

The whole situation was brought to a head when George Eastham's proposed transfer from Newcastle United to Arsenal was blocked by the Tyneside club's board, who insisted that he would play for no club other than their own. However Eastham's so-called 'slave contract' was ripped up in the courts by Judge Wilberforce, who deemed it to be a restraint of trade. Thus Eastham and the PFA changed the transfer system for ever. Back then I don't think anyone envisaged the system we have now where players can agitate for moves to earn huge contracts and spend each season at a new club, but it was a very necessary change to what had been essentially a feudal system.

The abolition of the maximum wage meant Johnny Haynes of Fulham and England became the first professional footballer to earn a basic wage of £100 per week, a salary awarded to him by the Chairman of Fulham, Mr Tommy Trinder, himself a star of variety, TV and radio, who understood that entertainers such as Haynes had to be paid their worth. I also think that Trinder understood the news value of making his captain the highest-paid player in the country. Haynes made hundreds of appearances for Fulham before he hung up his boots. In later life he retired to Edinburgh, and sadly was killed in a car accident in October 2005.

By the way, this fine player was responsible for Sunderland's own Stan Anderson not winning more than two England international caps during his career. Both men were similar in style and had loads of time on the ball to sweep 50 yard cross-field passes into the path of the left winger or sliding a defence-splitting pass through the eye of a needle for a forward to take in his stride. It is probable that Stan was better in the air and got into the opposition penalty box more regularly than Haynes. However Johnny was one of the 'Brylcream boys', who advertised the product in every publication at that time. For those of you who are a little younger than me, Brylcream was the equivalent to hair gel today. Haynes was also playing his football in London under the noses of the FA councillors who selected the representative teams in those days. There was only going to be one outcome, Stan Anderson missed out on his fair share of caps. Stan is not one to bear grudges, however, and he can now be found fit and well playing his golf off a single figure handicap in the south Yorkshire town of Doncaster.

The abolition of the maximum wage was a financial milestone in the game and must have focussed the minds of football club directors as the players' salaries were bound to rise which would undoubtedly eat into the bottom line profits which had been in the black for many a year. Previously gate receipts more than covered the outgoings on salaries at most clubs in the Football League. You don't need to be good at maths to know that a 30,000 plus gate at Roker Park, Sunderland or any other stadium up and down the country at that time equalled a huge profit. Where did the money go? Certainly not for the building of new grandstands and stadiums. Despite the tragedy which had occurred at Bolton's Burnden Park in 1946 when 33 supporters were killed in a crush as barriers collapsed under the strain of the massed crowds, there was only a pittance being spent on a minimum of maintenance at most grounds throughout the old Football League, solely and perversely to satisfy local safety and building regulations of the time. The tragic repercussions of this unregulated and blinkered attitude were to surface later at Hillsborough and Bradford in the mid-1980s, along with the Ibrox Park disaster in Glasgow on New Year's Day 1971.

The £100-a-week footballer evolved quickly. In late 1961 Jimmy Greaves cost Tottenham Hotspur £99,000 when he returned from his brief sojourn in Milan. The price was set to ensure Greaves would not suffer from having the tag of being the first £100,000 footballer weighing heavily around his neck. But within a few months that first £100,000 transfer took place when the mercurial Denis Law moved from Manchester City to Torino in the summer of 1961. Law would also become the first man that an English club paid over £100,000 for when he moved back from Italy to Manchester United for £115,000 after just one season overseas.

It would be a while before the first £1 million transfer of a professional footballer would take place, but it eventually happened when Nottingham Forest manager Brian Clough bought Trevor Francis from Birmingham City in February 1979. There is no doubt that this football revolution was the catalyst for the shape of the game as it is today. Maybe they have something to answer for with £20 million now regularly being paid for players who cost nearly as much again in salaries and signing on fees. That inflation has upped the cost of watching top flight football in this country, pricing out and alienating too many supporters.

Sunderland had gone on a brilliant 14 game unbeaten run in the old Second Division from October 1960 through to the New Year, including ten wins in 11 matches. Ian Lawther, the young Northern Ireland international, was in prolific form, netting 14 goals in as many matches, coinciding with the introduction of a huge bull of a boy, the 6 foot tall and 14 stone Scottish youth player Willie McPheat alongside him in attack. Willie displaced the diminutive veteran Ernie Taylor, who had starred for Blackpool in the 1953 FA Cup final, as Alan Brown, known to us all as Bomber, sought to zest up his line up with new blood.

McPheat, who sadly would be denied a long, glittering career through injury after being scythed down by Bobby Collins of Leeds United in August 1962 ending him as a top class player, added drive and youthful energy to the forward line and chipped in with a goal every two games. As you can imagine, with us riding high in the Second Division at this time and the probability in the close season of us all being able to negotiate new contracts, possibly on the back of promotion at the end of the 1960/61 season, morale and anticipation was high.

As a Sunderland first team regular when the ceiling was lifted I was earning the maximum £20 per week, with a bonus of £2 for a win and £1 for the draw. Remember the average weekly wage in Britain at that time was around £15. I appreciated how fortunate I was as my father was still working all hours under a railway wagon on Liverpool docks for £10 per week!

In the end our form slumped and we finished 6th in the table, but one day in early summer 1961 Sunderland's emerging young team were called after training to manager Alan Brown's office at the top of those daunting stairs at Roker Park. We were to learn what sort of new contracts we would be offered for the coming season, the first since the maximum wage was lifted. There was always a hint of menace when climbing the steps to see the manager. Remember, Alan Brown was a fearsome figure and he was unflinching over money matters. As I trod up the stairs to wait my turn I had a figure in my mind, which if he got close to meant I would be happy to put pen to paper on a new contract for another couple of seasons.

Our captain Charlie Hurley, an Eire international, was first into the manager's office ahead of me. Time dragged on as he negotiated his deal, eventually the door opened and out he came. Passing me on the stairs he remarked that he was happy with his deal. I was to hear later on in life it was £80 per week. Nearly five decades on, some of his old team-mates won't be too happy to hear of the salary he negotiated. Meeting up with Charlie in 2008 he told me not to forget to add his appearance money to the basic, sorry chaps!

Following in next to see the manager, I succumbed to the pressure of Alan Brown's presence and threatening tongue, signing a new contract at £40 per week. This did mean I doubled my salary and in addition there was generous appearance money and bonuses on offer. I was actually delighted to have such a substantial increase and was never interested in what others in the team negotiated for themselves. I certainly knew that the majority of my team-mates would be hard pressed to obtain a better contract than mine. I was immovable at left back and so was generously rewarded through my contract's appearance money clause as I missed only a handful of games over the next five seasons.

The first impact of my new contract was that we could afford our own home. A number of players were at this time living in rented, club-owned houses, but during 1961, after Valerie and I were married, I became the second player at the club to purchase his own house after big Charlie Hurley. Our acquisition in Dykelands Road was bought for £2,150. We sold it for £2,300 when I moved to Whitburn in 1964 after picking up a promotion bonus. What a contrast this was compared to how my father, during his bookies runner days all those years ago, had amassed his deposit for our family home in Liverpool!

In fact the increase in wages from 1961 lifted footballers far above the average working man in terms of earning capacity. This meant I felt I had to help my parents in any way I could, so whenever Valerie and I visited my parents' home in Fazakerley I used to leave some cash in amongst the washing up, so when Mum came to wash the dishes after our last meal she would find some paper money. It all started as a mistake after I inadvertently left a five pound note on the kitchen worksurface. Mum thought it was for her and that it had been deliberately placed amongst the dirty dishes by me. So started a game which was played out on every occasion we visited home. After we had said our goodbyes Mum would do the washing up and there, amongst the dishes, was a little something for her. Dad never ever mentioned this loving charade played out between mother and son. He was a proud man and probably felt a little demeaned by the fact that at times in his working life he was not able to provide enough money to keep house and home together. There was no union to fight his cause when he lost his job after forty years working for the same company close to Liverpool docks.

The cash floodgates were now open and many years later all and sundry were stepping through them to fill their pockets and boots. Who would have believed that those early skirmishes between the Football League chairman and the PFA would eventually lead to Frank Lampard earning over £6 million a year and Ricardo Kaka of AC Milan becoming the highest paid player in Europe on £7,458,750 a year? In fact the Brazilian playmaker was doing so well he could afford to turn down the huge wedge on offer from the Arabian owners of Manchester City in January 2009. How times have changed.

5 Old Big 'ead

THE SUMMER of 1961 saw the £48,000 club record signing of centre-forward Brian Clough from Middlesbrough. Clough had been a prolific scorer for the Teesside club, notching 204 goals in just 222 matches. Clough came with a reputation as a barrack room lawyer and the players at Middlesbrough had apparently signed a 'Round Robin' which was handed to the directors of the club with the threat that there would be a dressing room mutiny against the presence of Clough if his ways were not curtailed. The directors decided on the soft option and sold their greatest goalscorer to their arch rivals up the A19.

Despite Clough's presence, Sunderland's season started badly with a 3-4 defeat at Walsall, who had just been promoted from the Third Division. Alan Brown took this defeat very badly and was spitting bricks in the dressing room after the game. He locked the door and verbally slaughtered some of the senior players, new signing Clough included. During his seven year reign at Sunderland Brownie would often provoke a reaction from senior players who he wanted more from, or use the tactic if he had decided to force them out of the club, something I was to experience at a later date.

Brian Clough could be a plausible sort when he wanted to be, but he had a huge ego, as well as an antagonistic attitude towards those he decided he could not abide. He justified his ego with his reputation as a goalscorer, which he made sure went before him. He was tolerated within the Sunderland dressing room as he was going to be our bread ticket. The theory was Clough would score goals and win us matches. As it transpired he notched 34 in 43 games in his first and only full season at the club.

But we still weren't winning regularly enough to challenge for promotion from the Second Division. Five defeats from the first eight games cost us dearly, as in the final game of the 1961/62 season we needed a victory at Swansea Town to win promotion. The match was utterly vital to the outcome of our season and a good deal of controversy surrounded it after Charlie Hurley was approached by a couple of prominent members of the Swansea team he was familiar with. They suggested that because Swansea had nothing to play for they wished to offer us a below par performance and both points in return for some money. Quite rightly the offer was rebuffed by Big Charlie, but we still failed to beat a Swansea team now annoyed at our lack of acceptance of their 'hospitality'. The 1-1 draw cost us promotion by one point, so we returned to Wearside a Second Division club.

For Charlie it must have been a harrowing journey home to the north east, knowing that he had been offered the chance to nod his head and ensure his team would be promoted. I wonder how many times in later life Charlie pondered on what was a lucrative temptation?

A similarly disconcerting experience had occurred only two weeks prior to that Swansea game. On 14 April 1962 we had played away at Luton. Brian Clough, who was captain for the day as Stan Anderson was injured, came in to the dressing room and beckoned a few of the more senior players outside onto the side of the pitch. I was included in his pick. Clough told us he had been approached by a Luton Town player who was prepared to influence the game in our favour for monetary gain and he wanted our opinion. We concluded very quickly that the offer be refused. In my innocence I had thought the football world was straight. This myth was now well and truly shattered. At least we still won this game, 2-1.

Those instances were not the last time that an approach involving opposition players was made to stitch up a game over the next few years. The offers were always rejected. Certainly that was not the case elsewhere. It undoubtedly went on. The Jimmy Gauld match-fixing court case, indicting Peter Swan, Tony Kay and David Layne in season 1963/64, was a prime example of what was happening in the game at that time. It wasn't rife by any means, but it was there below the surface amongst unscrupulous players and, I believe, at board room level.

CHARLIE HURLEY may have been voted 'Player of the Century' by doting Sunderland supporters, while in a previous era Len Shackleton was accepted as the ultimate in skill and entertainment. However for sheer brilliance as a goalscoring centre-forward, as well as being one of the most colourful and extrovert of characters that football has ever seen in bringing unprecedented success to both Derby County and Nottingham Forest as manager, Brian Clough was a one off.

Having heard of Clough's arrival from Middlesbrough in the summer of 1961 it was understandable that two young centre-forwards Nicky Sharkey and Ian Lawther, who had tasted first team football, would be disappointed. Between them they had scored a significant number of goals, but Alan Brown, our inscrutable manager, opted for experience over the promise of youth. Lawther, at 22 years of age, had scored a commendable 44 goals in 83 matches, but was sold to Blackburn Rovers for £18,000 to offset the Clough transfer fee. If only the board had allowed Alan Brown to keep Lawther, what a forward line to choose from, with Nicky Sharkey waiting in the wings. That was another lost opportunity in my book.

Clough soon learned about manager Alan Brown's short fuse, as we stood together in a team group on our Cleadon training ground one bright sunny afternoon shortly after he'd joined the club. Brian and the rest of us were waiting for our instructions from the Bomber for our first pre-season training session. A public path ran parallel with the playing area and a passer by on a bicycle slowed down to get a close up view of our very expensive new player. Being a Sunderland player was always a shared experience with our passionate supporters, who were and still are also one of the team. Any new face joining the club was, in their eyes, an addition to their football family. Clough needed no introduction as he was already an established star with an international pedigree.

"Hello Brian and good luck," the man with the bicycle shouted. Clough without hesitation waved back to his admirer, bringing the odd nudge from some of the lads, and a wink and a nod as the players knew what was coming. The tell tale sign of the level of our manager's annoyance was the size of the throbbing veins on Alan Brown's neck standing out like bloated sausages.

"Brian, can I have your autograph please?" shouted the man.

Cloughie took four steps towards his new admirer, but didn't get any further. Brownie erupted and, with eyes popping, said to Brian, "Go over there, sign his autograph and tell the bloke to bugger off. If he doesn't you can stay and stand with him."

The lads knew the score. Within minutes of pre-season training starting another new addition had found himself in the vice-like grip of discipline that was Alan Brown. Clough was dumbstruck – not something that happened much in his life. His jaw dropped with astonishment. Brownie was determined to imbue his strict discipline on the egotistical star. Later in his football life Brian pronounced that moving from Middlesbrough to Sunderland was "like moving from Butlins to Belsen". The statement,

I think, was rather far-fetched, but we took his point that Alan Brown's ring of discipline remained unbreakable.

I have often wondered if that was the fleeting but significant moment when the Brian Clough we came to know as a disciplinarian manager later in life was shaped. He certainly instituted his own iron discipline and a no nonsense approach to establishing who was in charge at each of his clubs. It was a moment in management which you witness and then can grasp and use it to your advantage. I certainly caught and used that moment in my managerial career!

Brian was a penalty box striker, who rarely ventured out to the wings. He asked for the ball to be put in front or beside him in and around the box and he would do the rest – which invariably he did. He had a short backswing and was blessed with powerful quads that could generate so much power in his shots. That ability was little seen in those days as we never worked with weights.

Clough had scored 34 goals in his first full season for Sunderland as we fell short of winning promotion by failing to win that final game of the campaign at Swansea. The 1962/63 season had begun well, however and by the halfway point, propelled by Clough's goals, we sat in second place, four points behind Chelsea and three ahead of third-placed Plymouth, having beaten Don Revie's Leeds 2-1 at Roker Park in the last game before Christmas. Everything seemed set fair for us to return to the top flight, but fate was about to intervene.

On 26 December 1962 Sunderland hosted fifth-placed Bury, who were leading 1-0. Then came the defining moment in Clough's playing career, indeed life, and a moment in time which finally broke any bond of friendship which may have existed between him and I. I punted a long ball downfield which Clough, quick off the mark as ever, thought he could get to before Chris Harker, the Bury goalkeeper. He didn't quite manage that, and there was a collision which caused Clough to go to ground. In the heat of battle Bob Stokoe, the player-manager of Bury, having no idea of the extent of the injury that Clough had suffered, tried to pull the centre-forward to his feet, while suggesting to the referee that he was feigning injury. Stokoe was far from the truth as the cruciate ligament damage proved to be extremely serious and Brian was carried off on a stretcher.

Not only did we suffer defeat in the aftermath of that sickening collision and injury to our star goalscorer, but Sunderland then lost 0-3 in the reverse fixture at Bury three days later. Almost immediately afterwards the big freeze of 1963 took its icy grip on the entire country. Football ground to a shuddering halt for almost two months as grounds remained unplayable with road and rail routes blocked by snow and ice. If only it had come a week earlier Clough would not have been injured and I am certain we would have won promotion in season 1962/63. Clough had scored 24 goals in 24 matches up to that devastating injury.

After nearly two years of rehabilitation and dedicated work to rebuild his knee, Brian's attempted comeback saw him play his last three games in September of 1964, all at Roker Park. Firstly we drew 2-2 with West Bromwich Albion, then he scored against Leeds United, a goal which proved to be his last for Sunderland, and finally he played against Aston Villa. Far from this being a triumphant comeback, Clough was a footballing physical wreck. His unstable knee was in tatters, with gross wastage of the quads and upper thigh area. In addition his general physical condition was poor after eighteen months of mental torture and overindulgence, which eventually contributed to his downfall later in life. His playing career was over – and Brian did not take it well.

I always felt that Brian partially blamed me for him sustaining his injury. The relationship which we had prior to the Boxing Day incident always hung by a thread. Thereafter we hardly spoke, except for me to enquire of his well being while he was recuperating. Sadly, over the following three years that Brian remained at the club he indicated his dislike for me on a number of occasions, believing that I was a part cause of his career-finishing injury as I had kicked the ball down the field leading to his clash with the opposition goalkeeper. I never felt that he forgave my unwitting role in that incident.

When writing about Brian's demise one can only feel sadness for the man and his family. He was undoubtedly denied a greater place in Sunderland folklore by his injury. In the short time he donned the red and white striped jersey his goal scoring record was astounding. In all competitions he scored 63 goals in only 74 appearances. I would defy anyone to find me a centre-forward in the history of the post-war game who could muster a record of that standing.

Undoubtedly Clough became all the more driven to succeed in management because of the premature curtailing of his playing career. He felt as if the recognition which should rightfully have come his way had been denied him, not least because his fledgling international career was cut short after just two caps. Both Bob Stokoe, who had accused Clough of play acting in the immediate aftermath of the clash, and myself were ostracised, ignored and suffered from Clough's biting tongue.

Whilst recalling Brian's demise as a top class player in the writing of this book my eye caught an obituary in a national newspaper. It was of

Kurt Vonnegut, a satirical writer whose life was shelled with numerous tragedies. He himself as a prisoner of war in an underground bunker survived the fire bombing of Dresden by the Allies in February 1945, which killed 135,000 people. He wrote an account of his experience in *Slaughterhouse-Five* which became a bestseller. His mother was an alcoholic schizophrenic who committed suicide. His father died in dubious circumstances and his son was also a schizophrenic. His sister died of cancer and her husband died in a train crash – now that's what I call tragic! The point I am trying to make here is that a footballer's individual problems pale into insignificance alongside those of life itself, unless they are death-related as in the sad case of Phil O'Donnell the Motherwell captain who collapsed and died on the Fir Park pitch in December 2007.

How can you compare the loss of a football match or even a career in the game against the devastation of losing your entire mobility or life within a split second? In March 2005 Matt Hampson, an England rugby union under-21 international, went down in a scrum at tight head prop at an England training session. The scrum collapsed and Matt has never walked since.

Daniel James was another promising rugby player who suffered similar spinal injuries, rendering him tetraplegic, unable to move any part of his body bar the tips of his fingers. Daniel could not move following his accident and he eventually felt compelled to end his life, describing his condition as being imprisoned inside his body. He committed assisted suicide in a Swiss clinic in September 2008.

Brian Clough not only walked again after his knee injury, he strutted the corridors of professional football at the highest level of his profession.

A postscript to the depths our relationship plunged during Clough's attempted rehabilitation was that I refused to play in his Testimonial game after he had slammed me and the team in a speech to the Sunderland Rotary Club at an event at which I was a guest of the Chairman of that club. I walked out of the room during Clough's tirade at the team and me in particular.

An indication of the disharmony that Clough caused amongst the players was that a majority of them, on hearing of the abuse Brian had given them at the dinner, joined me in refusing to play in his Testimonial. However Brian solved the problem with a generous sweetener offered to all except me. It was in the form of cash-in-hand appearance money – a 'bung' for them to play in his game. Suddenly I was left isolated and especially disappointed that some of my closer colleagues had taken the money above a principle. I lost my first team place because of my stance on that principle, then regained it three games later. Parity, I believe, was restored.

Brian Clough never forgot his working class background. He was born a socialist and a reformer, but with a Tory approach to free enterprise and acquiring wealth. He was also a great admirer of right wing Wolverhampton South West MP Enoch Powell. In many ways I think Clough was actually a capitalist wearing the wrong colours. Brian was rightly proud of his upbringing on Teesside amongst a large family from a working class background. He made sure that during the bitter miners' strike in the mid-eighties he was up front in showing his support towards those he considered his own. His people loved him for these public shows of support for their causes, and Brian, true to those Socialist principles, would continue to do anything he could to help.

Brian made it clear to me he was a staunch Socialist one early winter's day in 1961, during his prolific first season at Roker Park, when he visited me at our home in Dykelands Road, Seaburn. He brushed past my wife Valerie with his usual brash swagger as she opened the front door for him and strode like a flash into the lounge, to stand warming his backside in front of the coal fire. He and I had agreed we should thrash a few problems out as the stand off between us was palpable and as professionals we could not allow our differences to come between the pair of us to such an extent that it would affect the team.

He opened the conversation by talking about his Socialist principles and the hard upbringing he'd had amongst a large family. My father, who was also a staunch Labour man, would have loved to have been in on the conversation, but for me, a Tory supporter, it was falling on deaf ears. I am convinced if he had entered politics as a Labour candidate Clough would have gone to the top of the tree. The Labour half of the country would have loved him. In fact pretty much everyone would have loved him. Eventually I managed to wean him away from the theme and on to the real reason for him being in my house, the clear the air meeting. We tentatively agreed to put our differences behind us for the good of the team and ourselves. An uneasy truce was settled upon and he departed my home, thanking Valerie for the refreshments she had laid on.

An example of Clough's common touch happened during his support for the miners in the 1980s. Whilst he was manager at Forest he joined thousands of pit workers and their supporters on a march one Saturday morning before a big game in the old First Division. As the march passed through a small mining village in the vast Nottinghamshire coal fields, a man in his early twenties shouted over to Clough, "Hey Cloughie, lend me a fiver."

Brian spotted who'd shouted and made to where the man was standing and retorted, "Young man, 'never a lender or a borrower be', William Shakespeare." Clough then turned on his heels and re-joined the march. When Brian had marched further, but was still within earshot, the young man shouted over to him, "Hey Cloughie!" As Brian turned around to locate where the voice was coming from, he continued, "'F**k off', DH Lawrence."

Brian asked Alan Hill for a fiver to give to the young miner for his "bloody cheek." Alan told me he never did get his five pounds back.

Alan also told me another great example of how Clough was a true man of the people. On this occasion he was sitting outside a pub having a beer with Cloughie during a Centurian Walk which they were taking part in to raise funds for an electric wheelchair for a young girl from Nottingham in 1983.

A lad came walking past, "Ay up 'tis Cloughie, in't it?"

"Mr Clough to you, young man."

The boy replied, "OK, Mr Clough, I wondered if I can bring my granddad to see thee?"

"Yes you can, but don't be long," replied Clough.

Ten minutes later the lad returned with his granddad, who was obviously blind, saying to him, "Mind the cow shit, granddad" as he guided the old man round the cowpats on the lane. On reaching the group the boy said, "Granddad, if you reach out your arm you can touch him." On seeing the man was blind Cloughie gave him a huge hug. The man's face lit up.

"I am touching my hero and today is my Golden Wedding anniversary. Will tha come and meet my missis and have a drink with us?"

Brian said he would stop at the pub for another ten minutes, but this turned into two hours as by this time the whole village had learned Cloughie was in there and they all wanted to meet him.

Alan also told me that Clough fell out with Peter Taylor on that same Centurian Walk on the Yorkshire Moors. Staying overnight at a small hotel Alan had rung his wife who had told him that Peter Taylor (who by now had left his job as Clough's assistant at Forest to become manager of Derby County) had signed John Robertson, one of Clough's main players and a left winger who been an integral part of the dual European Cup success and scored the winning goal in the second of those finals. Alan returned to the table and passed the information on to the rest of the party, which included the club doctor, Albert the bus driver and a police inspector. All present were all too well aware that Brian would go barmy when he found out. By this time Brian had already had the news broken to him by his wife Barbara and he came back to the table fuming. In his hand was a full bottle of Bell's whisky. Clough banged it on the table and said, "Do you know what that bastard Taylor has done? He has signed Robbo without even ringing me. After all I have done for him after all these years! I shall never speak to him again."

And he didn't. In actual fact that was something Alan believes that Brian always regretted, especially since Peter Taylor died seven years later without the once inseperable colleagues ever having spoken in that time. Clough once confided in Alan at a later date, "You should always be man enough to make up with a friend and not leave it too late." But Clough did not on this occasion. He attended Peter's funeral and said he was sorry that he had not been man enough to make things up with Peter before he died.

There was a postscript to the Robertson transfer story. When asked to comment by tabloid newspaper journalists Clough told them that he would only give them the true story if they donated wheelchairs to local hospitals. Apparently Alan lost count of the number of chairs that were subsequently donated.

BEN LYONS, a life long Sunderland fan asked the question in the autumn 2007 edition of the club magazine *Legion of Light*. 'Why was Brian Clough never appointed manager of Sunderland?' I can now tell him and thousands of other supporters why he never returned to the club he flirted with for so long. Supporters were never made aware that an approach was made for the maverick Clough not once but twice by Sunderland's board, but on both occasions it was he who was rebuffed because of his outrageous demands.

The first occasion came when, on 1 November 1972, Alan Brown was dismissed after his second spell at the helm and Clough was invited for interview. The board saw this as the opportunity to bring in the people's choice as the new manager. A clandestine meeting was set up by the Chairman Keith Collings at Holmfirth in West Yorkshire at the home of Alan Martin, the son of former director Billy Martin. Other board members in attendance were Jack Ditchburn, the Vice-Chairman, and Ted Evans the son of former Director Lawrie Evans. It was established that Peter Taylor, who was Clough's assistant at Derby County where they had just succeeded in lifting the First Division title, would remain outside the meeting ready to be involved if agreement could be reached between Clough and the board. The meeting opened up with Clough firmly establishing his ground with the board in telling them that the team bus would be out of bounds to the Directors of the club. In addition other demands of his were brought to the table. In Keith Collings' own words, "I was asked for things that I did not think were right." It is said that Peter Taylor's gambling debts were mentioned. Overall the impression left by Brian was not a very complimentary one.

Early on in the meeting Clough was asked by Ted Evans, "what is the most important relationship within a club?"

"That's easy Mr Evans, it is between the manager and the chairman. And I will tell you what, Mr Chairman, if it doesn't work then you're the one to go."

With no common ground between the board and Clough the meeting broke up. Clough had scuppered the opportunity to become manager of Sunderland with his demands and some of his caustic retorts. Ultimately for the Sunderland board this was another lost opportunity although it is difficult to see how they could have appointed Clough after that.

Brian Clough was an old-school manager who ran his club as he wanted to. His attitude was always 'take me as I am and lump it'. He was allowed to function like this by those chairman who enjoyed the success he brought them precisely because the brand of football he produced won unprecedented trophies and brought supporters through the turnstiles.

After Clough had lifted two European Cups, two league titles and four League Cups, a second attempt at bringing him to Sunderland came during Sir Tom Cowie's reign as chairman in the mid-1980s. I am told that Cowie arranged a meeting at a service station in the Midlands with a view to Brian becoming manager of Sunderland Football Club. It is said the meeting lasted less than ten minutes as Cowie found him to be "one of the most arrogant men he had ever met".

Clough turned up late, dressed in a tracksuit in readiness for his afternoon game of squash and made Tom Cowie aware that there would have to be a 'Golden Hello', if you like. The meeting was quickly curtailed.

I have to ask the pertinent question: was Brian Clough ever seriously interested in coming back to Wearside where he was revered as a player? His standing in the game was such that he had made it to the top without him having to prove himself all over again at Sunderland. My personal assertion is that he could not risk another failure like that which he experienced at both Leeds United and Brighton. In the north east he remains and always will be an icon despite the fact his greatest achievements lay elsewhere.

Clough's success is often put down to his unique philosophy and his ability to man manage, keeping his troops fresh and on their toes. The same applied to his backroom staff as well as his players. Alan Hill, who had been a decent goalkeeper in his time at Nottingham Forest, became a trusted friend of Brian's after being recruited to Derby County as Youth Development Officer. On his first day at the Baseball Ground Alan was told by Clough to "Look, listen, learn and ask questions."

One day he decided he would do exactly that.

"Gaffer, what are your thoughts on formations and coaching drills?'

Clough replied, "Don't f****** ask me about formations and coaching."

Alan was taken aback. "But Gaffer you told me to ask questions."

"Aye, I did. On formations: there is only one formation and that is 4-4-2, are you listening? Then what you do is you buy a quality goalie, centre-half and a great centre-forward. Then you get eight other decent players and tell them when the whistle blows to start the game. Then tell them they have to play as one until the referee blows for half time and the same until full time. If you can do that, pal, you won't go far wrong."

On coaching, Clough's pet subject was "don't do any, just let them play. Tell your goalie to stop the ball going through those white posts, tell the centre-half to just head the ball and your two full-backs to just defend. Midfield players pass the ball and if they cannot pass then give it to somebody who can. Centre-forwards? Just score me the goals like I did. That's coaching, so don't ask me any more questions. It has always worked for me." The lesson was over and Alan never asked another question.

A master psychologist, it is said that Clough once negotiated a new contract before one of the many European Cup nights at the City Ground as he walked across the pitch with his Chairman and the gathering crowd started to chant his name as he ambled around the pitch. Clough knew when to put the pressure on and when he had the chairman in his pocket.

I really admired Brian's attitude to gathering wealth as he squeezed every penny out of his employers on the way up and took everything he was entitled to when at the top of his managerial profession. Football is an industry at its worst short on patience and long on ruthlessness, so whilst you are riding high you must make the most of it. Good on you, Brian. I could have learnt a salient lesson from you if we had been on speaking terms!

I shall end my chapter on the late great Brian Clough with a story told to me by then Derby Secretary Malcolm Bramley. In March 1969, Brian Clough's Derby County were closing in on the old Second Division Championship. Malcolm Bramley was a friend of the Reverend John

Tudor, minister of Queens Hall Methodist Mission, a large church near the centre of Derby. Rev Tudor had arranged for a Sportsman's Service to be held at the church and a week before the event he attended a match at the Baseball Ground to meet with Clough and Bramley to discuss final arrangements for the service.

The Directors' Box at the Baseball Ground was close to the dugouts and every word uttered by the managers and coaches could be clearly heard there. During the first half, Clough took exception to a two-footed tackle on a Derby player that went unpunished. He leapt to his feet and bellowed at the linesman, "what's the use of having a bloody flag if you don't wave it?" John Tudor smiled and said, "That's my sermon sorted for the Sportsman's Service".

On the evening of the service, Clough had arranged to pick Bramley up to drive to the church. Ten minutes before the service was due to start there was no sign of Clough. Bramley rang him and he said, "oh f**k, I forgot all about it, give me five minutes". Clough duly arrived at Bramley's house and then drove at high speed to the church. All the parking spaces were taken. Immediately across the road from the church was the Derbyshire Royal Infirmary, so Clough simply parked in the section reserved for ambulances and left a note on his car windscreen saying 'Brian Clough is in the church opposite if you need the car moving. Call me if you dare'.

Clough and Bramley raced over to the church and arrived just as the first hymn was beginning. The church was packed and there was a good turnout from Derby County players, directors and staff, together with various representatives from other sports. When the time arrived for the sermon, John Tudor told the story of Clough screaming at the linesman. "What's the use of having a flag if you don't wave it?" He then proceeded to give a wonderful sermon based on the theme 'what's the use of having a church if you don't talk about it, what's the use of having a faith if you don't show it?'

As the sermon finished, Clough leant forward and said to Reverend Tudor as he sat back down. "Vicar, that was f**king magnificent". What Brian didn't realise was that he had spoken near to the microphone, so the whole of the congregation heard his words.

There was a deathly silence . . . and then, suddenly, applause broke out. It must have been the only occasion ever that a church congregation has applauded someone for swearing in church! It was certainly one of the very few occasions anyone can remember Clough looking embarrassed. But away from the microphone he confided to Bramley: "Dropped a bollock there didn't I? Oh f**k it, they all think I'm God anyway!"

When the service ended, Clough apologised to Reverend Tudor for his bad language, put his hand in his back pocket and produced £100 in notes. "Here John, put that in your swear box."

We may not have seen eye to eye for much of our professional life together, but there is no doubting Brian Clough was an incredible man.

6 **Psycho**

23 DECEMBER 1961 was the day my school sports master Idris Jones' words sprang vividly to mind. It was a pivotal moment for me as I ran out at Stoke City's Victoria Ground to play directly against the legendary Stanley Matthews, 'The Wizard of Dribble.' I was thrilled to be given the opportunity to play against the great man, but regrettably the experience did not turn out to be a happy one. This was the same man who I had watched on our black and white television screen destroy Bolton Wanderers eight years earlier in that pulsating, never to be forgotten Wembley Cup Final of 1953, the same year as the Queen's Coronation, Sir Gordon Richards winning his first Derby, the ascent of Everest, England's Ashes and, in football, a record seventh League Championship to Arsenal. In addition Matthews had been feted in becoming the footballer chosen to appear on the front page of the inaugural *Charles Buchan's Football Monthly* in September 1951, which sold at 1/6 (7.5p in today's money). It was so popular with the football public that the publication ran for 20 years.

I recalled Idris Jones' words of nearly a decade earlier telling all our school team to go to Goodison Park to watch Matthews play against Everton as it could be the last time we might have the opportunity. It was understandable that he should encourage us for what he thought would be Stanley Matthews' final Merseyside appearance, as it turned out he was about 12 years out in making that sweeping statement.

Nicky Sharkey was Sunderland's twelfth man on that day and takes up the story.

"It was a very hard playing surface and although it was an afternoon game the temperature was close to freezing. I was the 'Bagman' on this particular day and was looking forward to seeing Stan Matthews play. My vision of him was of an old man of nine stone wet through. He looked like a bag of bones, had stilted spindly legs and wore a jersey that looked twice as big as it should have been.

Within the first ten minutes Stanley tried to take Len on the outside. My recollection of the incident was of a shout or more of a squeal. Then I saw Stan flying through the air and landing on the cinder track in front of the Boothen Stand paddock. Len once again had nailed his prey.

Stan hobbled around for the remaining 35 minutes of the first half and then did not come out for the second half. My vivid recollection was of the team bus waiting to depart and being stoned by a few hundred angry Stoke City supporters. We certainly had to run the gauntlet that night. Len had a lot to answer for."

After the game was over Mum, Dad and my brother Albert were waiting outside the ground for me. There was no players lounge for families and friends as there is today. As I came out of the dressing room into the cold winter's air there was the usual clamour for autographs, but there was also a hostile atmosphere towards me for putting Stanley out of the match. I vividly remember Mum grabbing one of the youngsters' autograph books and writing, 'I am Len Ashurst's Mum. Best Wishes, Elsie.' I wish I could trace that autograph book today. Dad wasn't best pleased at what had happened to Matthews as I had denied him the opportunity to watch his son play against the great international legend, the 'ageless wonder' who was Stanley Matthews.

Worse, the game ended in a 0-1 defeat for us despite having a man advantage for most of the 90 minutes. In fact I was not proud at all at the way I had treated Sir Stanley and the guilt has remained with me to this day.

Stanley was knighted in 1965, whilst still playing in the First Division in his 50th year. He had played his first game for Stoke City in 1932 and ended his amazing 33 year football career when he appeared in Stoke's colours for the final time against Fulham on 6 February 1965, five days after his 50th birthday, his team winning 3-1. He had obviously fully recovered from his altercation with me in the December of 1961.

The Matthews incident could be linked in with another one of my moments of youthful petulance a year previously. It was in September of 1960 away at Portsmouth and involved a press photographer by the side of the goal that Sunderland were defending. Our goalkeeper Peter Wakeham could not take his full run up because of the photographer sitting on a small stool in line with Wakeham's path. Despite numerous requests he refused to move. I then lost patience and my composure, pushing him off his stool and flinging it up the running track surrounding the pitch. Then, using the strap on his camera for leverage, I slung it high in the air on to the field of play! There were no digital cameras in those days and as the camera bounced on to the edge of the penalty box twenty yards away it fell apart with bits and pieces, including his photo plates, flying everywhere.

I had lost my rag, which cost me a booking from the referee for ungentlemanly conduct. We also lost that game 1-2, to register our first defeat of that 1960/61 season. In addition I was fined by Brownie, who was near to violence towards me in the dressing room after the game, probably more because of the defeat than the camera incident. Knowing The Bomber, if he had been faced with a similar situation he would probably have done the same himself! I also had to pay the costs of new equipment for this freelance photographer.

'Ashurst and McNab' slips nicely off the tongue. I am often reminded by former colleagues and adversaries that there was no tougher pair of left-sided players in the game at that time. I do feel that does not do us justice as we could play a bit as well and, after all, tackling was and still is the basis of a defender's job.

We were 100% committed to our cause, as were our supporters, whose devotion to the team and its colours was bordering on an addiction. One day these two incredible forces collided. It was a Friday morning before a matchday and we were one short for a casual five-a-side game at our Cleadon training ground. Charlie Hurley asked a bystander by the name of Derek Watson loitering on the public pathway by the pitches, if he would make the numbers up. The bloke was stunned to be involved and started tearing around trying to make an impression on us. With a game the next day we kept the ball moving and kept well out of his way. That was until this guy tackled Jimmy McNab – hard. Of all of us the fan had certainly chosen the wrong one to pick on. A few moments later Watson was nursing a swollen knee cap and needing medical attention. That was Jimmy, God bless him!

It was very rarely sweetness and light in training as Alan Brown demanded the best from his players in everything. There was never a quiet five-a-side when the likes of Johnny Crossan, an assassin-in-waiting, and McNab, who was always happy showing his colours, were around. With them, Ashurst, Irwin and right-half Martin Harvey, who did not flinch a tackle either, flinging themselves around, Hurley, as the artist, generally stepped aside and watched his team-mates drawing blood!

There was licence in those days to give a bit of a kicking in games to those speedy wingers who were giving you the runaround as referees were a lot more lenient. Back in the Sixties, of course, the laws of the game gave you licence to tackle from the back, side and the front. Thank goodness I was a full-back, much easier to give it out than to avoid it, especially when the ball was between myself and the opposing forward! They call it a 'fifty-fifty' ball, but such challenges usually ended up with my victim suffering at least an ankle or a leg injury to the delight of my doting Roker Park supporters. To be honest the rules of the game in those days offered a near licence to kill!

Having since retirement met some of those players who manfully took the treatment I dished out, I have occasionally felt a pang of shame when reminded of the injustice of the physical contact of yester year when the laws of the game were couched all in favour of the defender. I was pleased to find my adversaries were all in one piece when we met up. I can also take solace from the fact that I was never sent off and additionally have never ended anyone's career with a tackle. Very few footballers continue to hold a grudge against their fellow professionals and if they do then they are probably not worth their salt. The one exception to that rule should be when an injury was inflicted by a premeditated and a deliberate career-finishing attack.

They were very different times and ones in which it was accepted that the physical side of the game was far more acceptable than it is today.

HAVING WOUND down his career with two, largely unsuccessful, seasons at Sunderland in the late 1950s, Don Revie returned to Roker Park as player-manager with Leeds United on 8 October 1960. Brownie, who had taken something of a dislike to Revie during his time at Sunderland, wound us up before the game and specifically picked out Revie for personal attention. "Whoever is closest to him . . ." was the way he ordered us to deal with him. Jimmy McNab and Len Ashurst would not disappoint our manager. Very early on in the game, somehow my over-exuberance found my left boot hovering a few inches from Don Revie's face as he lay on the ground in front of the main stand by the players' tunnel. He had gone down in a tackle from my fellow assassin Jimmy McNab, who had taken him off by the knee. A snap decision was required; do I engage, as the consequences would inevitably result in scarring Don Revie for life as well as me being sent off? I went against the immediate impulse coursing thorough my veins and pulled away, much to the disappointment of a packed house at Roker Park and probably to the annoyance of Alan Brown.

In fact that went a bit against the grain. By now I was 21 years-old and amongst opposition players I had become known as 'psycho', a turn of phrase used latterly for a complete and utter head banger. My tackling was ferocious to the extreme, I had no fear and was not averse to confrontation on the field of play. In fact I probably thrived on it as I wanted to win so badly.

The hatred which had developed between Don Revie and Alan Brown during the former Manchester City centre-forward's time at Roker had come to a head in an acrimonious clash between the two men in November 1958. We were playing an away league game at Rotherham United early in our first season after relegation as Brown sought to build a new team hungry for the fight. In the euphoria of a rare 4-0 away victory Revie had chosen his moment to ask the Bomber if he could go off to see some relations locally and not travel back on the team bus with the rest of the players. Alan Brown flatly refused, probably knowing he would provoke a reaction from Revie, as was often his wont. A verbal slanging match ensued at which stage Revie lost it. He pushed Brown into a corner of the dressing room and as the two of them traded blows, Stan Anderson who had not played in the match because of injury, Don Kitchenbrand and Charlie Hurley dived into the action and eventually parted them. Revie unwittingly got his wish to see his relations granted as Brownie immediately banned him from the team bus, the club and heavily fined him.

In fact Revie was never to wear a Sunderland jersey again as he got the job as player-manager at Leeds, where he would build a dynasty and become incredibly successful, shortly afterwards. Brown and Revie were to face each other on numerous occasions in the future with their respective teams.

Brown was a hard man, something which all the players had confirmed to them, if they didn't fully realise it already, when, after having dealt with Revie in the Millmoor dressing room, with blood splattered all over his face, he faced the speechless players: "If anyone else starts any trouble then you know what you will get."

He departed the dressing room, slamming the door behind him, at which point the players erupted in laughter and incredulity at what we had all just witnessed. Colin Grainger, a man of dry wit and a left winger of little physical notoriety with famously good looks unspoilt by much physical contact, broke the ice with a famous line: "I was just about to get stuck in to him when you lads stepped in."

Whilst in the Second Division for those six seasons in the late 1950s and early 1960s, Sunderland visited many towns like Rotherham which had a local industry unique to themselves. Scunthorpe United was for steel, Stoke City was the Potteries, Grimsby Town had its fishing port (and a pair of kippers given to you after the game), and Ipswich Town and its surroundings yielded beer hops as well as agriculture. Then there was Lincoln City for the potato industry, Liverpool for its humour and musical talent, while Middlesbrough boasted the massive ICI plant and associated chemical industry. All of these places had decent football stadiums. Except Rotherham. The Millers' ground, called Millmoor, was a whole different, stark world to me. On three sides behind the terraces steel mills spewed smoke and industrial particles into the air throughout the game. Behind the fourth terrace a busy railway line carried a freight train, belching steam and smoke, past the stadium every few minutes.

Even worse were the dressing rooms, bath facilities and toilets. A primitive bathing and shower facility sprayed you with brown-stained water, which could be either freezing cold or scalding hot, and would swing intermittently and without warning between the two. It was also the only ground that I can remember that had all the players' toilets outside the dressing room, along a cold concrete path towards the terraces so you were open to the elements as you ran the gauntlet of abuse in the Yorkshire accents of the home supporters: "Going for a shit? You are shit yourself . . ." and so on. Toilet paper was a sheaf of newspaper torn up and hung as loo roll, I never checked, but I doubt that it was *The Times* or the *Telegraph*.

Alan Brown had an irrational hatred of us playing golf. If he knew we had arranged a game he would keep us back for afternoon training. Conversely if he heard that we had been playing golf then he would call the culprits upstairs and verbally wipe the floor with you. I cannot ever remember the team having a game of golf which had been organised by Brownie and his staff. At most other football clubs this was a regular, or at least annual, occurrence.

One day Dickie Rooks, Martin Harvey, Ian Lawther and I were playing Whitburn Golf Club. As we were playing the back nine a four ball of elderly gents were walking down the fairway parallel to us. Dickie Rooks, a jovial lad who played golf like he played centre-half, all muscle and brawn with average ability, hit a fairway wood off at a right angle. The ball flew towards the old boys, ricocheted around their golf trolleys, then ended up back on our fairway 60 yards in front of us. The boys, including myself, were convulsed in laughter and we apologised, thinking no more of it. Imagine our surprise then when we finished our round and found on our return to the club house two senior members of the committee waiting to tell us to leave the course immediately and never to return.

That was in the days when there was a waiting list at golf clubs and a joining fee to pay – that is if you got past the 'Black Ball' system that existed not only at golf clubs but also many other closed organisations where membership was to be kept exclusive. Worryingly for us if a letter to Brownie had arrived at the football club we would have been in deep trouble, so we issued copious and grovelling verbal apologies and drafted a personal letter to the gentlemen who we had put the shits up and it was quickly posted off. Thankfully Brownie remained unaware of the incident, so we got away with it.

To a certain extent the hatred of golf was merely an extension of Brown's tendency to want to control everything and everyone. There were plenty of other examples. Harry Hooper, a former England 'B' cap signed from Birmingham City, was a fantastic footballer who oozed class, but he fell foul of Brownie's zero tolerance stance on not toeing the line. He liked to live the life and Brownie didn't appreciate that. Harry was a good-looking fellow who was to be sometimes found in the medical room when a female star appearing at the Empire Theatre, Sunderland was in for some treatment from club physiotherapist Johnny Watters. On this particular occasion it was ballerina Dame Margot Fontaine who was taking advantage of the facilities and there was Harry sitting on the end of the medical plinth flexing his quads as Fontaine watched in amusement. She knew the score and had seen plenty of this kind of behaviour all before I'm sure. I imagine her choice was vast! I thought, 'Harry you're not tilting at this one are you?' He was, and he failed.

I think that Harry had a raw deal at Sunderland. He was constantly left on the sidelines by Brownie, being replaced by the young Jimmy Davison and eventually by Brian Usher, who, surprisingly for one so young, did an excellent job in our promotion season of 1963/64.

Harry wasn't alone in living in fear of being on the sharp end of Alan Brown's tongue. All the staff and most of the players were frightened to death of the manager, so much so that not one player dared to tell him over a long period of time that he had a piece of cotton hanging down from the back of his light coloured mackintosh. Whenever we met at the railway station or were getting on the team bus there it was dragging along the floor as he walked away from you. It was a constant source of amusement to the lads and remained that way for months until one day it disappeared, his wife Elsie had obviously dealt with it.

Reflecting back to that dressing room mix of young and experienced professionals at that time, I was probably looked upon as an 'Odd Bod'. I was into antiques, hardly a normal pursuit for a footballer. Along with my colleague, experienced left-winger Jackie Overfield, I was often rushing off to a house sale around the Sunderland area to buy pieces of silver and antique furniture. In addition I was into stocks and shares and was a member of one of the earliest Investment Clubs in the country, formed at the old Roker Hotel by Jack Parker, one of the directors of the football club, along with several local Sunderland businessmen.

I also made the most of any spare time we were given when on away trips. It was nearly always an overnight stop when playing away from home, so I made sure that time was used to my advantage. When in the capital I sought out my former Liverpool Schoolboys manager Tom Parry at his London suburb home to inquire of his welfare and to say 'Thank You' for the start he had given me in 1953. Tom was in good health and was thrilled to see me as he had followed my career to date.

For me London was a feast of culture with galleries and the theatre. I particularly enjoyed the National Gallery in Trafalgar Square or the British Museum in Great Russell Street. As a cultural contrast there was also the occasional trip to the White City for a greyhound meeting, a case of letting your hair down after a Saturday afternoon match against one of the London clubs. A visit to a night club would then also be on the agenda. For players nowadays it would more likely be a Tapas bar followed by an evening at a pole dancing club! Not for us. Before we left the hotel we would be forcefully reminded by our manager of our standing in the game and society. In addition we had a train to catch next morning at 9am prompt, a journey that took all of six hours on a Sunday.

Museums and churches were visited around the country. I was particularly fond of Exeter and Lincoln cathedrals. Liverpool has two magnificent cathedrals, the Anglican and the wonderful Catholic buildings, which, much later, held the solemn remembrance service for the Liverpool supporters who were tragically killed in the 1989 Hillsborough disaster. On that occasion great credit went to manager Kenny Dalglish who held his composure throughout the service and was a credit to himself, his family and Liverpool Football Club. I also visited the city's Walker art gallery. Plymouth had its famous Hoe, Swansea the Gower Peninsula. However not every city had delights to offer. Nottingham, Leicester and Derby, for example. I had no wish to venture out and stayed put in the hotel. Back then there was no statue of Brian Clough in the centre of Nottingham to draw the crowds.

My team-mate George Herd also made use of the away trips, although in an entirely different fashion. He took bets on himself being able to walk down the stairs to the hotel foyer on his hands. Many supporters will remember his back flips and hand springs in celebration of winning promotion against a stubborn Charlton team at Roker Park in April 1964.

George had a particular way of setting some unsuspecting mug up for a bet. At the top of the staircase he would wobble disconcertingly until his victim was convinced that he would never get down to the bottom without collapsing. He never did and often would put his act on two or three times in the space of 30 minutes winning his bet each time! Sometimes there would be other Football League teams staying at the hotel. This was right up George's street as the gullible footballer is often ready to part with his money on ridiculous bets.

Another way I stood out from my team-mates was that whilst the lads read the *Mirror* and the *News of the World*, I constantly had my nose in the pink *Financial Times*. In fact to this day I still prefer *The Times* to the tabloids. Hardly the reading matter of a 'Psycho', you might think, but then I was mellowing and maturing by that stage. After all I was a senior member of a team with serious promotion ambitions to pursue.

7 The Nearly Men

O N THE football front a promising young Sunderland team was being knitted together at Roker Park by Alan Brown and a game that I vividly remember from that time came at Leeds Road, the then home of Huddersfield Town, on 8 December 1962. Jim Montgomery's famous double save at Wembley in 1973 has never been bettered, however, in my opinion, that day in Yorkshire Jim gave the most compelling overall goalkeeping performance I have ever witnessed. Huddersfield centre-forward Len White would, I am sure, testify to this as he held his head in disbelief at Monty's shot-stopping heroics. Shots and crosses from all angles and distances were kept out. However my abiding memory is of the three close range shots by White from inside the six yard area which Jimmy parried to safety as we enjoyed a 3-0 win.

Montgomery's introduction into the team was a decision taken by Alan Brown under duress, as pressure was exerted by captain Stan Anderson to replace Peter Wakeham, the previous incumbent, between the sticks. The manager was forced to concede that Monty should be in the side, and for Brownie this was a rare occurrence! Jim proved through time that it was a brave and correct decision and, who knows, if the change had been made sooner in the season then promotion may well have been achieved earlier than it eventually came along.

Brian Clough scored two of the three goals in the victory at Huddersfield and left-winger George Mulhall, who had joined the club at the start of this season from Aberdeen, netted the other. Johnny Crossan also played in the game after signing from Standard Liege a month before. That victory left us in second position in the Second Division table at the halfway point in the season. We were three points behind leaders Chelsea, but one ahead of Stoke in third and Bury in fourth. With such quality players assembled by Brownie, we had not been in a stronger position to sustain a major promotion challenge since relegation from the top flight in 1958 – that was until Boxing Day arrived, three games after victory at Huddersfield, and that career ending injury robbed us of Brian Clough.

An unusual, staged bonus had been put in place for the players at the start of season 1962/63. It was based on the team being in a promotion spot after each group of ten games in the season, growing by £250 each time. Being in fourth position on each occasion meant we missed out on £250 each after the first ten matches and another £500 after the second batch of games. Our 29th league game of the season was against Norwich City at Roker Park and by now we had got ourselves into second spot. As this was a game in hand we knew that a win would guarantee we'd be in the top two at the end of our 30th game on the Saturday at Grimsby, which of course meant we were playing for an extra £750 bonus against the Canaries.

Once again the dark side of football emerged from the woodwork as before the match one of the Norwich City players approached Charlie Hurley and I in the players' corridor. They had heard we were to receive this huge bonus if we took the two points and this particular player was suggesting to Chas that a number of the Norwich City team would be prepared to throw the game for some remuneration. Not for the first time Charlie was confronted with a dilemma of principle and once again in front of me an agitated captain refused to accept to bend.

After Clough's injury three months beforehand young striker Nicky Sharkey had been reinstated to the team which was still fighting on three fronts, having also reached the FA Cup fifth round and the League Cup semi-final. Frankly the way things had panned out merely fired us up further for a match we were already desperate to win, for the two points on offer which would take us closer to promotion as much as the money. 42,393 spectators at this evening game saw us hammer Norwich, who had won their previous three games 6-0, 5-0 and 2-1, by the incredible score of 7-1. It was a sublime performance against a team which plainly couldn't be bothered after we had rebuffed their offer and Nicky Sharkey made history by equalling the club's all time record of five goals in a game.

The irony was that Nicky, for some reason, had not signed the bonus agreement between player and club at the start of the season, and so consequently was not due to receive the extra bonus that all of the other players were entitled to. He was promised the bonus in a new contract for the coming season. It never materialised and in essence he is still owed the money on principle. Now that would be a gesture 45 years on! He tells me the match ball, which he kept in honour of his feat, has had an offer made upon it for £3,000! He is tempted.

As the season wore on Stoke City came strong and would eventually be crowned champions with 48 year-old Stanley Matthews incredibly scoring the goal which clinched their promotion and the title, while we went on a run of just two wins in the next ten games. Three successive wins, against Southampton, Swansea and Luton, sent us to the top of the table. However we now had only one game remaining. We were one point ahead of Stoke, who had two games in hand, and four ahead of Chelsea, who had two games remaining but a far better goal average. As it happened the fixture list presented another dramatic twist as our final game of that season saw us entertain Chelsea at Roker Park needing only a draw to send us into the First Division.

Tommy Docherty, the manager of Chelsea, gambled by playing the huge mountain of a man called Frank Upton, normally a centre-half, at centre-forward to unnerve our defence and Charlie Hurley in particular. The ploy succeeded as Upton caused chaos at a first half corner and the ball bounced across the six yard box to hit little Tommy Harmer in his 'privates' and dribble over the line for the only goal of the game.

Try as we might we couldn't force an equaliser which would have guaranteed promotion. For the second successive season in a row we had failed to get the last ditch results which would have seen us into the First Division.

Harmer had recently moved from Spurs to Chelsea for £20,000. When asked after the game by the press what he thought of his new signing as a player the Doc, never a man lost for words, replied: "I'm not sure what I think of him as a player but I do know one thing and that is at the moment he has got the most expensive pair of bollocks in football."

8 **Back in the Big Time**

SUNDERLAND'S 1963/64 promotion team had a steely mental attitude which had been ground into us over the previous experiences of the past three or four seasons when we had missed out so narrowly on promotion. That attitude demanded that we win. Money was never a prime mover. We knew we would receive our rewards if we earned it out on the pitch. As if to prove that point the directors tightened up our contract for the new season by writing in a bonus of £1,000 per man to be paid only if we won promotion. There was to be no staged performance bonus for this season.

Alan Brown continued to tinker with his team which had come so close over the previous two campaigns and during August 1963 Stan Anderson, our talisman and tactically astute captain, was sensationally transferred to arch rivals Newcastle United, the deal being concluded shortly after the season got under way. Stan had been at the club for more than a decade, making a club record 447 appearances in the red and white shirt. Brownie had once more seen off another senior professional who he wanted to replace with a younger player. In this case the starlet was Martin Harvey, while Charlie Hurley took over the permanent captaincy of the team. The team now had an average age in the mid-twenties, when that which had ben relegated five years earlier had been closer to thirty.

We began the season well, winning six out of the first eight games, and drawing one of the others. Our only defeat in that sequence was an inexplicable 0-2 loss at home to Northampton Town, a team who we would gain revenge on by knocking them out of the FA Cup at the third round stage.

We then stumbled, not winning in four, including being knocked out of the League Cup at the first stage by Swansea. In many ways that defeat allowed us to concentrate on picking up vital league points, rather than looking forward to rounds of the cup as we had the previous season when our campaign had lasted until the semi-final in April.

A spurt of four wins on the trot took us to the top of the table in mid-October. My personal contribution to the team that season was that I played in every game throughout the promotion campaign, including six FA Cup matches and that League Cup tie at Swansea. Montgomery, Crossan and Mulhall would also be ever present.

In addition, during that run of victories in October, my goal against arch rivals Newcastle United in a 2-1 win was professionally satisfying, as we were down to ten men with Hurley off the pitch having stitches inserted in a head wound at the time. I can now honestly reveal that the free-kick from some 30 yards out was an intended cross into the penalty box. Not only that but the goal was scored with a borrowed left boot. I was playing with a broken toe and so needed a larger, size eight left boot, which I borrowed from one of the lads. Charlie, having not witnessed the goal, refused to believe that I had scored. Even to this day he has his doubts! Could someone dig out some archive footage from somewhere?

Our desire to win was insatiable – never better exemplified than by us getting the better of our bitter rivals Leeds United during the course of that season. We drew 1-1 at Elland Road in a fierce encounter on Boxing Day and then won 2-0 at Roker Park two days later.

When Leeds United were mentioned on Wearside during the sixties and early seventies there would inevitably be an immediate intake of breath. The two clubs were fierce rivals for nearly a decade, culminating in that unforgettable FA Cup final battle in 1973, which Sunderland under Bob Stokoe won 1-0. Whenever the clubs met during that period there was high anticipation at the guarantee of controversy, excitement and invariably a hatful of bookings plus a sending off or two. More importantly, on show would be a multitude of committed and talented footballers.

It was common belief within the game at that time that Leeds under Don Revie were imbued on the training ground with the will and ability to 'look after themselves' on a football field. Well, we were up for the fight. In fact the two games over the 1963 festive season were near blood baths. The Elland Road fixture was played on a rock hard, frozen pitch, so all of the players decided to nail longer, leather-capped discs on to the soles of their boots then file and cut away a couple of layers of leather so exposing the nails for the dual purpose of a more secure grip on the surface and inflicting some damage on the opposition. This task could only be completed after the boot inspection by the match referee, who at that time came in to the dressing room ten minutes before kick-off to check that footwear was legal. Once he had departed, the room became akin to a cobbler's workshop as feverish activity with hacksaws and files took place.

At Elland Road there was a concrete surface in the passageway leading on to the field of play. As we departed the changing room all the Sunderland team were scuffing their feet on the rough concrete floor to further expose the nails through the leather stud. Leeds' players were doing the same. What followed over the ninety minutes was open warfare between two highly charged and passionate teams. The aftermath of a 1-1 draw was gruesome, with all twenty outfield players having lacerations from ankle to thigh. If the pitch had been a battleground then both treatment rooms looked like a wartime casualty ward after 90 minutes.

The return game at Roker Park two days later was just as fierce a tempestuous, bitter battle. At 2-0 up with minutes remaining Jimmy McNab tackled and 'finished off' Leeds's right-winger Jim Storrie, who had flown into a tackle trying to 'do' McNab. As Storrie lay on the stretcher surrounded by his team-mates he asked Bremner, who was itching for a fight with the perpetrator, "What happened?"

Bremner retorted in typically gruff Scots, "three things, Jimma pal. You chose the wrong bloke, you were too late in the tackle ..."

"What's the third one, Billy?" asked Storrie.

"You're f***** for the rest of the season."

With minutes to go in the game everyone within earshot saw the funny side of Bremner's comment. This incident caused quite a bit of mirth at Leeds United's training ground during the following weeks as the usually relatively tranquil Storrie's first attempt to be a 'hitman' ended up with him in casualty.

Billy Bremner, never one to be bowed, had his own back in the dying seconds of the game, although interestingly not on the perpetrator of Storrie's injury, but on me. The opportunity arose when he spotted me coming in to him on the halfway line to win the ball from behind. He backheeled the ball and in the process left six studs facing into my inner thigh. He drew blood – lots of it. The six inch scar remains to this day. But all was fair in love and war and the injury didn't keep me out of our next game. In my opinion Bremner did not need the dark side to his game as he was such a talented player. But he was also the toughest competitor you could ever come up against, never asking or giving any quarter.

Three points from those two games against Leeds left us on 36 points from 26 games, just a point behind the Yorkshire club at the summit of the table going into the New Year, but level on points with Preston North End, who would prove to be our main rivals for one of the two places on offer which would take us back into the First Division.

In addition to pushing for promotion we also went on a six-match FA Cup run, reaching the quarter-finals. Having seen off both Northampton Town and Bristol City in the early rounds, the fifth round draw paired us with Everton at Roker Park in February 1964. We hadn't had much success at Goodison Park over the years, so it was imperative that we settled the cup tie at home. As it was Everton we were playing, I was reminded of my younger brother Robin who had made the front page of the Liverpool Echo in 1962 with a young man's prank on the night before a Merseyside derby game between Everton and Liverpool.

Robin with his pals from the pub: 'Chips' Hines, Tommy 'the Print' Donnelly and 'Taffy' Griffiths, who were all mad Liverpool supporters, decided that they would climb into Goodison Park over the wall near to the church of St. Luke. Their mission? To paint the goalposts Liverpool red. A full tin of Cardinal Red paint was produced from the Ashursts' garden shed. This was the first league derby game in 12 years between these two teams from opposite ends of the religious spectrum due to both of them having had spells in the Second Division, so it was a massive match, surrounded by hype and anticipation on Merseyside. If the prank were successful it would make its perpetrators celebrities across the city.

As they climbed the wall under the cover of darkness the lads realised, on hearing voices coming from close by, that they were not the only spirited supporters around. It took a while for them to realise it, but these fellow Scousers had already taken up station on the St. Luke church roof overlooking the ground, bagging a great vantage point from which to watch the game the next day. Robin and his buddies eventually made it inside the ground and managed to paint the goalposts and crossbar at both ends of Goodison Park in the red of Liverpool Football Club. Sadly the local paper was only printed in black and white at the time, so the photograph which featured on the front of 22 September's *Liverpool Echo* does not reveal the true level of the desecration Robin and his fellow pranksters managed to inflict on Everton. However, it did, predictably, cause total uproar!

Bill Shankly's response to a local journalist who questioned him on the incident was, 'it seems like psychological warfare to me.'

With the game stirring up interest not only on Merseyside but throughout the country, it was to be a match that was covered on national radio and television. Commentator Kenneth Wolstenholme, who three years later would be making football history at the World Cup final at Wembley, was heard to remark to his TV audience, "If you think the goalposts are an off white, they are in fact pink, as some Liverpool supporters climbed into the ground overnight and daubed them with red paint." The groundstaff's frantic efforts to restore the natural white colour had not been entirely successful!

Incidentally the match which all Merseyside had waited a long time for ended up a 2-2 draw.

Robin was always a bit of a scamp – a rabid lifelong Liverpool supporter, made poor financially by his blood-red commitment to his team. One such an occasion was the European Cup semi-final in May 1965. Robin, who was then in his early twenties, bunked off work without telling the Gaffer and hitch-hiked all the way to Milan, arriving on the morning of the game. Once there he was spotted close to the stadium by a Liverpool reporter who, on hearing the story of the intrepid traveller, took his photograph and duly relayed it back to the *Echo* offices, where they made a splash of it in the evening paper. Robin was befriended by a local couple, taken back to their home and provided with a ticket for the game. Yes, he'd travelled all that way without one!

Liverpool had built a 3-1 advantage from the first leg, but Milan turned the deficit over with a 3-0 win to go through to the final 4-3 on aggregate.

On his return to work Robin was invited into the Boss's office and, although giving a convincing pack of lies as a cover, which included a doctor's sick note, his story was blown apart when his boss produced the paper with the photograph of him on the back page. Nice try, Robin!

Speaking of Scouse wags, Jimmy Tarbuck, who is still going strong as a fine entertainer today, was a big draw in the sixties and, along with my pal from our early Liverpool Football Club days Stan Boardman, who had also been a trainee, arrived on the Friday before our FA Cup tie with Everton at Roker Park in February 1964 and asked to train with the team. Stan was and still is a real Scouser, while Tarbuck has been living in the South for most of his life and mixing with a different set of people than he left behind on Merseyside. Jimmy is still a Scouser at heart like Stan and can be seen at Anfield and elsewhere watching Liverpool. Being Liverpool born I was thrilled to see them in the flesh, as I had moved to Wearside and had missed that great era when Liverpool produced a host of entertainers for screen and stage.

Tracksuits and kit were produced for the pair of them and the boys had a kickabout with the two stars of stage and small screen. Boardman had been in the same 'C' team with me at Liverpool, so was not a bad player at all, but he spent the entire training session bombarding us with Liverpool humour. He regaled all who were listening with tales of sharing a bath with me after training at Liverpool's Melwood training ground, telling them, much to my embarrassment, that he used to stick his big toe up my arse as we sat in a bath for two after training.

The Everton cup tie was won with great difficulty 3-1 with McNab, Hurley and an own goal from Dubliner Mick Meagan. My father was amongst the 62,851 spectators who packed the ground. He thoroughly enjoyed his weekend. The result was a double treat for my Dad for, as a Liverpool fan, he had taken numerous bets from his Everton pals back home on Merseyside.

When the FA Cup draw was made many years ago it was only broadcast on the radio. It was alleged that Sam Bolton, the chairman of Leeds United, used to put the black ball with his club's number on into the freezer overnight to make sure it was pulled out as a home draw. I don't know if it's true, but a stat for you is that between 1963/64 and 1967/68 Leeds came out at home in 12 out of 16 FA Cup draws. Syd Collings our chairman was at FA Headquarters to make the sixth round draw in 1964. He obviously did not have a trick up his sleeve as he drew out his own club Sunderland at . . . Cup holders Manchester United.

We were not daunted at the task, however, and played superbly well at Old Trafford. In fact my memory of this 3-3 draw and the two subsequent replays entitles me to call the game the 'Match of My Life.' We took the lead through a George Mulhall header just before half-time, and then went 2-0 up when Johnny Crossan netted straight after the restart. This was now dream territory, although we were brought back to earth when a harmless-looking cross came into the box and both Jim Montgomery and Charlie went up for it. Charlie actually beat Monty to it and flicked the ball past him. I remember standing near the edge of the box, helpless, watching it dribble over the line.

It didn't knock us back too much, though. Within five minutes we'd won a penalty after Crossan dribbled past three United defenders before being brought down. He picked himself up and from the spot beat David Gaskell in the United goal. United were riled and we were forced back onto the defensive for much of the rest of the game, although I never felt hugely uncomfortable. But they boasted stars such as Bobby Charlton, George Best, my direct opponent, Denis Law and Nobby Stiles in their side, so they weren't going to take this ignominy lying down. ,

During a break in play for an injury to Jim Montgomery close to the end, with Sunderland leading 3-1, referee Arthur Holland was chatting to Johnny Crossan, telling him that he had been over to Ireland recently to take charge of an Irish League game. At the same time I was telling George Best, who had moaned at me for 83 tough, physical minutes, that United were 'gonners'. I liked to work on my opponents' mental strength as well as their physical. Johnny asked how long to go, and Holland's response was, "it's all over, Johnny. There's only seven minutes left." How wrong he was. Bobby Charlton and George Best scored United's two goals in the final four minutes of the game to draw level at 3-3 and rescue a seemingly impossible situation.

Charlton's goal came after Monty had been fouled and hurt going for a cross. He was whacked heavily on the head and concussed, but because these were the days before substitutes were allowed he had to carry on. Shortly afterwards United won a corner out on the wing and it was slung into the penalty area, right under the bar. Normally any goalkeeper would grab it without a second thought, but because of Monty's injury he could not come out and claim it. Instead Bobby got his balding head to it and flicked it into the net. 3-2 and the tension was enormous.

I distinctly recall Best's late equaliser. I had always prided myself with doing well against Best over the years and that day was no exception. I thought I had a damn good game, but he then went and showed his genius by coming up with one moment of magic which squared the tie. Normally heavily right-footed, on this occasion Best cut inside and hit a left foot shot which went through a sea of legs in the muddy Old Trafford penalty area and beat the still-dazed Monty. It was gutting. All the more so that just a couple minutes later the whistle went to end the game.

The replay on the following Tuesday at Roker Park proved another thriller as once again Manchester United clawed their way back into the tie with another late Bobby Charlton header to draw 2-2 after extra time.

As dramatic as this game was, it was overshadowed by the massive attendance packed into Roker Park and the chaos which surrounded the efforts of the team to gain access to the players' dressing room and for what the spectators had to endure regarding their safety. I remember an hour and a half before kick off I walked up from the Roker Hotel along with my team-mates. This was normal practice as it supposedly stretched the legs. It was difficult to make progress towards the ground as all the side streets were packed with thousands of people, desperate to see the match. I had to climb on to and over parked cars' bonnets and roofs to eventually make it to the players' entrance.

In fact this night could so easily have been the forerunner to the Hillsborough disaster. The police estimated that nearly 100,000 people were in and around the ground. Two people were killed as the huge metal exit gates at the Roker End were forced open through crowd pressure. It would appear that one of those who died was trampled as the crowd surged forward to gain access, while another died of a heart attack amidst the hubbub.

Despite thousands failing to gain access to what turned out to be another epic clash, the open gates allowed thousands of people to gain access without paying and the crowd was so vast they had to be accommodated on the running track that surrounded the playing area. Supporters had also climbed the pylons of the floodlights and sat themselves on the top of the grandstands. It was estimated that there were over 75,000 in the ground, however the official attendance was 46,727 paying spectators. The Roker end terracing that stretched high into the sky accommodated thousands of extra people that night and must have been very close to disaster. Eighteen years later it was deemed to be unsafe by the local council safety officers and had to be slashed in capacity to less than half of what it once held. It was ironic that the attendance bonus written into our contracts would have given us generous reward as we should have received £5 per thousand over 50,000, but we missed out as the official attendance was below the threshold.

Malcolm Bramley, who was assistant secretary at Sunderland at the time, opened the ticket window alongside the players' entrance an hour before the kick off and saw through that grilled window a thousand desperate faces of supporters contorted in despair at not being able to get into the ground, fighting for space so as not to be crushed, taking refuge on car bonnets and roofs, as well as climbing the drainpipes of the surrounding buildings and on top of lock up garages. He quickly and sensibly shut the window up again and disappeared into the bowels of the main stand, handing the tickets for players and staff families to a couple of burly club stewards and asking them to deal with them.

The following morning the ground looked as if a bomb had dropped. The players were ordered in by Alan Brown to stretch off and then discuss the game, as well as the all important league match against Middlesbrough three days later. When we arrived we found the ground littered with tons of paper, straw that had protected the pitch from the frost until kick off and general rubbish scattered around. Crush barriers at both ends of the ground had been bent and twisted under the pressure of bodies and hundreds of shoes that people had lost in the crush were lined up in the players' tunnel by groundsman Jack Drydon.

That second drawn game meant that we had to go off to a neutral ground for a third meeting between the two teams, and Huddersfield Town's Leeds Road was the chosen venue. The match was another sell out. Once again we took the lead in the tie, this time thanks to a Nicky Sharkey goal, but our joy lasted only a few minutes as United equalised and went on to run out comfortable 5-1 winners. The effort had wiped us out.

Sixteen goals over three games meant five hours of superb entertainment for over 160,000 paying spectators. Unfortunately in that second replay all the action was at the wrong end of the pitch.

For me involvement in professional football as a player or as a manager encompasses more than the game and the result, it is the journey to and from a match, the build up of adrenalin and the elation or despair in the aftermath! This adage of mine could aptly be applied to the three games against the highly talented and mighty Manchester United of the time.

During the Cup run we kept up our great league form, winning five and drawing the other two of our league games, and, after drawing 0-0 at Middlesbrough in early March, we headed the table, a point clear of Leeds and three points ahead of Preston. No-one else was in the hunt. Two clubs would achieve their dream and one would fall by the wayside. We were now a group of steely, battle-hardened footballers, determined after two successive, heart-breaking late failures that we would go up this time around.

Losing 0-1 away at Newcastle United in mid-March was more of a parochial disaster for our supporters than it was to us as we made amends the following week by trouncing third in the table Preston North End 4-0 then followed that up with another win 2-0 against Rotherham United at Roker Park, watched by an astonishing crowd of 56,675. Promotion was just a nudge away after we drew 0-0 at Southampton and we confirmed our First Division status the following week with a 2-1 victory over a stubborn Charlton Athletic at Roker Park in the last home game of the season.

The scenes at the end of the game were remarkable as we, along with our doting supporters, celebrated our return to the top flight. It seemed appropriate that George Herd and Johnny Crossan should score the two goals. They were two fabulous footballers who had been instrumental in scheming and plotting against the best of defences in the league and had weighed in with a hatful of goals between them. George performed his hand stands and back flips on the pitch to the delight of all as the team took its plaudits with a double lap of honour. I wish I could have bottled that day for posterity as it was my first and only success as a Sunderland player.

9   The Brown Bomber

UNDER RESPECTIVE managers Alan Brown and Don Revie, Sunderland and Leeds United were expected to push on and take the First Division by storm after winning promotion in 1964. It still hurts me to this day to say that Leeds did exactly that both domestically and abroad, sweeping all before them. Sunderland, however, went into almost terminal, self-induced decline. The reason was obvious. Our manager Alan Brown bitterly and incredibly departed the club a few weeks after the glorious promotion season ended.

Brownie had formed an unbreakable bond with his players. We understood him as a man who knew what he wanted. He was on the verge of achieving it too, with us in harness alongside him. His departure was a disaster as he exited the club as quickly as the bubbles in the promotion champagne disappeared. Another historic lost opportunity.

To understand why on earth this could be allowed to happen at such an important moment in Sunderland's history, you have to look back at Brown's career at the club and the way things had developed between himself and the board in what was a sometimes tempestuous relationship.

On 30 July 1957 Alan Brown had arrived as Sunderland manager from Burnley, where he had spent three largely successful seasons, finishing in 10th, 7th and 7th position respectively in the First Division. He had a reputation of a no-nonsense approach as well as a belief in building his teams with young players. He was ahead of his time as a football innovator as well as being highly thought of at the Football Association as a forward-thinking coach.

Brown arrived at Sunderland after falling out with Bob Lord, the belligerent chairman of Burnley. Lord was one of a dying breed of pre-war Lancashire tycoons, who had made his fortune in the world of butchering. Lord told Brown that Sunderland had asked for permission to approach him to become their manager. Brown was reluctant to make the move until Lord told him that there was no option: "I suggest you take it as you will be getting the sack anyway," he said. Lord could see a tasty compensation package for his club and most managers are easily replaced.

One of Brown's masterstrokes when he joined Sunderland was to persuade the board of directors to purchase a piece of land from Ralphie Holmes, a local farmer, along the Whitburn Road at Cleadon on which to build a training ground. The board agreed to his request and the Cleadon training ground was established, burying for ever the archaic training methods in use since time began of running around the track at Roker Park and up and down the huge steep terraces at the Roker end of the ground.

He developed the team, taking the twin disappointments of failure to clinch promotion on the last day of the 61/2 and 62/3 seasons as spurs to improve his side rather than crushing blows, and eventually succeeded in returning his team to the top flight.

Then, at the very height of his Sunderland managerial career, he departed over a dispute regarding his salary. Despite his integral role in the success of 1963/64, Brown was denied the same £1,000 promotion bonus that the players had received. He had also asked the board to sell him the club house near the training ground in which he was living. Most of the senior players of the promotion-winning team had been given the option of purchasing their rented club house at the original price the club had paid, with the player paying the legal costs. But for some reason Brown was also denied this privilege by the board. He must have made a number of enemies in the board room along the way or they had considered his salary sufficient reward for what he had achieved.

This decision was the last straw for him and, although he gave the board every opportunity to change their minds, Brown found he had no option but to resign and take up the offer of the manager's job at Sheffield Wednesday, who had finished fifth in the First Division the previous season, but whose manager Vic Buckingham had departed before the season's end in mysterious circumstances following the conviction for match-fixing of three of his players.

The director's machinations must have been long and hard in the Sunderland boardroom over Alan Brown leaving the club. They had played the brinkmanship card and lost. For us players it was a difficult pill to swallow as we knew we had lost our guiding light, and the driving force behind our success. Indeed, in his second season at Hillsborough, Brown guided Wednesday to Wembley for the 1966 FA Cup final.

I am utterly convinced that if Alan Brown had remained as manager of the club he did not want to leave then we would have been knocking on the door of Europe along with Leeds United a few years down the line. As it was, this famous club was self-driven once again down the road to another period of mediocrity and eventual relegation.

The fact that Leeds United could not beat us in the league in 1964, yet under Don Revie went on to enjoy a decade of near domination touching every corner of Europe with massive success, told me a story. In my opinion Alan Brown's departure was a serious misjudgement by the Sunderland Football Club board of directors. It is the only time in my footballing career that I reflect upon and say, 'if only'.

We as players respected our club and our public. We dressed up to the nines more often than not with collar and tie. I have always believed that dressing up was part of the job. If you are in the public eye as a professional footballer, then you must act and dress appropriately. At times today it seems that anything goes. Many clubs have given in to lower standards of dress to keep their players happy. It is reassuring to know that my own Sunderland Football Club still holds true to our standards today and you have to be dressed accordingly to gain access to the main areas of hospitality and certainly the boardroom and its surrounds. Those standards were imbued into me at an early age by Alan Brown. He was a man who demanded the highest standards of his players and also of himself.

That came to a head when one day Alan Brown walked into the dressing room after training and told us to sit down and listen. He then informed us that he had been touched by a "Man of Faith" from a Christian movement and that the following afternoon we would all be visiting the New Theatre in Newcastle on a team outing to watch a show about a worldwide movement for moral and spiritual renewal which had been formed by a Frank Buchman in 1938. We thought he was off his rocker!

The following afternoon there we all were sitting watching this play about giving your soul to God. We were the only ones in the theatre. Brownie must have asked them for a special midweek matinee for the footballers. We didn't have a clue what we were there for and none of the players were converted. How could we be when the following Saturday we were to be seen kicking six lumps of shit out of an opposition player? Without asking us, the price of the ticket was taken out of our wages. No-one dare argue about it.

All the more shocking then that shortly afterwards Alan Brown summoned thirteen local and national journalists to his house with the promise of a great story. He proceeded with great courage to inform them, in front of his wife Elsie, that he had been unfaithful to her and asked her to forgive him. In addition, he opened his heart to the assembled scribes, telling them that he had been a real bastard towards them in the past and wanted to apologise for his past behaviour, for not allowing them to do their job properly because of his belligerent and unhelpful attitude towards them.

This was a private moment in a brave man's life which he was now going to share, in some cases with strangers and certainly a few enemies who could quite well belittle him in tomorrow's headlines! Only one let him down, a journalist from a national newspaper, who printed and enlarged upon the details of what was essentially a private story. But that was one too many for a man who had proffered his heart. He never forgave that man and neither would I have done.

Many years after Brown had retired I arranged to call on him at his home in Bodmin. Valerie and I had the opportunity to make a detour on our journey home from a holiday in Cornwall, during a summer while I was Newport County manager. I knew from the grapevine that Alan was not in the best of health and this would probably be the last time I would see him. It was a red hot day and the meeting point was on a slip road off the main drag close to his home. Valerie and I were an hour late having been unavoidably held up by a traffic accident. Even after all the time that had elapsed since he was the boss, I once again felt the butterflies in the pit of my stomach as I fretted about what he would say. I knew for certain what he would be thinking. But, this being a social occasion, he kept that to himself.

We pulled in and there he was, where he had promised to be, standing ram rod straight at the side of the road with the aid of a stick in the blistering heat as disciplined as ever!

We parked up and he showed us through a gap in the hedge to a row of fairly new, terraced bungalows. I never found out whether he owned his home or if it was social housing and warden controlled. The bungalows were certainly well kept and quite formal. Once inside the house, which was neat and tidy, there was Elsie. My mind went back to that moment in his life many years before when he opened his heart to all, at his Cleadon home and particularly Elsie, his loyal wife. I found it gratifying that she had remained alongside him over those long and rather sad decades.

This was the same man who had harboured a guilty secret with inner turmoil, who eventually found it too much for him and had to be honest. This was the Brownie with the fiery temper and rasping tongue which could strip wallpaper when needed, a man with a massive inner strength and who was, in his time, physically as strong as an ox. He was also a man who sadly had been denied the football success to which he was entitled because of the injury to Brian Clough in December 1962 and the injustice of the Sunderland board in the summer of 1964.

I have occasionally traced the whereabouts of former teachers, tutors or mentors who have helped me to progress my career, I have never been disappointed in what I have discovered. This visit however was tinged with sadness. A man who had been at the very top of his profession was now brought to his knees both physically and mentally by the passage of time.

During our conversation I quite clearly picked up the fact that Elsie and him were very hard up. I was moved when he told us that the flowers adorning the sideboard were from Brian Clough. Surely this was testimony to the man's contribution to the game and particularly to those who had passed his way as players under his care. I had been one of them and I was, with this visit, paying due diligence to the influence he had on my career. I was tempted to offer him and Elsie some money, but I thought I knew what the answer would be from a man of huge pride. Was I correct not to? I shall never know.

As we chatted I managed to tease from Alan the real reason he had departed from Sunderland, of the board's refusal to match our bonuses or his offer to buy his house. I had never heard it before and was shocked.

As Alan showed Valerie and I to the door, leaving Elsie in her chair, I thanked him for everything, giving him a warm shake of the hand and pulled him towards me for a first and final hug. We stepped outside and the door closed behind us. He probably thought the hug was a little crass, I hope not but I will never know.

A few months later a phone call to my home in Monmouth from a tearful Alan Brown told me that Elsie had died. He was obviously devastated by this loss and soon afterwards he also passed away.

Valerie and I made the long journey down to Bodmin to pay our respects to the man who had given me my start on the senior professional football ladder. His funeral was sparsely attended, no more than a dozen people. His two daughters, son Ian and close family were accompanied by a few football people: Colin Symm, Ian Branfoot, Sam Ellis and Jack Whitham, along with Lawrie McMenemy, saying farewell to a man who had missed out on the rewards of his hard work and yet would still have been the envy to many of his peers.

I knelt and said a prayer for his life and then walked out of the crematorium into the sunlight with Valerie on my arm.

10 **The Bacardi Years**

OUR FORM during the early part of our first season back in the First Division was nothing short of disastrous. Sunderland FC was a managerless team spiralling out of control as it slipped into the relegation zone. It took nine league games until we registered our first victory and then until mid-November for our second. That came totally out of the blue immediately after former England international left-back George Hardwick was appointed manager. George later told me that he had rung Chairman Syd Collings and offered himself as manager promising that he would lead the club to a safe position in the table, which he did. George was a breath of fresh air in and around the dressing room, a handsome fellow with the looks of Errol Flynn from the silver screen. He was a man who could never pass a mirror. He oozed confidence.

He made an immediate impact on the team as we won that second game of the season 3-2 against Burnley. Further success followed as the team started to improve its form. Hardwick's flamboyant approach rubbed off on the players and particularly myself as I proceeded to play the best football of my career. Some scribes suggested that I should be considered for a full England call up. The team finished in a very respectable mid-table position. George Hardwick had delivered and along the way had installed the broken Brian Clough as youth team coach, so setting Clough off on his managerial career.

As a reward for the all-round efforts of the staff, the board of directors took us off to London to attend the 1965 FA Cup final between Liverpool and Leeds United. On the Friday night before the game we were entertained at the Cafe Royal for dinner. Chairman Syd Collings made a profound speech in thanking the players and in particular the manager for his achievement in pushing the team in to a respectable position in the table. On the Monday Hardwick was sacked by the board.

On arriving as manager in November 1964 George had moved from the traditional office at the top of those stairs to his private office in the old gymnasium at the Roker End of the ground. He had made himself comfortable with some cosy reclining chairs and a settee along with his office desk and filing cabinets. Rumour was rife in the dressing room amongst the players that his sacking was because of his philandering. Evidence of chicanery was that the lights often burnt late into the night in that comfortable office and, in addition, the wooden flooring that had been laid in his office was pit-marked with stiletto heel marks. This was apparently the evidence that sealed his fate.

Hardwick, a man of style and pedigree, departed the club a bitter and disillusioned man. That second idiotic act from the board in successive summers paved the way for what I consider the most disastrous period during the thirteen years I was a Sunderland player.

Ian McColl's appointment as manager spelt disaster for the club. McColl had been one of Scotland's classiest footballers in the 1950s, an era in which the Scots had boasted numerous players of star quality. He had managed Scotland's national team for five years, but wanted to try his hand at club management and so accepted the job at Roker Park. Originating from the Rangers stable, McColl was a quiet unassuming type, probably a nice man to know socially. Conversely, in my opinion he did not have the skin to be a manager, let alone to handle a character like Jim Baxter, who became his first and fatal signing for the club. To say he was in stark contrast to the disciplinarian Alan Brown would be the understatement of the century.

I read of Baxter's signing from Rangers in the summer of 1965 when I was in London on a finance course, which I had decided to undertake as I was keen to pursue an insurance business outside of the game. My immediate reaction was delight at the prospect that one of the greatest players that Scotland has ever produced would be coming to Roker Park and would be playing left-half in front of me. But hold on, surely he could not take Jimmy McNab's position at left-half? Yes he could, and did. McNab was history.

Bringing Jim Baxter to Sunderland was Ian McColl's biggest mistake. Wonderful player though he was, Baxter's arrival split the dressing room down the middle with Charlie Hurley's group of players, who had been together for many a season, forming the basis of the successful promotion team, on one side of the dressing room and Jim Baxter's followers on the other. It doesn't take much to upset the very fine balance and pecking order of a dressing room. Baxter's arrival wrecked Sunderland's. Worse, Baxter brought a new culture of drinking in to the club. Football's history is littered with players who have been ridden by drink. Baxter's exploits became legendary.

In addition there was also the religious element in the equation. McColl came from a staunch protestant background, so the catholic personnel within the club were sidelined. I would like to think that Ian McColl dropped players from the team for the correct reasons, football reasons, but there were too many illogical decisions taken over the following 18 months. Two of the Catholics in the dressing room, Sharkey and McNab, played a mere handful of games in the McColl era, while Charlie Hurley was grudgingly retained as captain for a while until a lad called George Kinnell, at 29 years of age, was bought from Oldham Athletic to replace, of all people, Hurley at centre-half. It was bad enough that Kinnell, in my opinion a decidedly inferior player to Hurley, was being preferred, but George was also Jim Baxter's cousin. McColl's thinking, apparently, was that his presence would comfort the not so 'Slim Jim' and make him feel at home. The reality was that the drinking culture continued.

Dressing room disruption followed as Baxter attracted his followers and manipulated the manager for his own ends to the detriment of the team and its followers. Pre-season training in the summer of 1965 was a farce, as John Mortimer, our first team coach, was constantly upset by Baxter, who simply did not want to put the work in and avoided training whenever he could. In addition Baxter, a personable sort when he had not taken a drink, constantly encouraged others to follow his lead. I felt as if we were constantly fire fighting and all this lead to dressing room bust ups between Baxter's cronies, and those who cared. Sir Matt Busby was asked around that time why he had not signed a player of Baxter's class for Manchester United. His reply was cutting, "I did not sign him because I did not want my young professionals and apprentices at the club listening on Monday morning to what Jim Baxter had got up to over the weekend."

The first home game of that 1965/66 season was against Sheffield United on Saturday 28 August. Playing against me was their powerful right-winger Alan Woodward, a player who had always given me a thorough test in the past. Having gone through a pre-season fighting my corner with the manager over football issues, this would be a real examination. I was not wrong!

Although we won 4-1 in front of 42,127 spectators, Woodward scored United's only goal. To be honest he, along with two other of their right-sided players, ran me ragged. No winger in the past had ravaged me as he did this day, not even the great George Best had achieved that distinction. But it was because my new left-sided partner, Jim Baxter, barely lifted a finger to help me stem the tide of Sheffield's right-wing attacks. He had been given the freedom to play his game by the manager, leaving me completely exposed.

Perhaps predictably, Baxter, shorn of any defensive responsibility, scored two goals in this his home debut, the perfect start for him. He was brilliant on the ball and had the vision of a radar screen, but sadly the leg break he had suffered a few seasons previously whilst a Rangers player had slowed the man down and the excesses of the high life had taken their toll on Baxter's body. He simply was not the player he had been in his heyday at Rangers and in my opinion Sunderland had bought a 'Pup'. In spite of the fact that Baxter scored 7 goals in 36 games in his first season, Sunderland's fans soon saw through it all and we ended up with 30,000 fans watching the team for the last game of the season, a drop of 12,000 at the gate. Sunderland supporters are no fools when it comes to judging the game and the players within their squad.

After that opening game of the season, I allowed the euphoria from the 4-1 win to subside and then got in to Jim Baxter about him buzzing off upfield and leaving me stranded facing two players. I was used to the comfort of having the tenacious, reliability of Jimmy McNab in front of me. Baxter shrugged his shoulders and told me not to worry. Big Charlie Hurley, as captain, listened to this exchange and accepted the situation for the time being as Baxter had scored two goals and, more importantly, the team had won their opening match on that bright summer's day. However the dark clouds in the dressing room were looming on the horizon.

A short time after the match finished I was upstairs, outside the manager's office determined to voice my disquiet over being left with two and three men to cope with, whilst Jim Baxter wandered all over the field enjoying himself, and Woodward's consequent goal. I recalled that Sunderland had a player named Len Shackleton who royally entertained in the 1950s, but that the outcome for the team in that era was a first ever relegation from the top division – a one-man team that had led to inevitable dressing room discontent and terminal decline. I could see it coming again.

I knocked on door. There was a delay and then a curt "come in" saw me face to face with Ian McColl. Being a man of few words he stood looking at me from behind his desk waiting for me to open up the conversation. I was elsewhere as I stood in front of him staring open-mouthed at the huge amount of cash piled on the manager's desk only an arm's length away. Gathering myself, I spilled out my disquiet at having to do Baxter's work defensively. However McColl wasn't interested. He blanked me and, without uttering a word, he beckoned Jim Baxter from behind a screen that had been in the office for many a year. Baxter had obviously nipped upstairs before me and slipped behind the screen as I had knocked on the door.

Baxter looked me in the eye and said, "Lenny, get used to it as it won't change. Just give the ball to the 'Claw' and I will look after you." The Claw was a reference to his brilliant left foot which had unlocked many a tight defence over the years. Sadly at Sunderland we were only to see spasmodic flashes of Baxter's flawed genius.

I walked out of that office astounded at what I had seen and made my way down the stairs. I knew, as my football question had not been answered, things for me at Sunderland under the McColl/Baxter regime would never be the same again. In addition the one thing I was nearly certain of was that Baxter was receiving illegal payments outside of his contract, which presumably would have been authorised by the chairman. That could be the only explanation for the huge pile of cash on McColl's desk. I decided I had to keep what I had witnessed secret and not tell the dressing room as mayhem would have ensued. It was a secret that weighed heavily upon me.

The whole issue of Baxter's signing did not please me, particularly as, at that time, Football League rules allowed a player moving from one club to another to be entitled to 10% of the transfer fee. Baxter's fee was £72,000, so he would have earned a substantial sum of money. But on top of this he had pocketed an illegal payment, something which he later admitted to me during another attempt to belittle me.

At a later date it was revealed that Syd Collings, a man who, as a member of the Football Association Board the following summer would stand next to royalty as England received the World Cup at Wembley Stadium, and his vice-Chairman Lawrie Evans had travelled to Glasgow together to clinch Baxter's signature. After initially turning down his demand for a £20,000 'sweetener', they had succumbed to Baxter's demands for a sizeable payment of £17,000 to secure his services. The money on McColl's desk was part of that sum, paid out of income from a huge 42,000 attendance for the opening game of the season. It was not too long before the board realised that this was and always would be a bad investment. Had they also forgotten that a decade ago in the fifties Sunderland Football Club had hung its head in shame because of being found guilty of making illegal payments, with directors being banned from football for life and having to resign their positions?

THE 1965/66 SEASON saw the introduction of substitutes in the Football League. Right-winger Mike Hellawell had the dubious distinction of being Sunderland's first unused substitute when he was on the bench away at Leeds United on Saturday 21 August, a match that Sunderland lost by 0-1. It was not long before I had the feel of a number twelve on my back. It was for a home game against Burnley in November of that season as McColl had seemingly decided I was to be ousted from the team. Maybe it was because I knew too much after my visit to his office.

Numerous other players from the 1964 promotion team had their doubts regarding their position in the team because of the probability of an influx of Scottish players in to the club led by Baxter and orchestrated by McColl. The talented George Herd, a skilful inside-forward, who, along with the brilliant Johnny Crossan, had been at the vanguard of our successes over past seasons, was immediately put in his place by the new manager who told George, "You won't be 'The General' any more. Jim Baxter is to be the man who pulls the strings. You are now one of the soldiers." Despite being a Scot himself George was also sidelined as he had crossed McColl while on international duty for Scotland. The new manager had obviously not forgotten this.

Although the manager was determined to keep me out of the team, the directors, knowing me and my history as a player and believing in my ability, denied him any extra funds to replace me with a new signing. Instead McColl turned to in-house players to usurp me. There was my close friend and colleague Jimmy Shoulder, Alan Black, another signing from Scotland, John Parke, Jimmy McNab and Martin Harvey. All of them were tried at left-back and McColl even tried Jim Baxter's relation George Kinnell. To be fair Parke and Harvey had a fair amount of success in the position, but on their own admission they were never at home there, both of them being naturally right-footed players.

Whenever my position in the team was threatened I drove myself to the limit during training sessions, particularly when I had any sort of opportunity to impress the manager and coach John Mortimer. I tore in to my team-mates in practice to win my place back very quickly. I figured that if contenders were injured then they couldn't be selected and another challenger would be seen off! But McColl was stubborn in his resolve to avoid picking me and it would seem ours had become a hate relationship.

The icy relationship that prevailed amongst certain members of the team was often broken with dressing a room prank or an amusing Jim Baxter antic. One such occasion was an away game at Stoke City. Trentham Gardens was our overnight stop. The travelling director was Stanley Ritson, one of the more senior directors of the board. When he retired for the night he would place his rather large boots outside his bedroom door for them to be cleaned by the night porter. On this occasion Baxter took the boots from outside Ritson's door, attached some bunting to them and floated them on the huge lake in the surrounding gardens. At breakfast time as the lads came down there they were bobbing along in the middle of the lake with a Union Jack protruding into the air as a sail. Stanley Ritson came to breakfast in his bare feet, unaware that his footwear was floating away.

Pre-match team talks were a farce as McColl had a propensity to silence and was reluctant to speak up. It got to the point that bets were taken amongst the players as to how long it would be before he opened his mouth. George Kinnell kept the stopwatch and always sat at the back of the room so as not to be seen. The record from John Mortimer calling for silence and McColl speaking was twenty three long seconds. He would sit there for an age as he tried to summon up the inner courage to open his mouth, his embarrassment all the more exaggerated as he rocked backwards and forwards in his chair like a slowly-ticking clock or as if stricken with some sort of affliction.

What a contrast, I understand, to Bob Stokoe's team talks, often held before training took place when the manager would lead a prolonged discussion about all things pertinent. I have been told there were some sharp lads in that team who regularly brought in subjects of little importance deliberately to keep the conversation flowing. Eventually Bob would look at his watch and decide there was only time for a five-aside, which the lads revelled in, and not any form of fitness or stamina training. The bottom line is that it some how worked, as silverware sat on the sideboard in 1973 thanks to that marvellous victory over Leeds United in the FA Cup final.

It was an away game at Leicester City on the 21 January 1967. I was on the substitute's bench again. I was never used during any game when I was a substitute for McColl, I wonder why? This match was Bobby Kerr's fourth full appearance for Sunderland's first team. There were far greater things to come for Bobby Kerr, who would become a hero in that Cup-winning side, than Leicester City away with it pissing down with rain on a cold winter's day in January. The game was won 2-1.

McColl's dislike for me manifested itself on this particular day. Having not been involved in the game, I quickly showered and made my way into the players' lounge, which was a small cramped room inside the Filbert Street ground and where I held deep conversation with Leicester striker Derek Dougan about PFA business as we were both reps for our respective clubs. After finishing talking to The Doog I moved outside to board the team bus at the agreed time only to find it had departed without me. Eddie Plumley, the secretary of Leicester City, asked the police to flag down the Sunderland team coach and inform them that one of their players had been left behind. I am told that Ian McColl, on being told who had been left stranded, instructed the bus driver to proceed on the journey home. I was naturally livid when the Leicester police told me of the outcome. This was pure vitriol against me.

I had to make my own arrangements through taxi and train for my journey back to Wearside. It left me plenty of time to ensure that this incident hit the national and local headlines. It did not suit McColl or the football club as I indicated that I would be putting in an expense claim for the costs that I had incurred. Coincidentally Dougan, on behalf of the PFA, took up my cause with the club and I was eventually paid the expenses I was entitled to.

I was by now so disillusioned at the way the club was being run that I put in a written transfer request, which immediately attracted Wolverhampton Wanderers to table a substantial cash offer of £45,000 for me, but the board turned it down. I then received a phone call at my home asking if I would like to become a Leeds United player. As I've said earlier, Leeds under Don Revie were now one of the best sides in Europe and were enjoying plenty of domestic success. The caller was the secretary of the club and I indicated that I would jump at the opportunity if it materialised. It was, of course, technically what they call 'tapping up'.

It didn't happen as once again the board were not prepared to sell me to the club's fiercest rivals outside Newcastle United.

Sunderland were invited to tour Canada and North America in the summer of 1967. Unfortunately from my point of view I was not chosen to travel to a part of the world I had never been to and have never visited since. I wanted to be there, unlike Charlie Hurley, the now ex-club captain, who had requested not to be included for personal reasons. I was distraught when told by John Mortimer that I was on standby and would not be travelling. As it turned out it was a professional and PR disaster for the club.

Before they departed on the ill-fated tour, the Sunderland squad were kitted out in new suits for the official part of the trip, then before their departure I was privy to Ian McColl laying down the law to all the players over behaviour and the level of intake of alcohol during the journey as well as throughout their stay in North America, reminding them all that they were representing the club and country. Which country was it, England or Scotland?

"No alcohol"! This was akin to taking your breath away for Jim Baxter and his cohorts. Baxter, nicknamed 'the vampire', flew at the manager and threatened not to make the journey, immediately McColl relented and told them, "OK, you can have beer only." That was all they wanted as the door to debauchery was now fully open. The management had caved in once again.

Whilst in America stories abounded over the drink problems, the trashing of bedrooms, aeroplane hostesses and stewards being abused. I was told players urinated in the swimming pool of the top class hotel they were staying at, and then chandeliers were damaged in the Georgian Towers Hotel in Vancouver, Canada as drunken players swung on them as they rampaged along the corridors. Indeed Sunderland Football Club would still be receiving bills six months later for the damage done to property whilst the team was over there. The football was secondary to the entertainment and the alcohol abuse.

Pre-season 1967 was a disgrace as over the four weeks before the first game Jim Baxter did his best to act like Lord Lucan, avoiding training whenever possible. He had come back from America grossly overweight and he turned up for pre-season training determined to upset the whole of the club. This could not go on! Finally the board acted. Baxter was sold to Nottingham Forest in December 1967 for a fee of £85,000. However, slightly strangely, Sunderland eventually obtained £100,000 as the Chairman of Nottingham Forest was desperate to make an impression and join the 'Ton Up Club' and so paid the six figure sum. I am told by a former director that the deal was concluded in a night club, obviously when alcohol had had its influence. Baxter once more received another huge signing on fee and so over a period of less than two seasons had pocketed around £35,000 in signing on fees alone and in the process destroyed the ethos of Sunderland Football Club's dressing room.

McColl's final signing was Geoff Butler, a left-back, there's a surprise! Butler arrived from Chelsea for £65,000. McColl, whose time was running out, had once again tried to replace me. Butler made the first team on just three occasions; one league game against Burnley in January 1968 and the subsequent two FA Cup matches against Second Division Norwich City. McColl was sacked after the Canaries dumped us out of the Cup at the third round stage. His expensive final signing averaged out at almost £22,000 per game. The board of directors had run out of patience.

McColl had cost me nearly 50 league and cup appearances over two and a half seasons, and in the process had humiliated me in the dressing room by not selecting me when I was still the best left-back at the club. He also piled more ignominy on me as he made me train with the reserves and the youth team, humiliating me further by excluding me from the close season tour to America, taking instead my perpetual understudy Jimmy Shoulder, a lad I respected both personally and professionally.

I know I have been damning towards this former manager, however remember it was he who ostracised me. The truth is I signed no contract with him during his tenure, it was Sunderland Football Club who employed me.

11 **Return of the Bomber**

ALAN BROWN returned to manage Sunderland for a second time in February 1968, taking over a club that had been devastated by the two and a half years of Ian McColl's reign. Brown once again stripped the dead wood out of the dressing room and gradually introduced younger players into the team. It worked that season as he somehow kept us up, winning six of the last 12 games to dig ourselves out of the relegation mire.

1968/69 was a much more sedate affair, although not after a record 0-8 defeat at West Ham United in mid-October. We eventually finished 17th, comfortably clear of the relegation zone, but it was clear things were not working. Brown still maintained that ruthless streak of his as players were made aware on numerous occasions that if you stepped out of line you would suffer the consequences. Even the late Ian Porterfield, McColl's brilliant signing from Raith Rovers was blackballed from the team for having a boozy festive season party in his own house. Brownie had a phobia against anyone who touched alcohol, a total contrast to the previous regime. The word was passed back to him through Billy Elliott, one of his coaching staff, that there had been a walloping party at Ian's house near The Barnes Hotel in Sunderland. Ian quite rightly refused to apologise for something he was entitled to have in the confines of his home. Alan dug his heels in, declined to relent and shunned Ian for many months. Eventually Brownie wrote Porterfield a letter to ask him to come and see him. It transpired that peace was made between them and 'Porter' was restored to the team. But that was the way Brownie did things. Like it or not, most players respected him for it.

Knowing I wanted to consider a career in coaching after my playing career had finished, Brownie allowed me time off on a Friday to coach the police cadets and the prison warders at the grounds of Durham College, an invaluable experience as you could have as few as half a dozen and as many as thirty. You never knew how many would turn up for the session, but it was a great grounding for management.

In 1968 the board of directors granted me a testimonial match to acknowledge my ten years of service to the club. I had been denied a game by the previous management, so as soon as Alan Brown was installed he set a date for the late summer just after the season started. Annoyingly it was put back a number of times as the team's league position was precarious. Eventually it was fitted in during the November with a strong Newcastle United side as the opposition. Unfortunately sleeting rain and bitter cold spoiled the night. Allied to our poor league form, the match turned out to be a complete financial flop. In comparison to the cash questionably dolled out to certain players during the McColl reign the £800 pounds I perfectly legally received from the match was a pittance.

Another player to feel the cold shoulder of Alan Brown's discipline was Calvin Palmer, a blond-haired, seasoned professional who had been the returning manager's first signing when joining from Stoke City for £70,000 in February 1968. Palmer turned out to be an expensive utility player who cost the club on average £2,000 per game, as he played only 35 times.

Ironically Palmer was hoping to make an impression on his return to his former club in September 1969 when Brown's strict code robbed him of the opportunity. The Friday night before the game we all as a team went to the local cinema to see, would you believe it, *The Sound of Music* – hardly the kind of film you'd expect to see twelve healthy young men watching on a Friday night! At least we were not paying the admission for this questionable experience or for the sugary sweets with which we were plied during the evening to generate energy for following day's game.

The cinema in Stoke was certainly up market to the one I attended as a boy, which was a near fleapit called the Rio in Fazakerley, Liverpool. In those days we waited outside in all weathers as young teenagers to ask an adult to "take me in, please.' We were utterly oblivious to the possibility of laying ourselves open to the temptation of those preying on children.

Like all of us, Palmer had seen the film on numerous occasions, so after just five minutes he got to his feet and walked out, despite protestations from trainer Billy Elliott. Brown's response was predictable. When he found out that Palmer had walked out of the cinema, he immediately dropped him from the team and suspended him for a week without pay. Palmer went home that evening, making the major mistake of spreading the news of this bust up across the Sunday sports headlines. The papers made a meal of the issue and the public ate every crumb of it. Outraged, Brownie made sure that Palmer never kicked a ball for

Sunderland again. He remained out of the first team for two years or so before joining Crewe Alexandra in October 1971. Alan Brown had effectively destroyed Palmer's career in one fell swoop.

As a footnote we lost the game the following day 2-4, probably much to the delight of the disciplined Palmer who was sitting at home somewhere in the Potteries.

That was the 11th game without a win that we had gone since the start of the 1969/70 season. We did somehow manage to win the next two matches, against Nottingham Forest and Spurs, but then another 11 league games elapsed before we won again. Brown clearly wanted to shake things up, so Palmer simply gave him the ammunition to jettison him from the team, which was headed downwards back to earth faster than Apollo 11, the successful moon landing spacecraft of that year.

There have always been diverse characters in every football dressing room; an odd or a singular one, a player with a complex character or appearing somewhat different. Graeme Le Saux in his book *Left Field* exposed the resentment, jealousy and suspicion of one who bucked the trend in a dressing room full of professional footballers, many of whom have come from a humble background and have tended to have limited horizons. I was never a partygoer or a womaniser. My fitness and integrity came first. I love the Last Night of the Proms and the concert from Vienna on New Year's Day rather than drinking or carousing, and with interests as varied as other sports, antiques, the stock market and insurance, as well as brewing my own beer (waiting for it to ferment when most footballers would have been necking the stuff!) I probably fitted into that Le Saux-type box! Jealousy and resentment is sometimes just below the surface in a football club. Fortunately I was not aware of this in Sunderland's dressing room amongst the 1964 promotion team. Regrettably it was the case in later years.

In fact only recently Micky Horswill pointed out to me that the inkling I had about how my behaviour was viewed by other Sunderland players was correct. He deemed me 'different' and told me that I was talked about in the dressing room as being rather singular. Micky is also 'different'. A well-liked cheeky chappie, who does much good work for charity, he was a member of that 1973 Sunderland Cup final team that upset the odds at Wembley. He is now the third member of 'The Three Legends,' a two-hour evening programme on Century Radio in the North East of England. The insatiable appetite in this part of the country for anything to do with soccer has thrown up, in my opinion, a programme of dubious entertainment value and opinionated rubbish. True, it is occasionally amusing and sprinkled with interesting facts, but for me more often than not it is a futile waste of precious time. However, the programme retains a loyal following who continue to enjoy the air time it occupies. It's just not for me. It has now been running for over seven years. Along with Horswill, Bernie Slaven, an ex-Middlesbrough striker, is an integral member of the team. The programme is hosted by the legendary Newcastle centre-forward Malcolm Macdonald, a goalscoring machine from the golden age in soccer that has now gone for ever. In my opinion as a host he seems to me to sometimes be in need of the occasional wake up call. Perhaps the zip of a different talisman heading the show would enhance the attraction of the programme. With a salary of up to forty thousand pounds a year that person would not be hard to find!

DESPITE ALAN Brown's attempts to stem the tide, the 1969/70 season culminated in relegation. Needing two points from the final game against Liverpool to overtake Crystal Palace and stay up, the team put in a meek performance and were beaten 0-1 at Roker Park. I did not play in this game as I was injured. I happened to be standing in the medical room after the match when I struck up a conversation with the wonderful Bob Paisley, then Liverpool assistant manager. He was sharing a noggin with our amiable physiotherapist Johnny Watters, and I recalled to Bob how I had cleaned his boots at Liverpool when I had been a ground staff lad many years before.

Johnny Watters had worn the white overall at Sunderland for two decades. He was from the green end of Glasgow, and possessed a mischievous sense of humour that lifted any injured player out of his injury-inflicted torpor. Along with Dr Scott, the club doctor, who incidentally was the stepfather of actor James Bolam, they were at times a double act worth paying to listen to. Both of them were heavy smokers. Johnny loved his pipe and the Doc smoked cigarettes. Bear in mind that this would be while they worked on injured players. Pipe smoke filled the air and ash was dropped into the talcum powder with which their magic fingers worked the injury. Johnny's private patients, which he took in on an afternoon after the players had gone home, were subjected to the same conditions.

Ike Spain, a local businessman who had a club foot which looked as though it had been honed in the local shipyard, once came in to have a minor adjustment made to it and some treatment for a sore spot on his ankle. I remember him undoing this huge boot, dropping it on the floor and sitting up on the plinth waiting to be treated. The mischievous Watters gave me and a couple of other players the wink and put a number of medical items on a tray alongside Ike. There was some liniment, bandages, scissors, a kidney dish and a pair of bottles which contained blue and green coloured liquids. It looked a bit like a scene out of a Sid James farce and Ike looked on in growing trepidation each time a new item was laid out, his eyes growing wider and wider as the thought of what might be about to happen to him ate him up. The whole rigmarole took ages as Johnny played the thing to the max. He finished his performance by producing a huge hypodermic needle, which was laid alongside the kidney dish. Ike, his eyes now as bulbous as a fish's, flipped, jumped off the plinth forgetting his boot was not attached and fell arse-over-tit on to the floor. It was the last time he ventured in for treatment and it is certain that Johnny lost a client, his payment and his usual bonus of a brace of pheasants – all just for the laugh. They don't make them like Johnny Watters any more!

At just 31 years of age it was becoming increasingly apparent that I would become the next victim of Alan Brown's predilection for shipping out older pros. My final first team game for Sunderland was at Coventry City in a 1-1 draw. A few months earlier I had been privileged to break that classy footballer Stan Anderson's club record of 447 league and cup games for Sunderland. I held the record at a total of 458 games for a few years before it was broken in turn by legendary goalkeeper Jim Montgomery. I'm proud to say, however, that no-one else has overtaken me.

In late February 1971 Alan Brown called me upstairs to his office to tell me (Brownie never 'informed' anyone, he told them) that he had given permission for Hartlepool United to speak to me about becoming their player-manager. He also made it quite clear that I would be a reserve team player for the rest of the season and that I would not be having my contract renewed thereafter. So it was done and dusted, talk to Hartlepool or be on the dole in three months. This was Alan Brown's way of doing things. It was no different to what I had seen happen to dozens of other players down the years. In actual fact it was far more humane. At least he had sorted something out for me.

Alan Brown was sacked by Sunderland in November 1972, with the side languishing in 14th position in the Second Division. He was replaced by Blackpool manager Bob Stokoe. However let us not forget that less than seven months later, six of Brown's youth prodigies, plus two of his masterful signings in Dick Malone and Dave Watson, were lifting the FA Cup at Wembley. It is fact that Alan Brown had a hand in contributing to arguably two of the best teams to have worn Sunderland's colours since the 1930s, that FA Cup team and the 1964 promotion side.

Generally we former professional footballers and managers are a hard-bitten lot, but nothing gets to us more than the genuine warmth of supporters. I was lucky enough to experience plenty of that during my time playing for Sunderland. But the fans on Wearside are special. They remember things so vividly and are so happy to give of themselves. I'll give you an example. After attending the Sunderland versus Stoke City game at the Stadium of Light on the 13 March 2007, as I was wending my way home along with thousands of others from this evening match, a supporter moved alongside me, turned to me as he walked by and said, "how are you, Len?"

"Fine, thank you," I responded and shook his hand. It costs nothing after all!

"Thanks for the pleasure you gave me," he continued. "I used to watch the 1964 promotion-winning side, they were the most enjoyable Sunderland team ever." Then my new-found friend melted into the crowd.

A lump came to my throat. After watching a dour game, has there ever been anything other in recent years when Stoke City come to Wearside, his mood could have been tainted and his remark simply a desire for better days, I will never really know. But for me to hear so unexpectedly that all the sweat and effort in that red and white striped shirt so long ago was appreciated . . . it was a special, fleeting moment amongst my own.

12 An Honest Bastard

THAT FATEFUL morning when Alan Brown, manager of Sunderland, called me to his office at the top of those stairs at Roker Park in March 1971 and informed me that Hartlepool Football club had asked if Sunderland would release me to become their player-manager he told me I had something to offer the game in management. Although I had passed my FA Preliminary Coaching Badge, when I eventually finished playing the game I had set my mind on becoming an insurance broker, in partnership locally and then eventually to re-train to become a broker on the money markets. But Brownie's comment meant something to me and got me thinking. All the more so that it was this tough, terse man who had given me, for him, a glowing recommendation. At 31 years of age, I still had something to offer as a player, so player-manager sounded pretty good to me!

I slipped down the A19 south to Hartlepool, an hour's journey on a single carriageway coast road in those days, passing through the bleak colliery villages and small towns which were the heartland of support for Sunderland Football Club. On match days thousands used to plough their way from these parts to Roker Park to watch idols of the past such as Raich Carter, Len Shackleton and local lad Stan Anderson, then latterly Charlie Hurley and the great promotion team of the early sixties which I was a member of.

On reaching the outskirts of Hartlepool I stopped the car to gather my thoughts and have a look at a town I had never visited in 13 years of living in the North East. I was not impressed with the back drop, in the distance there was the massive ICI Teesside plant, which employed nearly 20,000 people. That chemical giant was belching out tons of what we now call greenhouse gas. The foreground was little better, a haze-filled sky blanketing what appeared to me, an era gone by. As I descended the gentle slope into the town, I spotted the Victoria Ground in the distance with the telltale floodlight pylons standing proud in the sky. On arrival I noticed a defunct old stone-built cinema. I didn't know it then, but this would have a significance for me and the club at a later date.

I parked up in Clarence Road alongside the only entrance in the 8 foot high wooden fence running the full length of the dilapidated grandstand. I pushed open the players' entrance and after glancing at the pitch and the surrounds I found myself immediately turning left through another door into the Board Room.

John Curry, the Chairman of the club and a local counsellor, dressed in a dark sombre suit, was sitting at one end of a huge table. He was 61 years of age, an easy-going, bespectacled bloke, who looked closer to 80. I learnt and realised later why he looked so old – the huge financial problems at the club were swamping him. Those same cash problems would nearly cut short my managerial career at a later date.

During the drive down I had grown in stature at the prospect of becoming one of only 92 Football League managers in the country. I would be able to sit at the same table on equal terms with not only my mentor Alan Brown, but other esteemed names in the game at that time: Bill Shankly, Ron Greenwood, Bobby Robson, Bill Nicholson, the colourful Malcolm Allison, my former contemporary from our Roker Park days Brian Clough, as well as Don Revie, the man that my left boot had hovered over at Roker Park a decade before.

I had made my mind up that I would take the job if it was offered to me, however I had not bargained for the state of disrepair of the ground and the paltry salary which was on offer to me. It suddenly struck home to me. This club was amongst the bottom three of the 92 clubs that made up the Football League. On top of that the Victoria Ground was a run down relic from the past. In addition they were a racing certainty once again just a few months down the line at the end of that 1971/2 season to have to apply for re-election. It would be the 10th application in their history, a record that might spell the end of Football League soccer in the town of Hartlepool.

John Curry and I sat down in this board room of little history, one salutary small china plate adorning the walls. We were underneath the grandstand on Clarence Road, the coal trains from those same pit villages and towns that I driven through on the way in were snaking their way past, shaking everything to their foundations. The one commemorative plate hung on the wall jigged from side to side, never falling off. I imagined it had been a fixture there for years pinned to those dark, dank walls as the coal wagons made their way to the bustling Hartlepool dock area and then on to industrial Teesside.

Everything I saw of the ground and its surroundings should have deterred me, but it didn't. I now had my managerial blinkers on! Curry was at his persuasive best, as he opened up about how we could change the fortunes of this ailing club. With his chairman's hat on, he assured me he would not meddle with the playing side of the club, team selection, training and coaching as well as the firing and hiring. I thought to myself that was encouraging. Brownie had stressed to me only hours before to make sure I was in charge or I should not take the job. He also added some of the wisest words ever uttered to me in my life, that if I was appointed to, "make sure you are a bastard, but an honest bastard."

Chairman Curry also told me there was a silver lining around the corner in the way of a new dual carriageway to run through exactly were we sitting, and with local council grants we would soon have a new grandstand and dressing room facilities, offices and a board room. That was thirty eight years ago as I write and Clarence Road is still there and unaltered to this day. Hartlepool United Football Club have since built a modern structure in place of that grandstand and appear to have lost the habit of finishing at the bottom of the pile.

Curry never once asked me what I had to offer the club. Someone had marked his card about me, and it appeared the job was mine from the start. Maybe they had tried a dozen others and they'd all turned the job down. On the stark evidence so far, they would not have been wrong!

Having put pen to paper for a basic wage of £88 per week, two pounds a week less than what I had been earning as a player at Sunderland, I drove back to my home in Whitburn and told Valerie of this great, 'not to be missed' opportunity. She was bathing our two young children Jane and Roger. "How much is your salary?" Valerie instantly asked. That spoiled the day, as I realised I had selfishly taken this job for me and not for us, which I have to confess, was often the case throughout my football managerial career.

It transpired that John Curry had been alerted to me by Len Shackleton, who at the time was filling the inside page of the *Sunday People* with all sorts of football gossip. He thought I was management quality and had a decent record as he had been responsible for setting up Brian Clough at the same club a few years before. I like to think it turned out over the coming years that he wasn't wrong. Len Shackleton at that time was pretty much the major conduit for many of the transfers and the occasional managerial appointment to and from the north east clubs. I now consider that he was an unpaid forerunner of the present day agent. Len certainly got his payback from my appointment as Hartlepool boss as over the next few seasons I fed to him many an inside story surrounding the big three in the north east and my own club. The exchanges between us were generally in the club house or on the golf course of South Shields Golf Club of which I am still a member. Shack always played during the week, never at the weekend because, as he put it, "I never play golf on my day off." That was typical Shack. In addition I became a contributor to 'Shack's Club', as I supplied an occasional letter to his Sunday paper column under the fictitious name of Tom Moody, who was my father-in-law and a grand bloke as well. The best letter of the week entitled you to join the club.

I concocted a letter in Tom's name and he duly received an exclusive Shack's tie and £5 for the contribution and in addition was invited to the end of season drinks party thrown by *The People* newspaper, but only on one condition – that under strict orders from 'Shack' he kept quiet about being my father in law, so as not to cross the sports editor who would not be best pleased at this flagrant piece of nepotism.

With it all happening so quickly there was not even a farewell drink with my former team-mates. There was no time for a family break or to even catch my breath as I was introduced to the playing staff on the Monday morning, 8 March 1971, exactly two days before my 32nd birthday. I'm pretty sure that made me the youngest manager in the Football League then.

The day before that Monday morning I had spent quietly with my family and Valerie's parents Tom and Sally Moody at their home in the rural village of East Rainton in County Durham. It was always a good eating house and this day was no different as roast was the Sunday norm. Once the table was cleared away, I suggested we have a run out to Hartlepool in my white Triumph 2000 to show everyone were I was to be found as from tomorrow onwards. We all piled in to my car, our children oblivious to their future.

Arriving at the ground, no one was impressed and Tom, always a Doubting Thomas, could not believe what he saw. He must have been tossing over in his mind the comparative grandeur of Roker Park some 30 miles north. As we stood there, the adults open-mouthed and silent, the children excitedly running around on the grassless pitch unaware of the significance of the moment, it crossed my mind that maybe I should quit before a ball was kicked. Now that would have caused a stir! But no, the youthful ambition once again took over. I desperately wanted to be sitting amongst those privileged 92, even if it was under the sword of Damocles – re-election!

There were no club blazers and flannels at Hartlepool, just a pile of old training kit, which was dumped on a table in the middle of the dressing room on a Monday morning. Whatever you grabbed you kept for the week, so get there early on a Monday or end up with the scrag ends. It was kit peppered with holes and the entire dressing room area was filled with the smell of carbolic soap, the abrasive substance which when liberally applied rubbed away the skin and gave you a rash around your bollocks!

That same well-worn table, which held the kit on a Monday and the tea and oranges on a Saturday matchday, would often be thumped at a later date as I laid into one of the unfortunates in the dressing room who had not been born with what it takes to make it to the big time. There were plenty in the Hartlepool squad all being paid a pittance, but happy to be called a 'Pro'. Amongst some of those never-have-beens, there was a young tall, skinny, raw-boned lad, who had plenty going for him, mainly his appetite for work and his desire to learn from an old professional like me. His name was Bill Green, a young centre-half who was later transferred to Carlisle United in a bizarre deal before making his name at West Ham United.

On Wednesday 10 March 1971, two days after joining the club, I lead my team into battle for the first time, away at Southend United, who were a few places above us in the league. It was a round trip of over 700 miles to the first of many grounds that I had never been to on my football travels as a Sunderland player which I would visit with my new club. What's more we travelled down on the day of the game in an outdated bus without toilet facilities, then made our way back immediately after the match. Overnight stops were unheard of at this club. I remember thinking very early on this was amongst a dozen other things that I wanted to change. We never made our pre-match meal in the afternoon before the game as traffic was heavy and we missed the scheduled time of 4pm at a fast food outlet along the A127 so we pressed on to reach the ground 45 minutes before kick-off, arriving only just in time to hand the team sheet in to the referee at the mandatory 30 minutes before the game kicked off at 7.30pm.

We all tucked in to some pork pies and sweet tea at the caravan café on the car park at Roots Hall. I paid for this most singular of pre-match meals and then claimed my expenses from the club, which I received some months later when they had some spare cash floating around. These first few days taught me what the game was about at this level, I had been 'cosseted' at the big club on Wearside for the past thirteen years. This was the real world and I realised that my football life would be very different from now on.

Obviously this was not the best preparation for my first game, however the adrenalin kept me going as I read out my first team selection. One comforting thought for me was that I had inherited my former team-mate George Herd as my first team coach and I was glad to have him around to share the load. Needless to say we started the game slowly and ended up losing 0-2. To compound the misery of the result and the long journey home, the defeat dumped us to the bottom of the Fourth Division. We arrived back in Hartlepool at 6am the following morning. What had I let myself in for? "Happy thirty second birthday Len!"

I realised that we were a certainty to have to apply for re-election and that I would be telephoning my newly-found friends in the game, my fellow managers, for their club's vote in June at the Annual General Meeting of the Football League. Although we won our next match 2-1 against John Bond's Bournemouth, we ended up in the bottom four of the Fourth Division and little Hartlepool – never a winner since their inception way back in 1908 – now had the threat of expulsion from the league hovering over their heads that Saturday morning, 5 June 1971.

The dinner at our hotel on the Friday night before the meeting felt as if it was the last supper as pessimism prevailed amongst our group. I awoke next morning after little sleep. On my mind was one thing only, the future of the club, or more to the point the future of Len Ashurst after just three months as a manager. I entered the escalator on the fourth floor and amongst the football fraternity making their way down for breakfast was a diminutive-looking chap who recognised me and proffered his hand wishing me, "all the best for your re-election". As soon as he opened his mouth his north east accent gave him away. He introduced himself as Russell Atkinson, an ardent Sunderland supporter from Westoe Colliery. He was at the hotel taking part in a national safety competition with The National Coal Board. "Good luck," he pronounced as we departed the lift.

"We'll need it," I thought, with the likes of Hereford United and Wigan Athletic breathing down our neck, itching to win election, and deservedly so, into the Football League. Big Ron Atkinson and Ron Saunders had heard the exchange and both shook my hand, then with a pertinent nod of the head Atkinson spat out a none too hopeful message, "You're up against it, Len, but all the best." My buoyancy for our survival was dissipating fast! We were at the mercy of other club chairman of the Football League. Quite frankly I did not think they would be bothered. Indeed some would hardly know where Hartlepool could be found on the map and would certainly have never have set foot in the place. What interested the bigger clubs was how the money from media rights and advertising would be distributed for the coming season, with all of the major clubs fighting their corner for a bigger share of the pot. In that

The England youth team to play Switzerland at Brighton's Goldstone Ground in 1958. I am fourth from left.

The closest I got to a full England cap was playing for Young England against the full side in May 1961. Our team featured starlets such as Bobby Moore and Terry Paine.

ENGLAND v. YOUNG ENGLAND

ENGLAND - TEAM MANAGER W. Winterbottom
(White shirts, blue shorts, red and white stockings):—

Goalkeeper :	R. Springett (Sheffield Wednesday)
Right Back :	J. Armfield (Blackpool)
Left Back :	M. McNeil (Middlesbrough)
Right Half Back :	R. Robson (West Bromwich Albion)
Centre Half Back :	P. Swan (Sheffield Wednesday)
Left Half Back :	R. Flowers (Wolverhampton W.)
Outside Right :	B. Douglas (Blackburn Rovers)
Inside Right :	J. Haynes (Fulham) (Captain)
Centre Forward :	G. Hitchens (Aston Villa)
Inside Left :	J. Greaves (Chelsea)
Outside Left :	R. Charlton (Manchester United)
Reserve :	B. Miller (Burnley)
Trainer :	H. Shepherdson (Middlesbrough)

YOUNG ENGLAND - MANAGER/COACH : W. Wright
(Red shirts, white shorts, white stockings):—

Goalkeeper :	E. Macedo (Fulham)
Right Back :	J. Angus (Burnley)
Left Back :	L. Ashurst (Sunderland)
Right Half Back :	J. Kirkham (Wolverhampton W.)
Centre Half Back :	R. McGrath (Newcastle United)
Left Half Back :	R. Moore (West Ham United)
Outside Right :	T. Paine (Southampton)
Inside Right :	F. Hill (Bolton)
Centre Forward :	J. Byrne (Crystal Palace)
Inside Left :	J. Robson (Burnley)
Outside Left :	G. Harris (Burnley)
Reserve :	J. Barnwell (Arsenal)

LEN ASHURST
Sunderland

Pictured just after joining Sunderland in December 1957 on the princely sum of £11 per week in the season and £10 over the summer.

The great Bill Shankly. He only ever spoke to me once, but it made such an impression when he told me, "Lenny, you should have been a Liverpool player, laddie."

Jim Montgomery might be most famous for his double save in the 1973 FA Cup final, but I saw him pull off countless stops just as good in the years we played together.

Charlie Hurley captained Sunderland throughout most of the 1960s and was rightly, in my opinion, voted Player of the Century by Sunderland fans for his contribution to establishing the club in the First Division.

Brian Clough was a goalscorer supreme – but didn't he know it. Our fallout over my part in the injury which finished his career was compounded by his big-headed antics and general unpleasantness towards me.

Nicky Sharkey was one of the players who made way for Clough when he arrived from Middlesbrough for £48,000 in 1961. Nicky's claim to fame is that he scored five goals against Norwich City at Roker Park in March 1963 to equal the club record.

I married my sweetheart Valerie on 13 May 1961 in her home village of East Rainton in County Durham.

Larking around after training. Above, in the showers with Nicky Sharkey, and left on the Roker pitch. That's me pulling down Charlie Hurley's shorts!

Mum and Dad and my three brothers wearing Liverpool colours before Sunderland's 2-0 4th round FA Cup win over the Reds in 1961.

Two of the Everton F.C. ground staff, armed with paint scrapers and paint remover, strip the thick red paint from the goalposts at Goodison Park before repainting them in time for the kick-off.

"Red" Raid During The Night On Goodison

Goal-Posts Found Painted In Colours Of Liverpool

Liverpool supporters struck the first blow in the "derby" battle during the night. When the Everton ground staff arrived at Goodison Park this morning they found the two sets of goalposts had been completely covered with bright red paint.

Four men were immediately put to work scraping off the thick oil paint and rubbing down the posts with paint remover in a battle to restore them to their former pristine condition.

Said one of them: "There's

no doubt who's responsible for this lot. They must have climbed into the ground about midnight last night. When we got here this morning the paint was completely dry.

SHINING WHITE SOON

The ground staff were confident that the goalposts would be shining white again in time for the 3 p.m. kick-off.

Mr. Bill Shankly, Liverpool's manager, was at the Anfield ground early this morning checking on the condition of Scottish International centre-forward Ian St. John, who is doubtful for this afternoon's game because of a toe injury.

Told about the goalpost incident he said: "It sounds like psychological warfare to me."

FIRST IN THE QUEUE

Two 16 - years - old Everton supporters were first in the queue at Goodison Park this morning.

They were Eric Wright, of 64 St. Anne Street, Liverpool, and Donald Walsh, of 12 Menai Road, Bootle, arrived at the Gladway Street-turnstiles at 9 a.m.—hours before they were due to open.

They certainly had nothing to do with painting the goalposts. "Red is one colour we wouldn't even touch," said Roy.

And the forecast of two Evertonians: "A 5-2 win for the Blues, of course."

once again.

Mr. McCoy has already written one song — "An American Sailor at the Cavern" — for charity, and is now writing a second for another charity.

Lagos. At London Airport he said: "This is a further stage in my tour of all Commonwealth countries. It is a fact-finding mission and I shall find facts."

operations. No pedestrians were allowed near the cordoned off area and police and firemen ensured that there was no smoking inside the gas filled area.

script for the film "Les Liaisons Dangereuses," won the French Goncourt prize for "La vie" in 1957. He was also a playwright and essayist.—(Reuter).

Three Liverpool supporters who began hitch-hiking to Milan last Saturday photographed after their arrival at the Milan stadium to-day. They are Robin Ashurst, aged 20, of 9 Grace Avenue, Fazakerley; 20-years-old John Leek, of 45 St. Bernard's Drive, Bootle, and Tony John, aged 23, of 100 Admiral Grove, Toxteth. They have not yet got tickets for to-night's match.

My younger brother Robin was always getting himself into bother with his antics. Here are two clippings from the *Liverpool Echo*, the first describing how he and some mates climbed into Goodison Park and painted the goalposts red before a Merseyside derby, and the second a picture of him in Milan for Liverpool's European Cup semi-final second leg when he had told his boss he was ill!

In the 1960/61 FA Cup we defeated Arsenal, Liverpool and Norwich on the way to meeting Spurs in the quarter-final at Roker Park. Tottenham took the lead but this photograph shows the 61,000 crowd's reaction after Willie McPheat scored the equalising goal in a 1-1 draw.

Our epic Cup tie against Manchester United in the 1963/64 season went to three games. We should have won the first two, but United pegged us back late on. Here I am clearing from Denis Law in the second replay at Huddersfield. We took the lead once again, but couldn't sustain it and lost 1-5.

Heading the ball clear. My fearless approach to playing the game soon earned me the nickname 'Psycho'.

"Ref, it was only a little tap on the ankles…!" I didn't get into that much trouble with referees, but here I am being booked. The chances are I deserved it!

Manager Alan Brown enjoyed two spells in charge at Sunderland, winning promotion in 1964 before sensationally leaving the club in the summer over a dispute over receiving a bonus for his feat. He was a very hard, stern man, but he knew how to keep footballers in line and put a good team together.

In fashionable Crombie coat

After 458 appearances and 14 years at Sunderland I realised my top flight playing days were over . . .

. . . and so in March 1971 I joined Fourth Division Hartlepool as player-manager. It felt like a different world!

Len Shackleton, my golfing partner, played a huge role in getting me the jobs at both Hartlepool and Sheffield Wednesday, where I moved after spending 18 months as Gillingham manager.

In October 1972 a fire burnt down most of the main stand at Hartlepool's Victoria Ground. Here I am inspecting the damage to the dressing room area. Hartlepool were not insured so I spent the next few days begging and borrowing kit, balls and cash donations to keep Hartlepool afloat.

One of the few great moments from my time in charge at Priestfield Stadium. Meeting Watford chairman Elton John before playing his team at home in the old Third Division. I am sharing the moment with club secretary Malcolm Bramley.

Joining Sheffield Wednesday seemed like my big break. They were a huge club, down on their luck and in the lower reaches of the Third Division. Here chairman Bert McGee (centre) welcomes myself and my trainer Tony Toms to Hillsborough.

RIGHT LADS, OFF YOU GO, AND REMEMBER, PAIN IS GOOD NEWS!

ILKLEY MOOR

FERRET

SURVIVAL KIT

Tony took the squad on a 'bonding session' up on the Yorkshire moors in January 1976 – which very quickly went down in local folklore and was celebrated by this cartoon in the local newspaper.

Following a successful stint at Hartlepool, Chris Turner became Sheffield Wednesday manager in 2002 after I gave him his debut as a young goalkeeper in 1976. He is now back in charge at Hartlepool.

After taking the job at Fourth Division Newport County in June 1978 I took the club to unparalleled success. We won the Welsh Cup for the first time in the club's history in May 1980. Here the team celebrates in the dressing room after the 5-1 aggregate victory over Shrewsbury Town. Goalkeeper Gary Plumley is catching the drips from my champagne!

Showing off the Cup to the massed hordes from the Newport Town Hall balcony.

Ashurst's Army rejoice at some long-awaited success in south-east Wales.

My daughter Jane and son Roger with the Welsh Cup. He couldn't resist wearing an England kit!

Undertaking the gruelling Cardiff marathon to raise funds for the Rookwood Hospital. I clocked the shoddy time of five hours and one minute, at least passing runner no. 446 in the closing stages!

My brother Robin tipped me the wink about a young lad from work at Ford Merseyside. He'd been attracting a lot of admirers at South Liverpool FC and I had to don a disguise to secure his signature. Here Aldo, who would go on to a fabulous career with Liverpool, Tranmere and Real Sociedad, scores the clinching goal in our 4-2 victory at Walsall on the final day of the 1979/80 season, which saw us promoted to the Third Division.

I was blessed with great strikers at Newport. Here the three of them, from left, Tommy Tynan, John Aldridge and Dave Gwyther, celebrate promotion from the Fourth Division.

In my first full season with Cardiff City we won promotion back to Division Two, where we'd slipped in my initial months in charge. Along the way I earned a Bell's Manager of the Month award.

Greeting my brother Robin in the Cardiff boardroom after beating Leyton Orient 2-0 to win promotion to the Second Division.

My triumphant return to Roker Park as manager proved a very difficult homecoming. We survived on the final day of the 1983/84 season, but were relegated the following campaign.

Tom Cowie was my chairman at Sunderland. He was a phenomenally successful businessman, but could not stir the huge sleeping giant that was Sunderland Football Club into action.

Taking my team to Wembley for the Milk Cup final was one of the proudest moments of my life…

…however I knew, even as I posed for photos alongside our youth coach Ian Hughes (left) and Chief Scout George Herd, that things were not right. The players were unhappy at the way their Wembley bonuses had been handled and I was unhappy at not being given tickets in the Royal Box for my family as Norwich manager Ken Brown had.

Signing Clive Walker from Chelsea was a fine piece of business. Unfortunately when it mattered most he missed a penalty as we lost the League Cup final. He had been magnificent during the run to Wembley, though.

A tearful Barry Venison, who I had made the youngest man ever to captain a team at Wembley, leads his players around the pitch. Little did any of the supporters know of the shenanigans which had been going on in the dressing room in the lead up to the game as Barry had been forced to black out his Adidas boots so our sponsors Nike did not notice. It was that or not play at Wembley!

I worked in Qatar from 1986-1988. Here I am eating a traditional 'Mutton Grab' meal with my hosts …

… while sometimes you would come across the most unusual of obstacles on the putting 'greens'!

Coaching in Malaysia in 1992 with my assistant Tajuddin Nor. I managed Pahang and we won the Malaysia Charity Shield, but I never did earn the gold ingot I was promised for winning the league, finishing second.

I was employed in Malaysia by Prince Tengku (here with the red and blue tie on). He loved football and kept close tabs on the team. Note the bodyguard and car in the background.

I coached Wakrah Club in Qatar from 1993-1995. Here I am watching a night match in Jordan. Alongside me is my Brazilian assistant Flamarion.

In September 1994 we undertook a tour to Baghdad, which was an incredible experience. This was the view from my hotel room in the centre of the city, looking across the river Tigris. Note the gun emplacement on the mound to protect the bridge.

While in Baghdad I went on a guided tour of the city and came across an underground bunker which had been bombed during the conflict a couple of years earlier, killing around 500 civilians inside. It was a sobering monument.

At the end of the tour we visited Gaza, but on the bus on the way out of Baghdad I had a lucky escape when a rock was thrown through the windscreen, killing the assistant coach driver just in front of me and striking me a glancing blow. Here you can see the dressing covering the cuts on my face as we tuck into some food in Gaza.

Having spent five years, from their start up in 1998, working within the Premier League Academy system, I can testify to the wonderful work they do – especially at clubs such as Middlesbrough, who have a policy of bringing through players into the first team. There are still many wrongs which need to be righted, however.

Sir Trevor Brooking is one of the most loved figures in the game. But I have to ask the question is he being effective in his role as Director of Football Development at the FA? Not in my opinion.

Ellen MacArthur's achievements in sailing far outweigh anything our footballers have done in the modern era. She is one of the sporting giants of our age. Footballers are mere cosseted pretenders in comparison.

sense, the game hasn't changed to this day. Just a few more zeros on the cheque nowadays.

Near the end of the morning agenda came the all-important (to me anyway) re-election vote. I can recall the voting slips being handed around the room. Then the Tellers collected the slips and counted them in the corner of the room in the presence of the auditor and four other representatives of the Football League and the clubs themselves. All I could think was "What are they contriving?" We waited for what seemed an eternity, but then fifteen minutes later the result was announced. Strong candidates applying to gain admission were Hereford United, then managed by John Charles one of the greatest players to grace English and Welsh football, along with the Lancashire club Wigan Athletic, who had been knocking on the League's door for some time.

I had done my bit towards the cause in lobbying by telephone most of the managers that mattered in the First Division, playing on the human element of this being my first chance in management and that when I joined Hartlepool in March my club was already down and out. The majority of them indicated to me their desire to help and said they would be speaking to their chairman on our behalf. However what they decided today might be another matter entirely. I was assured of one club's vote and moral support and that was my former club Sunderland, but we needed enough to finish in the top four clubs. Anything less and we would be out of the League.

The fact was that the bigger, southern-based clubs wanted the likes of Hartlepool, Barrow, Southport and Workington to go the same way as Gateshead had a few years previously by voting them out of the Football League. They considered we were sponging from the pot of money put up each year by the League, which was shared out on a pro-rata basis throughout the four divisions. Plus, of course, we were so far away from them. Of those four clubs from the North of England, only Hartlepool survives as a Football League club today. The influential majority eventually had their way.

Silence fell on the room as the result was announced by Alan Hardaker, the Secretary of the Football League. Wearing a pair of those black-rimmed reading glasses, in his Lancashire accent he pronounced, "Lincoln City and Newport County 47 votes each, both of these clubs are re-elected to the Football League." A pause followed, I don't know why, as Hardaker was never a man for subtle drama. "Barrow, 38 votes, are also re-elected," he continued.

The tension amongst our small group of Hartlepool officials was tangible. I glanced at my chairman John Curry, who was doubled up in his chair with the strain. Hardaker eventually announced, "and Hartlepool with 33 votes also retain their Football League status." John Curry was an ill man. He never moved. Finally he was helped out of the room to be attended by a doctor who was on hand, obviously for this sort of occurrence. Applying for re-election was obviously a health hazard.

For me this was a defining moment in my very short tenure as a manager. It meant that I was assured of at least one full season at the hard end of the game to prove my ability as an up and coming young manager. We were back in business, hand shakes all around and then it was to the bar for a brandy and port to settle a stomach that had been in turmoil for 24 hours.

The bar was filled with football people. I was in my element and on a real high. I was warned several times by experienced men to 'be aware'. Management is, after all, a profession that mocks any thought of longevity and loyalty. However I was enjoying the moment and milking the plaudits coming from fellow managers surrounding me at this trough of experience.

Alan Brown and a director of Sunderland Keith Collings came over to shake my hand and wish me "Good Luck". I had the feeling I would need it.

HAVING CLEARED out seven players at the end of the previous season, one of my first signings for Hartlepool for the start of the new 1971/72 campaign was a player called George Potter from Torquay United, closely followed by his Gulls team-mate Eric Welsh, a neat little right winger who turned out to be a crock with a serious knee injury.

A local paper reporting on the double free transfer signing of two team-mates made reference something along the lines, 'That both players were going to live together, as they had been doing in Torquay'. As you can imagine, neither player were too happy at the suggestion that they were a touch effeminate and asked me for my support, as they were going to take legal action against the paper – Defamation of Character, I believe they called it.

I indicated to them, through my connections at Sunderland, that I could access a suitable solicitor to take the case on their behalf. They agreed and added that they would give a portion of any settlement to thank me for my support, as they realised the case could mean that they may have to miss training to attend the courts. I wasn't going to say no to the generous offer. Four weeks later, on a Friday morning, an out of court settlement of £900 was made to them. True to their word I received a gift of £300 in cash. Amazingly, in four weeks, without moving away from my office desk and having made one phone call, I was given by these two Fourth Division players nearly half of the amount of money that I had received at Sunderland from my testimonial match after ten years of service to the club. Who was it that said it's a funny old game?!

Both players kept their places in the team: but entirely on their merits. I was backing my judgment on signing them, rather than their generosity towards me. Needless to say the reporter was quickly removed from the sports department of the paper, probably ending up scribing a few lines on the Hart Village Church Fete for the diocese magazine and the Womens' Guild events in the town.

An additional signing of mine for the new season, who was to go on to great things in an infamous but successful football management career, was a young left winger by the name of Neil Warnock. I signed him on a free transfer in manager Jimmy McGuigan's office at Rotherham United. That was a policy of mine. If I wanted a player to sign for me I always met them on their home ground or at a halfway house. I would never have convinced a player to sign for me if they had visited and seen the town and the surrounding area. Warnock and other players who followed him later concurred. I like to think Neil stored this away amongst his armoury of psychological ploys for his future managerial career!

I was desperate to improve conditions at the club as well as the playing staff, but with no budget to do so, resorted to some innovative thinking. Leeds United, with whom I had many a football battle against during my days as a Sunderland player, had won their first European trophy, the Fairs Cup, defeating Juventus on away goals, at the end of the previous season. I rang Don Revie, their manager, and asked if he could help us out by giving us some training kit. His positive answer sent George Herd and I hurrying down to Elland Road one Monday morning, where we were made to feel so welcome by Revie and his management team. We met up and joked with some our previous adversaries Bremner, Hunter, Charlton and co. over the situation at Hartlepool.

Within an hour of arriving at Leeds we were back in the car driving back up the A1 with a boot full of training kit and a back seat piled high with the white shirts of Leeds United. I knew what it would do for dressing room moral to have some decent kit – especially as it had at some stage been worn by some of the greatest players in the land.

We opened the 1971/72 season with a home game against Reading in appalling weather conditions with rain and gale force winds battering the town. This suited us as we knew those so-called 'Southern Softies' would not fancy it. We had done nothing to enhance the décor of the visitor's dressing room during the summer close season. In fact quite the opposite.

A week before that game I had instructed Harry Simpson, our grounds-man, to take out the 150 watt bulbs from the ceiling and replace them with 50 watt bulbs. A dingy visitors' dressing room as the away team walk in does nothing for the spirits. With water trickling down the walls from the unrelenting north èast gale and an old 'Kelly' stove in the middle of the floor to heat, or not, the room it was a dark, dank and unwelcoming place. Reading were, metaphorically speaking, one down before they kicked off.

I wouldn't put it totally down to the conditions which Reading faced as, after all, we still had to put the ball into their net, but a 3-1 victory was a very satisfying result. It was something of a high with which to start the rollercoaster ride which was to be my first full season in football management. On the following Wednesday morning my club received a letter from the Football League. Reading had filed a complaint about the facilities offered to them at the Victoria Ground – I didn't expect it would be the last!

This 1971/72 season was a season of two halves, bottom of the league at the start of the New Year with only 11 points from 20 matches, we embarked upon an astonishing run of games, winning ten of fourteen from mid-March, which saw the team soar up the table to finish 16th with 42 points from 46 games, with home gates trebling to 6,000 plus. That wasn't to say that the season wasn't a massively steep learning curve on just about every front. Looking back I realise I was put through the full spectrum of a football manager's life, with the exception of spending money on an incoming transfer deal or having the fulfilment of selling a player for a five figure sum, all in that one season. I realised very early on that managing at this level meant you had to have a skin of leather, the wisdom of Solomon and friends in the game that you could turn to in times of need, plus a huge slice of Lady Luck. I believed at the time that I had all of those attributes going for me. What also pulled me through was my stable and solid marriage and the stark realisation that there were four mouths to feed in our house in the village of Whitburn.

In that season I was really put through the hoop by a club gyrating between bankruptcy and self-strangulation. I knew the situation was always tight, but it became apparent that things were close to becoming terminal – and very quickly. On a Monday morning in mid-January 1972, as we sat bottom of the entire League following a 1-2 home defeat by Cambridge United, I was taking training along with George Herd at the Victoria Ground. Out of the corner of my eye I saw John Curry striding across the pitch towards me and when your chairman approaches you so early on a Monday morning, especially after a home defeat, you start to think the worst. His first words when he reached me didn't quell the uneasy feeling developing in my stomach: "We have a problem here, Len . . ."

Curry beckoned me to my office, sat me down and told me that the club was in dire financial trouble and unless we could find a four figure sum by Thursday it would cease to exist. This was pretty serious and immediate stuff.

"We will have to sell a player," he said, stating the obvious.

Fairly desperate, considering not many clubs will be looking to pay a great deal for players from a club propping up the entire Football League, I decided to start at the top and picked up the phone to Malcolm Allison, who was riding high in the First Division with Manchester City and had recently told Curry that he was impressed with our left winger Neil Warnock.

"Malcolm, it's Len Ashurst. I understand you were impressed with Warnock, our left winger, in the game at Chester. Would you like to make us an offer?"

Allison burst out laughing and retorted, "Len, I only bullshited your chairman to cheer him up and soften the blow of the heavy defeat." My heart sank and I could picture the cockney glint in Malcolm's eye as he spoke. I told Curry there was no deal.

"There is only one thing to do and that is to ring up Brian Clough at Derby County and ask him to help us," he said.

"Chairman, you will have to pick the phone up yourself as Brian and I are not the best of pals and if he does a deal to help us out it will be for you and Hartlepool United Football Club and not for me." The call was made and Brian agreed to see us at the Baseball Ground the next morning at 10am sharp.

We departed Hartlepool at 7am and arrived in plenty of time. We found Brian's office in the bowels of the club just before the allotted meeting time and Cloughie opened the door dressed in his famous green sweater, baggy grey tracksuit bottoms finished of with a pair of short Wellington boots.

"Ah, welcome John and come in," he said to Chairman Curry. Then, looking at me, he said, "You can piss off." What a put down. I was put in my place good and proper.

All I glimpsed of Brian's office through the half-opened door was a cabinet full of alcohol on the facing wall. I made myself 'comfortable' on a chair in the corridor underneath the grandstand and patiently waited. There was no hospitable cup of tea to pass the time away, and I was left alone in a cold and depressing concrete-walled area, which added to the ignominy of being shut out of the conversation between two men who were obviously very good friends. Finally, after about thirty minutes, I heard movement. Looking down the short corridor I saw John Curry beckoning me to join him as he made his way outside to the car park.

"Have we done a deal?" I asked.

"Get in the car and I shall tell you," he replied.

Once headed homewards the chairman told me that, instead of Warnock, he had persuaded Brian to buy Tony Parry, our centre-half who had played under Clough's tenure at the Victoria Ground in a deal worth £2,500. When we reached Hartlepool I was to go to the player's house to tell him of the deal and then drive him the next day to the Baseball Ground, oversee the negotiation of personal terms and ensure pen was put to paper. Once all the procedures were completed I was to return with the cheque. This sort of money would keep the club in business for quite a while.

It seemed straightforward enough, especially as I thought persuading Tony Parry to join Derby would be plain sailing as he was originally from the Midlands and had family living down in the area. Indeed Parry had been signed from Burton Albion by Peter Taylor during Brian Clough's reign. He was an amiable sort, sleight of build and a decent player, but someone who liked a drink. Unwittingly that meant he was to find himself at the centre of a saga which could have put Hartlepool out of business.

Upon reaching Hartlepool, I immediately made for his small terraced house close to the ground. The player himself opened the door and invited me in to a tiny, impoverished home. There was hardly a piece of furniture around and certainly no carpet on the floor. However there was a huge television in the corner of the room.

"Tony I have some good news for you," I began.

"What's that?" he replied.

Giving it the big sell I continued, "We have done a deal with Brian Clough at Derby County for your transfer. I will pick you up in the morning and we'll go down and complete the formalities . . ."

That was as far as I got as he broke in to my flow to tell me quite emphatically that he had a big problem with Clough. "I am not signing for him as he won't let the players enjoy a social drink." The deal was off as far as Parry was concerned. At that pivotal moment the club was slipping in to receivership. I pointed out to him that if he refused to go he would be out of work by Thursday night and on the dole with the rest of us. It didn't matter to Parry, who gave me another emphatic 'no'.

I rushed straight down to John Curry's house to inform him of the hitch.

"Leave it with me," he said. "I shall give you a call when I have spoken to the player."

The next morning I travelled back down the A1 to Derby with Tony Parry alongside me in the car. The transfer went through and I returned with a cheque for £2,500 to the board meeting which had been convened to welcome the salvation cheque into the club's bank account.

I never did get to see Brian Clough, other than that brief put down outside his office the day before. If I had encountered him when leaving Parry at the ground I would have been inclined to tell him he had chosen the wrong centre-half as Bill Green, a youngster of great promise, was the lad he should have signed. Nevertheless, with this gesture in buying Parry, Clough had re-paid a favour to his former chairman and club for putting him on the managerial path to unparalleled fame and fortune. It would have pleased him less to learn that also inadvertently he had saved me from the dole queue.

When I felt it appropriate I asked the chairman how he had persuaded Tony Parry to change his mind and agree to join Derby. A wry smile broke across his face. Removing his black, horn-rimmed glasses Curry replied, "Len, it was money. £200 of it."

I also wondered what agreement was reached on that Monday morning during the private meeting inside Clough's office, the office that I was never asked to step inside. I never did find that out.

Managing a club like Hartlepool meant you had to grasp any help you were offered. One day in the spring of 1972 we were told that the obsolete cinema which stood next to the ground was to be demolished. With the retaining wooden fence surrounding the football pitch near to collapse, this was seen as an opportunity too good to miss and we accepted the offer of the free granite blocks from the rubble. The demolition people even delivered them to the ground. Volunteers from the supporters club, Harry Simpson and I built two walls running the full width of the pitch behind each goal. Painted blue, they are still in position at today's newly refurbished and renamed Victoria Park.

It was also sometimes the case that I had to avoid a hotel or a motorway service station where the club had called the year before for a pre-match meal as the bill had not been paid by the club. On one occasion I was up tight over an away game at Crewe Alexandra as the players' pre-match meal was late in being served. I made my way through a couple of swing doors into the kitchen confronting the staff as to why? On berating the chef for being late, I was promptly put down by the manager of the eatery, who had arrived on the scene and suggested that I back off or we would not be having a pre-match meal at all, as the bill for the previous season was still to be paid! I retreated, wholly chastened by his cutting comment. Tap water, which cost nothing, was the drink of the day with that particular pre-match meal as we kept costs to a minimum. This was management on the breadline.

Given the importance of help in keeping the club going it was all the more silly then that around that time I fell out with George Herd, my assistant at the club and trusted friend and team-mate from our Sunderland days. Like many fallouts between close friends and colleagues it was over a minor disagreement over a training schedule, which should have been settled immediately by me. Instead I overreacted and created a problem which should never have existed. I had asked George to take the players for some Friday morning sprints whilst I tended to some office work. The admin concluded, I popped in to training only to find that the players had gone home. I instantly sacked George for disobeying my orders, only to discover that he had thought the ground too dangerous to work on as it was ice bound.

On realising my mistake I immediately tried to mend bridges, but Wee George was a proud man and walked away, leaving me with the mess to deal with. I had acted hastily, an impulsive and flawed angry reaction. It is something I was ashamed of for many a day until I linked up with George again after becoming manager of Sunderland in 1984. With this balls-up I realised that I had to learn the clever quirks of management as quickly as possible. Pleasingly, George and I have remained good friends to this day. I also later employed him as my youth development coach at Kuwait Sporting Club in 1985, where he remained for a six-year spell looking after the Arab side.

George's departure from Hartlepool left me running the sinking ship on my own, which hardly improved matters. A great example of this came when I attempted to boost our scrap against demotion from the Football League by signing Bobby Smith from Chester on transfer deadline day in March 1972 on the premise that if he helped us to finish outside the bottom four he would receive a bonus of £500.

An archaic system existed regarding the registration of a player's transfer between clubs. Smith's transfer forms had to be physically registered at Football League headquarters in Lytham by 5pm on deadline day. There were no high-tech electronics back then, no emails and not even any faxes. So on that March Thursday afternoon I arrived at Lytham with Smith's transfer documents five minutes before the 5pm deadline, having rushed by car from Hartlepool that afternoon. I knocked. No one answered, I knocked again. Still no response, and yet lights shone brightly inside the building.

Eventually, in desperation to have the player registered, I climbed up onto one of the huge window ledges of this fine Victorian building and started hammering on the window trying to catch someone's attention. They were giving me the cold shoulder. However I was determined to stay until there was a response. I think the staff had decided between them that if they ignored me long enough I might go away – I was, after all, only from Hartlepool Football Club. It was an impasse as far as I was concerned. But I would stand my ground until they registered my player.

With no one responding to my banging on the window at that front office, I jumped down and raced around to the rear of the building and climbed on the biggest window ledge I could access, peeking in though the window. There was David Dent, the secretary of the League, sitting at his desk. I knocked on the window and he turned round and was clearly astonished at my persistence. Slipping the window down he took the transfer forms from me and processed them there and then. Bobby Smith played the following Saturday and proved to be an excellent professional and a fine influence on the team in our battle to survive.

There were now just a couple of months to the end of the 1971/72 season, but at least we were on a decent run of form. Five wins in seven games, including a 5-0 home thrashing of Stockport, had seen us move out of the re-election positions, albeit on goal average only. Easter Monday, 3 April 1972, saw us travel to Barrow, a distant Cumbrian outpost, to visit fellow re-election candidates for a vital game. My journey with the team through picturesque countryside was spoilt by the pain emanating from my stomach. It was the pain of a manager under extreme pressure. Now I knew how my Chairman had felt at that re-election meeting nine months before.

Barrow was a grim place back then – and that's me talking as manager of Hartlepool! The club had knocked down part of two grandstands to build a speedway track to bring in extra income to the club, so we were open to the elements, which responded by whipping a gale in off the sea and teeming down with the biggest raindrops I have ever seen. The ball was so hard that it felt as if it had been sculptured in the local Barrow-in-Furness shipyard. When it was kicked out of play it rolled for miles across the adjacent field in the high wind. We contrived to lose the game 0-2, which was a crushing disappointment as Barrow now stood three points clear of us. We had missed a huge opportunity to haul ourselves further up the table.

However the overriding feature for me was the attitude of the FIFA referee in charge of the game, who I was meeting for the first time. His name was Jack Taylor and he was to take charge of the 1974 World Cup final in Germany which he handled brilliantly. It seemed to me as I handed the team sheet in 30 minutes before kick-off, that he was asking himself, 'Why should I be refereeing this Fourth Division re-election scramble at this outpost of the soccer world, when Manchester and Liverpool are just down the road?' I wasn't impressed, however Jack proved to be an utterly charming man when I met him socially later in life.

After that humbling defeat at the worst ground I have ever taken a team to in all my managerial career, we never looked back as we put together a sequence of five wins in six games which took us out of the bottom four re-election group to the safety of 18th position in the table at the end of that season. The last of those five victories was our penultimate game of the season away at local rivals Darlington, a crucial match which we knew if we won would make us safe from re-election.

I had announced my team selection at a group meeting before we departed on the short trip to Darlington. But on arriving at Feethams I found that the pitch had been hose-piped, leaving it a veritable mud heap of a surface. I immediately made a change to my line-up and dropped Nicky Sharkey from the team, replacing him at centre-forward with a lad called Willie Waddell, who I thought would be more suited to the playing surface. It proved a masterstroke as we won the game 2-1 with Waddell scoring one of the goals. We were safe.

Neil Warnock ended up in hospital overnight after the game with a sprained ankle and serious bruising to his spleen. He had complained to me at half-time, but to no avail as I sent him out for the second half with orders to "run it off". Bobby Smith collapsed in ecstasy as the final whistle was blown – it was either delirium at achieving our goal, or delight at pocketing that £500 bonus!

We had survived the re-election scramble – unlike Bobby Smith my reward was not a monetary one. I merely had personal and professional satisfaction for a job well done, although an added bonus was that I picked up the *Daily Mirror* Footballer of the Year award. The prize was a silver tankard, which was the first and only piece of silverware I was to win in over fifteen years as a player. It prompted me to prolong my career for another season. After all, I couldn't afford to replace me!

It was proved how vital it was that we had kept our heads above the dotted re-election line as those other serial members of that particular club, Barrow, found themselves voted out at the League AGM, being replaced by Hereford United. A 1-7 defeat at Exeter on the final Saturday of the season ended their Football League existence ignominiously. I am convinced they were thrown out because of the disaster area they had inflicted upon themselves in demolishing half of their stadium. Their passing was certainly not mourned anywhere outside south Cumbria.

In the summer of 1972 the telephone rang in my cramped office, which seemed as if it had been built around my office desk. It was a producer from Tyne-Tees Television. Out of the blue came a ray of light. They wanted to know if I would agree to my team taking part in a fitness challenge programme involving a number of different sports. The players would be pitting their fitness against a group of Royal Marines from Lympston in Devon in what would be called in today's world a Sporting Celebrity Challenge. I readily agreed. Television cameras at the Victoria Ground were a very rare sight!

There would only be one winner and it was the Royal Marines, who bench-pressed masses of iron, did one arm push ups for fun and leg-pressed 200kgs. With quads and thighs like tree trunks they could also sprint quicker than any of my professionals. I was duly impressed and wanted to know more.

Their leader was a guy called Tony Toms, nicknamed 'Tomsie'. I liked what I saw and decided I wanted him alongside me. I had managed without assistance for quite a while since George Herd and I'd had cross words. When I proposed this addition to the staff to the board they took some convincing. However they reluctantly agreed after my veiled threat that if they vetoed my request they would be looking for a new manager. Shortly afterwards Tomsie bought himself out of the army in time to join me for pre-season training. He proved to be innovative and invaluable. He was also brilliant in keeping dressing room moral high. In addition, he was the first man to change the diets of professional footballers in this country, twenty years before Arsène Wenger arrived at Arsenal, and he completely changed the training programme from that which we had all been used to over the years. However Tomsie arrived with some baggage – what Royal Marine wouldn't – which would surface very soon afterwards.

That summer, in a bid to improve the team within the confines of my miniscule wage budget, I had to make many changes in the playing staff. I knew that in this job I would be making difficult decisions many times throughout a football season and this time the unfortunate recipient of bad news was Nicky Sharkey, another of my former team-mates from that 1964 promotion-winning team. I told him that he was surplus to requirements. Nicky took it well, but I had now despatched to the dole queue a second team-mate from my Sunderland past.

We opened the new 1972/73 season with an opening day fixture at Lincoln City, who had been made hot favourites to win the Fourth

Division title. Our pre-match meal, influenced by Tony Toms, consisted of braised lamb in gravy with mashed potatoes and plenty of vegetables, followed by apple pie and fresh cream. The Chairman and his board of directors obviously thought we had already won the league! The lads were flabbergasted at the feast presented to them, which perked them up no end, and they went on to win the match 1-0. The players were delighted that steak was a meal of the past and were hooked for ever on the new regime. We won our first two league games and so leapt to the top of the Fourth Division table. Optimism flowed through the club for the first time in my seventeen months in charge.

Early on in the season the fixture list threw up consecutive away games at Torquay United on the Saturday and at Exeter City on the August Bank Holiday Monday night, which meant we stayed in Torquay over the weekend. This was when Tony Toms's baggage surfaced. We lost 0-1 on the Saturday, however I allowed the boys to go and enjoy themselves for a few hours in a local watering house. Since the professional game began, wherever there are footballers out on the town they soon attract the bees around the honey pot. This night was no different.

I hadn't hit the town myself, opting to spend a quiet evening in the hotel. I went to bed early, but was woken just before midnight when I was alerted by the night porter that one of the player's bedrooms now contained a couple of women. I was up to the room like a flash, bursting in to find white wine being poured. On confronting the two players I was told by one of them, "What is good for your right hand man has got to be alright for us." It appeared that Tomsie was also up to these tricks in his own room. I made sure that the two players got rid of their two female friends and then hot-footed it to Tomsie's room.

It was now well past midnight and as far as I was concerned this was now the day before another football match. I knocked on the door, but there was no response. The master key was obtained from the porter, but on gaining access it was obvious that Tomsie had been forewarned by one of the players that I was on the war path and had made a quick exit with his female friend through the window of his ground floor bedroom. I eventually tracked him down to the back of the team bus where I found a group of my players and the bus driver peeping through the back window at whatever he was doing on the back seat. Admirable determination, you have to say! Later I had a quiet chuckle to myself at what I had witnessed.

The next morning before breakfast it was made very clear to my new recruit that this was not the example to set at my club. Tomsie and I often had a good laugh in the dressing room with the lads when we related the story of that trip to Devon. It became more and more embossed with each retelling.

That weekend seemed to be fated as I experienced another first on the way back from our game at Exeter City. Having drawn the game 1-1 the players were in a buoyant mood as we made our way north on a team coach that had no toilet facilities, dodgy heaters and only one scruffy card table. It was hard work made no easier when the coach's engine broke down around the Bristol area. It was one o'clock in the morning and here we were stranded on the hard shoulder of the M5 Motorway.

Fortunately it was late summer and the weather was calm on this balmy August night. As the lads attempted to wave anybody down to hitch a lift to the nearest service station, a lorry pulled up and the Liverpudlian driver told the boys to pile on to the back of his open top truck and he would drop them at the Gordano service area at Bristol. Off they went, leaving me, Tony Toms and the bus driver to wait for the replacement transport that arrived an hour later. I can still see them now, professional footballers perched precariously on the back of a lorry, being driven away to who knows where. I'm pretty sure the driver was not insured to carry them and certainly we had never insured our players for such an occurrence!

Another trend of the football times was that some of the bigger clubs were making for the recording studios to record a club anthem or song. We decided to join them. Stan Launden of Radio Cleveland was a Hartlepool fanatic and he approached me to see if I would agree to the players cutting a record in a studio in Newcastle. Once again it was a case of anything to boost morale and to put us on the map. This quite novel arrangement went ahead, but like the football team it never climbed the charts. With a line in the song which went, 'that they put sugar in my tea,' it was an inevitable flop.

A far greater innovation was to follow in September 1972. Tomsie had only been with me a couple of weeks when he decided that he thought it would be good for morale if we all took a trip to the North Yorkshire moors on an overnight survival course. This was the soldier in him talking!

I couldn't believe what I was hearing when he explained that the players could only take one item of food, some water and certainly no money. There would be no canvas tents for overnight cover, it was to be plastic sheeting, and to keep us warm we were allowed sleeping bags, blankets or anything in the thermal line.

I was immediately on to the media to make sure that a freelance photographer was alerted to the trip and would accompany us over the moors to take the pictures that would be used to once again give us national coverage in the morning dailies.

On enquiring with the club secretary if the players would be covered for personal injury and loss under the Football League insurance scheme, he told me that it only covered them for training and during an official club football match. We kept that quiet and went ahead despite the risks. Could that happen today?

As player-manager I could hardly opt out of the trip, so I decided to link up with the one man who would definitely survive the night – Tony Toms himself. One of my players, Jimmy Shoulder, was to be teamed up on the moors with the veteran Bryan Conlan, a tough, hard-boned centre-forward who advocated not buying fitted carpets as he moved around the country so much from club to club. He was sharp enough to see that money could be made out of the trip. He brought a frying pan with his one item of food which was enough bacon to feed an army. Shoulder, my understudy at Sunderland for many seasons, brought sausages and between them they sold the English breakfast to the lads. Along similar lines Bill Green, unbeknownst to the management, had brought a cooked chicken for his item of food and had shrewdly stuffed its belly with milk chocolate bars.

In fact they all seemed to have the same idea. Amongst my squad was John Coyne, a 23 year-old from Liverpool, who brought with him as his one item of food a huge cooked chicken, which he had surreptitiously stuffed into his rucksack along with his protective clothing. We trekked over the Cleveland hills on that late Autumn afternoon and as the group climbed one of the many stone walls to reach our destination to bed down, John's bulky clothing opened up at the waist and out poured dozens of Mars bars. The rest of the boys waded in and helped themselves to the Scouser's grub.

Once we had made camp, the novelty of being under the blanket of stars with a backdrop of the pitch black night sky soon wore off when Tomsie revealed to the boys that they wouldn't be going straight to sleep, or sitting around a camp fire. In fact he told the players to spread out across the moors, hiding themselves wherever they thought they could not be found by him, stressing that the first four to be found would have their food confiscated and would have to rely on the good will of their team-mates for any scraps they were prepared to give them. Panic gripped the players as they scrambled around in the dark as the minutes they had been given to find a hiding place ticked by on Tony Toms's luminous compass/watch.

Time was up and the pair of us set off to find the first four lads. The players' stomachs would be churning over at the prospect of being in the first group to be caught. Tomsie could smell them a mile away and it wasn't long before he beckoned me over to a small gulley where he'd discovered four of the lads tucked away behind a small bush amongst the heather. They would have gone hungry next morning had it not been for the fry up which Conlan made them pay through the nose for.

It was surprising how many of the players, under these circumstances were frightened of the dark. Others had a hang up over creepy crawlies and field vermin. I was comfortable as Tony had made a cracking plastic-covered 'house', propped up with sticks, surrounded by heather and gorse from the moor. I had a great night's sleep and a hearty breakfast with the food confiscated from the four unfortunates the night before.

As well as being hungry, everyone had a tale to tell once daylight broke. I felt this was great bonding for the lads and we then broke camp and told everyone to make their way back to Hartlepool as best they could. There was no transport organised. It was hitch-hike or walk and report for training the next day. It transpired that Neil Warnock had rung a mate of his to pick him up and taxi him away. It was a smart move from a shrewd bugger, who hasn't changed down the years as he's made his successful way in the game. I found Neil an amiable sort whenever I met up with him in later years on the football circuit. I obviously never saw the other side of him as he ruffled feathers and attracted a reputation that did not endear him to many of his fellow professionals. You speak as you find in our game!

I had arranged that my part-time physiotherapist Tommy Johnson would pick us up in my car, but only after we had a full English breakfast at the nearest local café in Guisborough. Once again we had made back page headlines in the national press, which the dressing room talked about for many weeks after. The trip had been a success and there were no insurance claims!

Insurance reared its head in another way shortly afterwards. After returning from an away game at Newport County in October 1972 we had placed all our kit used during the game in the drying room ready for use the following morning, as I had instructed all the players to report for a training session in readiness for a home game against Gillingham on the Monday night. I was awakened in the early hours of the Sunday morning by the ringing of the telephone. At that hour I feared the worst kind of news of family and loved ones. However the conversation went something along these lines.

"Is that Mr Ashurst?"

"Yes," I replied.

"This is the Hartlepool chief fire officer. I have some bad news for you. Your dressing rooms have burned down at the football ground."

"That's great," I replied. "Have you salvaged anything?"

"Well it seems that you have lost all your football kit with the exception of a metal box which we have managed to recover which contains the football boots."

"Brilliant, I will see you first thing in the morning," was my response. I then went back to bed.

The reason for my joy was that here was a one-off, not-to-be-missed opportunity to build new facilities for the players. It was not to be, however, as on arriving at the ground early next morning Bill Hillen the club secretary informed me that the club had not insured the building against fire or theft. They had not been able to afford the premiums to cover such a liability. I was flabbergasted. We now had no kit or footballs and we were near bankrupt. In addition we had a game within twenty four hours against Gillingham.

The local police and fire officers made it clear to the club that they would not allow the fixture to go ahead because of safety reasons and it was agreed by the Football League that we would rearrange the fixture for the Wednesday night. Arrangements were made to hire two rooms at the local Leisure Centre for both Gillingham and ourselves to change in, facilities that were sheer luxury compared to what we had been used to at the Victoria Ground and a bus was hired to ferry the two teams to and from the ground.

With all our kit having been destroyed, I spent Monday morning ensconced in my office, which was underneath the old grandstand and so had survived the fire, contacting my friends and fellow managers in the game. Sunderland, Middlesbrough and Newcastle United all provided me with a start, not only promising cash donations but also delivering training kit, towels and medical equipment. Numerous other clubs were generous to the extreme. By contrast there was an emphatic silence from nearly all of the London clubs – in particular Arsenal and Chelsea who never responded at all, while Tottenham Hotspur's reply was 'Our need is greater than yours'. West Ham United, to their credit, were the only London club to help out, immediately sending a donation by return. Bobby Robson's Ipswich Town provided us with two sets of first team kit, one of which we used for the match against Gillingham. Remember Bobby is a north-easterner and is a man who never forgets his roots or his friends. I am honoured to be counted amongst them.

It was inevitable that with so much good will prevailing from our colleagues within the game, we would be sure to come away with two points and we did with a 2-0 victory over the Gills. The Ipswich Town blue and white colours inspired the players, along with an above average attendance from our own home supporters, turning out to show their solidarity with the adversity we were experiencing. The fire did eventually turn out to be a blessing in disguise as we had never been so well off for kit and equipment, while the generous donations paid the wages for a number of weeks.

The couple of old Nissen huts which had been the dressing rooms since the year dot had been destroyed, along with all that was in them, including the huge rats that had made their home underneath the building. Before the fire we had often found one or two scuttling around the place when we opened up of a morning. One particular morning a dead one was lying in the middle of the dressing room floor. Tomsie picked it up and, unbeknown to the players, while we were out training tied it loosely to the plug in a bath that could only take six people at a time. You can imagine the panic when the players stepped in for a good soak after their training session and the dead rat loosened from its mooring and floated to the surface. They had never moved so quickly in their lives!

Good will prevailed within the town and we were offered and immediately accepted from the local North East Electricity Board a huge pair of portable cabins, which were modified to our needs and became the dressing rooms and showering areas for the team. We felt as if we were in the lap of luxury. There was also enough room for me to move from my pokey office into the new facility. As it would not fit through the office door (something we couldn't fathom) Tomsie sawed my desk in half in order to move it out to the new building. He glued it together, but it was never the same again!

But the lack of insurance bit hard into our resources despite the huge generosity of people across the football community. The players were aware of the poverty and to their credit accepted the situation and got on with the job, but times were so hard that we re-cycled bandages and strappings and picked up the stocking tie-ups from the dressing room floor after a game to re-use for future matches. Wintergreen rubbing oil was substituted with a substance (I don't even know what) that we could buy cheaply by the gallon, and when we ran out of the 'magic' rubbing-in cream for the treatment injuries on the pitch Tomsie replaced it with a tube of toothpaste. The players were never any the wiser, proving that many injuries are in the mind!

We pinched and borrowed from everywhere and everyone. On our travels to the away games, I would often ask my friends amongst the opposing managerial staff for some form of medical equipment to help us through. The coup de grace was on a trip to John Sillett's high-flying Hereford United, who had just been elected in to the Football League. Tomsie found that the cabinet benches in the away dressing room were full of weightlifting equipment, so he decided to help himself to some of the weights and without me knowing placed them in to the skip for the journey north. After the game Tony, along with the twelfth man, pulled the weighted-down wicker basket along the passage way from the dressing room and out in to the front foyer. There he faced a problem as there were some steps to negotiate down to the waiting team bus. Tomsie, apparently without breaking stride, wrapped his huge arms around the skip, lifted it waist high and carried it down the steps and dropped it into the boot of the coach.

My team were using the weights on the Monday morning whilst Hereford United must have been wondering where the hell they had disappeared to. I was expecting a call at any time from the Herefordshire club, but fortunately the phone never rang. We had got away with this one. However I decided it was the last time we would tempt providence, as that kind of behaviour would get around the football scene like wildfire if it had come to light.

Desperate times meant we were also forced to re-use the same match ball for our home games. The last task for me before departing the ground on the day before a home match was to whiten the ball and re-touch the name 'Mitre' on it with a black felt pen. A new football should have been used for each game, but at £20 each they were a luxury we could not afford! On one occasion we went five matches with the same ball, but my fiendish plan was scuppered in mid-January when, late one Friday afternoon, having toiled over the re-touching for an hour or so, Harry Simpson burst in to my office and told me it had started snowing so we'd have to use an orange football the next day! The problem was we did not own an orange football and at that time we owed the local sports shop a small fortune for favours done in the past, so there was little chance of another hand out. A few phone calls uncovered a local business man who generously donated the orange ball to kick off the game the next day. Little did anyone know that if it had been kicked out of the ground on to the nearby railway line the game would have to have been abandoned as we had only had the one ball.

Throughout that 1972/73 season my team performed at the peak of its ability, and we made ourselves very difficult to beat. Despite that, with a couple of months to the end of the campaign, once again we found ourselves battling for survival both on and off the field. Two wins in 16 games had left us in 14th position, but just three points above the re-election zone in mid-February 1973. However I had every confidence in this group of players and four wins in the next six games saw us rise to 12th position. Our goalscoring record was remarkable in the fact that throughout the season we could not score any more than two goals in any one game. A couple of times we were heavily beaten away from home, but other than these two setbacks we did not concede many goals.

Safe from the spectre of re-election more than a month before the end of the season, I felt I could turn my mind to progressing the club further, rather than fire-fighting, literally or figuratively, as had been the case for most of my two years in charge.

Saturday 7 April 1973 was a red-letter day for all Sunderland fans. We were returning home after another tight away game at Doncaster Rovers, in which we had been beaten in the late stages of the match by the odd goal in three. That fixture coincided with the famous FA Cup semi-final between Arsenal and Sunderland at Hillsborough. As our team bus slipped on to the A1 northbound we were caught up in the flow of thousands of jubilant Sunderland supporters making their way north after their fabulous 2-1 victory. I looked out of the window of our coach at those deliriously happy fans and didn't know whether to laugh or cry. Here I was at a club teetering on the brink of financial meltdown, fighting a perennial battle against the odds to keep them from having to apply once more for re-election when I might easily have been in that other camp with a Wembley trip to look forward to.

Hundreds of fans held two fingers up at me as they recognised the Hartlepool team coach. I am not sure to this day as to whether that was an 'Up you, Len' sign or was it for the two goals their team had scored that day! I presumed and would like to think that it was an acknowledgment of Billy Hughes's and Vic Halom's goals.

In response I gritted my teeth and gave a thumbs up sign. What was particularly galling me was the knowledge that during the following week, when the entire city of Sunderland would be celebrating reaching Wembley, my new club would be once again being bled dry again by local millionaire and former Chairman of the club Ernie Ord. Ord was a diminutive, portly man and wealthy with it. A hard-nosed businessman, who had made his money in the town in the years after the war, he had been chairman of the club at the time Brian Clough was appointed as manager. I would like to have been a fly on the wall when those two started squabbling! The club at that time had been denied bank support, so they had taken on a loan, apparently for £7,000, from Mr Ord at a very generous rate of return. This was an enormous amount of money at that time, but add on the compound interest and you had a situation that was barely manageable. No wonder John Curry looked so ancient. It must have hurt Curry when Ord, with his head hardly visible above the huge steering wheel of his gold Rolls Royce, drew up outside the club offices in the town centre to pick up his monthly repayment.

Playing and managing amidst all this was becoming increasingly difficult. My fitness levels were not as high as they could and should have been as I could not do all the training as I had too many mangerial duties calling on my time. There were simply too many distractions and side issues to concern me. The season was coming to a difficult conclusion. On 21 April 1973 we had dropped down to 19th in the Division, still needing two points to be sure of finishing clear of the re-election places. We had just three games remaining and the first of those was at Northampton Town's County Ground. We went into the half-time break a goal behind and I remember thinking to myself as I walked to the dressing room, 'what am I trying to prove to myself? I am struggling to keep my playing standards up and then having to stand in front of a losing dressing room trying to lift a group of honest but average footballers.'

I had suddenly fallen out of love with playing the game and so I immediately substituted myself and decided to retire. I never kicked a ball again in a competitive match.

Having opened my professional soccer career with a home debut against Ipswich Town at Roker Park in 1958, I was finishing at this lowly unfashionable Fourth Division venue where cricket and football merged together at a shared facility. I was to hang my boots up on that proverbial peg of history. They were not the original shiny, toe-capped relics with which I had begun my career, they had long been dispensed with. These were the fabled football boots of an ex-player and his achievements, slipping into the past amongst the thousands of others that had gone before. It was nothing new to those who were watching from the terraces, they had seen plenty come and go down the years, both idols and journeymen of the past who had inevitably, eventually trodden this same path to football oblivion. To me this milestone in my life was at least my choice, a choice that I was pleased and relieved to make having played over 500 league games between my two clubs spanning fifteen years. I also thought myself fortunate to have only picked up a couple of minor injuries throughout that time. Sadly I never held a trophy aloft, however my personal cup was full to the brim with professional satisfaction and happy memories. It was, however, decidedly time to close the chapter.

As our financial needs were so great, I fed in to a national newspaper that my young centre-half Bill Green was to be sold to one of the big three north east clubs hoping to draw an offer from one of them. As it turned out Swindon Town offered me £12,000 for him, but it would prove to be a transfer deal with a difference that unravelled in the spring of 1973. I agreed to sell the promising young raw-boned Geordie centre-half to Robins manager Les Allen and Green travelled down to Wiltshire to complete formalities.

But then I received a phone call early the next morning from Allan Ashman, the manager of Carlisle United. Allan told me he would also like to sign the player and suggested that if I could coax Bill Green to return to the north east he would pay an extra £4,000 on top of Swindon's offer. £16,000 was a fortune for my club, so I immediately conjured up a fictitious story and lifted the telephone.

"Swindon Town Football Club," the receptionist answered cheerily.

"I would like to speak to my son, Bill Green," I responded.

"I am sorry, he is at the hospital having a medical. Shall I ask him to call you when he returns?"

"Yes please," I replied.

"It is his father speaking, would you ask him to call me on this number."

Not wishing to give my home or club number in case Swindon smelt a rat, I used a telephone number of a resident who lived close to the ground, popped round to the gentleman's house, sat and waited. Sure enough 30 minutes later a tentative Bill Green rang. I got straight to the point, "Bill, it's Len Ashurst. If you can manage to return to the north east without signing any transfer forms you will be a Carlisle United player tomorrow." Both clubs were in the lower reaches of the Second Division at the time, so there was little difference in playing standard, and I knew what Bill wanted was to remain as close to home as possible.

The next day Bill, having somehow extracted himself from a sticky situation in Wiltshire, was elated to be travelling the comparatively short distance from his home in Newcastle along the A69 to Cumbria. He returned a Carlisle United player and we were a comparatively well off football club. The nub of the story is that he couldn't understand who had left the original message at the Swindon Town office and thought it particularly strange as his father had died three years earlier! Bill was a huge success at Carlisle, starring in their promotion campaign in 1973/74 and their fantastic start to life in the First Division which saw them win their first three games to sit atop the Football League. Bill was eventually transferred to West Ham United for £75,000.

As well as the money from Green's sale, I also recouped £2,500 for Neil Warnock, my previous season's free transfer signing, who joined Aldershot. Financially the club had never been so well off.

I had become adept at the public relations side of my job, particularly enjoying my open house approach with supporters, that, having accommodated the local media over two difficult seasons, I was asked by Radio Teesside to take a slot on their Thursday night sports programme. This involved me reviewing the weekend fixtures of all the north east clubs and soccer gossip in general from in and around the area. I was in my element and thoroughly enjoyed the experience as it gave me the opportunity to promote Hartlepool Football Club and in addition to have a pop on the air at some of my critics. The programme went down well locally and I was offered a permanent position on the station. I was tempted, but nothing came to fruition as the media was a virtual closed shop in those days and a journalist's ticket was required for anyone working in the broadcast media. It was obvious that pressure was being applied to the Head of Programmes from the unions and so during the course of the 1973 season my part-time contract, which had lasted a year or so, was cancelled. After all we had plenty to focus our mind out there on the pitch. With us flirting once again with the re-election zone, we knew we could lay that particular ghost to rest if we could defeat Southport. The problem was Southport were top of the table. Luckily for us in the previous game they had clinched the title and so they had little to play for. Somehow we managed to come away with a 1-1 draw while Crewe lost at Hereford and so could no longer catch us. We were safe.

The summer of 1973 belonged to Bob Stokoe's FA Cup-winning team. Having finished my Roker Park tenure a couple of seasons earlier I was able to tap in to a huge favour from Bob, who brought his squad of players to the Victoria Ground for a pre-season friendly. Interestingly I had applied for the vacant manager's job at the same time as Bob Stokoe, but the Sunderland board had sensibly chosen experience over my youth and their choice of manager was vindicated with silverware in the trophy cabinet.

In spite of me instructing Harry Simpson to upgrade the away dressing room as best he could for Sunderland's visit, which effectively meant putting in some higher watt light bulbs to brighten the place up, it must have been a culture shock for the Sunderland boys. From a Wembley Cup final in May to Hartlepool for a pre-season friendly, with that bath in the corner of the dressing room which could only take six players at a time and the coke-fired stove whose chimney poked through the grandstand roof. The piss-taking and stick I must have taken behind my back as some of my former team-mates took in the surroundings. The Sunderland players all travelled through in their tracksuits – they had obviously heard that smart suites could be ruined! After the match Johnny Watters, the much-loved Sunderland physiotherapist, deliberately left mountains of his medical kit and equipment behind in the dressing room for my team to make future use of. It lasted for months.

In addition a week or two later Bobby Kerr, that tenacious little Scotsman who had recovered from two broken legs to lift the FA Cup at Wembley, came through for me again when he dropped in to have a photo call with the Cup at the Victoria Ground. We were inundated by supporters desperate to be photographed with the Cup and a bona fide hero, which raised more vital funds for us. Bobby to his credit stayed until everyone was satisfied. I will always remember and appreciate the 'Wee Man's' gesture.

Every close season the Football Association hosted regular summer coaching courses at Lilleshall. Having already passed my Preliminary Coaching Badge I was intent on completing my Full Badge, which at that time was the top qualification you could attain. Under the guidance of quality coaches such as Dave Sexton, Malcolm Allison, Terry Venables and Don Howe, who I was to cross later in my football life at Cardiff City, with hard work and devotion to the cause I could hardly fail. I was delighted to achieve the second highest mark ever of 97% for a Full Badge pass. All the trepidation on those Friday mornings in Durham City coaching the police cadets and screws encouraged by Alan Brown had stood me in good stead.

Life was never dull with Tony Toms around and our trip to Lympston Royal Marine camp for a week's pre-season training left me breathless. We did everything from carrying a telegraph pole across the mud of the River Exe, to scrabbling through a water tunnel littered with obstacles to be pulled out at the other end close to suffocation, to climbing up a sixty foot tower and jumping off with a rope to descend in to a deep pool of water at the bottom. That was the one challenge which petrified me. I reached the top of the ladder, took a look and then bottled it. I climbed back down, which apparently is much more difficult than taking the plunge. To this day I still get sweaty palms at the thought of it. Could you see present day Premier League players trying this one for pre-season?

The 1973/74 campaign began well for us with a 1-0 home victory over Brentford, but we then went on a nightmare run, winning just two more games before December to sit equal bottom of the division. Consecutive victories over Christmas against Scunthorpe and Workington set us on the road to recovery. We lost just three games of the next 20, including one run of five consecutive victories. After winning 2-0 at Torquay in early April we were as high as 9th in the division. This was heady stuff!

As manager of a football club you receive numerous requests to attend a myriad of functions and sometimes one pops out of the mail a little different than the norm! One winter's morning in 1974 a letter with an Armley Jail postmark stamped on the front of the envelope took my attention. It was from an inmate who was a Hartlepool supporter. His request was for me to give a talk to the prisoners, the covering letter from a prison officer confirmed that it was a genuine request. England World Cup winner Nobby Stiles was coming to the end of his fabulous career playing up at Middlesbrough, so I asked him to join me for the journey to Leeds. Nobby was a huge success as he related to over a hundred inmates tales from his Manchester United and England career. What you see is what you get with Nobby, a nicer person you could not wish to meet in football.

What shocked me during our visit was that on making conversation with the inmates I learned that they had committed the most heinous crimes, it seemed with no remorse. They would have to play out their lives inside the grim battlements of Armley jail with no chance of being re-educated and returned to the outside world. Nobby and I were duly humbled at the experience, although we knew we had fleetingly brightened the inmate's lives.

That 1973/4 season was a comparative success for me and Hartlepool Football Club as we finished in eleventh position in the table. What's more we had been able to return to all of our previous pre-match hotels and eating houses as all the bills had been paid by the money generated by those transfers. We had also been able to use a new match ball for all our first team games during that season. More importantly I received a salary increase. In addition the players never had to fret about whether their wages would clear into the bank on a Thursday morning. Times had changed for the better.

But it now felt to me as if my work here was done. In fact I was desperate to move on as I knew I had run my course as a manager at this impoverished club. This was the best it could possibly get, so I decided I should leave while the going was good.

Over three years I had worked morning noon and night to make my mark, with a hundred and one things to do in a week I hadn't had time to scratch my arse let alone lead a normal family life or take a holiday. I felt I had surely seen it all and done it all, touching every facet of soccer management except spending money on a player in the transfer market. In fact I had embraced in those three years more than most managers would in their careers as the vast majority never had the experience of starting at the bottom and having to apply for re-election, being within hours of receivership, telephoning fellow managers to scrounge kit and having their dressing rooms burnt down. Had Bill Shankly, Bill Nicholson or Bertie Mee camped on the moors in the middle of nowhere or put their players on the back of a lorry on the motorway? I knew the answer.

With the vagaries of professional football management being what they were even then, I was aware I would have to improve again next season otherwise it would be deemed to have been unsatisfactory – a laughable state of affairs really. So when the phone rang one morning in May 1974 the opportunity which presented itself was too good to turn down. It was Andy Nelson, the manager of Gillingham, asking me if I wanted his job. He was moving on to Charlton Athletic, after taking the Gills up to the Third Division. An interview was not necessary as it seemed my work had not gone unnoticed. I did not take too much persuading and departed the club taking Tony Toms with me, leaving Hartlepool in a healthier position at the bank and also in terms of playing squad and position in the table.

After clearing my desk and saying my farewells I arrived home and told Valerie that I had quit and we were on our way to Gillingham. "Where is Gillingham?" she enquired. Within days of the decision to move I was ensconced in my office at Priestfield Stadium, a room which was slightly bigger than the broom cupboard I had been used to at Hartlepool. We had purchased a house and chosen a school for Jane and Roger. There had been very little family discussion over the whole affair, as we had learned very quickly that football management sucked the blood from family life. I was on the treadmill and hooked on the adrenalin as well as the desire to succeed.

On reflection I was concerned that I had jumped ship too quickly in taking the first offer that came my way. Should I have focussed on a more prestigious move, not that one had ever come along, although I had probably not been patient enough? The concern I had uppermost in my mind was that I might be left on the shelf at Hartlepool to rot away to soccer oblivion. I had to take this chance and see where it led me.

It was a wrench to leave the North East after fifteen happy and relatively successful years. Valerie and I had been married in County Durham and our two children had both been born and bred there. In addition we were leaving behind Valerie's ageing parents as well as some wonderful friends in an area steeped in soccer tradition and friendly people. As we departed we knew we would return. This was home, but we just had no concept of when we might be back.

We closed the doors of our Whitburn bungalow in the summer of 1974, our car packed to the hilt with the belongings we would need to see us through a couple of days in our new house in Penendon Heath, near Maidstone, before the removal van arrived with all our worldly goods. With our children along with our pet dog in the back of our car we made our way south down the A1 and negotiated a river Thames bridge. We were now in Kent, but I didn't really know where I was going so I decided to follow a huge container lorry clearly heading for the A2 and Dover to cross the Channel. I ended up following it into Smithfield fish market in the City of London and then had to pay a cabbie to put me back on the correct road.

There was more drama to come as around eleven o'clock at night we located the road in which our new house was situated. The arrangement between the solicitors was that I would be picking the keys up from my new neighbour, but the said gentleman was not too happy at our late arrival and seemed quite pleased to tell me that there were no keys to be had – only a message from the vendor's solicitor to say the money had not been transferred and the keys were thus being withheld. At this late hour who was I to argue after an eight hour journey? Problem was, we had nowhere to sleep. There was only one thing that could solve the problem and that was to break in. So that is what we did. With a part-glass back door it was easy. All of us, including the dog, slept like tops, dossing down on the floor in the upstairs bedroom.

This was the manager of Gillingham Football Club of the English Third Division, technically breaking in to someone else's home. It seemed to me to sum up everything about my time at Hartlepool, so was this out of the frying pan and into the fire?

13 **Fire Fighting at Hillsborough**

I WAS RIGHT. I lasted just fifteen months at Gillingham and I realised pretty much immediately that I had jumped right into the Kentish fire.

The quality of family life was a drudge. From having dozens of friends in the north east to having none in and around our Maidstone home was hard for Valerie. We also had neighbours who would not speak to us and folk regularly passed us in the street without so much as a glance. 'Is this the South of England?' I thought to myself.

The Gillingham chairman was Dr Grossmark, a man high up in the Football League pecking order. He was the most singular of characters that I have ever met in or outside the game. Never did I see a smile cross his face. Whether we had won, lost or drawn a game mattered not. The same expression, which seemed to me to say 'you could have done better', was etched across his face.

Dr Grossmark was also the club doctor, but he would rarely actually lay a hand on an injured player, choosing instead to fix his eyes on the unfortunate lad lying on the treatment table before giving his prognosis after weighing up his own inner thoughts and the opinion of my physiotherapist. He ran the club on a tight purse string, sending Malcolm Bramley, the club secretary, round the bend with his cost cutting. The budget had to be adhered to at all times.

He deplored paying anything to players and seemed hell bent on paying less to his office staff. I remember one board meeting when Malcolm requested to employ an assistant to shed some of his enormous work load. When Grossmark was told the salary Malcolm intended paying, he replied, pan-faced as ever, "Malcolm, do what I do with my house maid. Pay her a pittance but let her steal things." End of meeting and Malcolm soldiered on.

The late Brian Moore became a board member, I believe solely because of his position as chief sports reporter for ITV. Brian was a Gillingham fan and a pleasant and popular individual, although a non-contributor to my cause as far as I was concerned.

Despite all that, things went splendidly on the pitch as I had moved up a league and was handling better players, such as Brian Yeo, Dave Chadwick, Damien Richardson and Dick Tydeman. Indeed we finished 1974/75 in 10th position, one of the club's best ever seasons in the Football League.

A couple of Gillingham players I recall for non-football reasons. Peter Feeley, a centre-forward, who scored numerous goals during his loan spell from Fulham, increased our attendances, so we were told by Grossmark that we had to sign him permanently as his arrival had brought significant money into the club. Feeley asked for £3,000 in cash as a signing on fee and to my astonishment Dr Grossmark agreed to give him the money to sign a two-year contract. Grossmark handed the money to Feeley in my office and then went ballistic. I thought he was going to have a fit as he took on a John Cleese guise. He knew he had gone right against the grain and was distraught at having given cash to a player against his principles. He departed my office frothing at the mouth. Feeley and I looked at each other and burst into laughter at what we had witnessed. Feeley told me he would be buying cottages in Ireland with the money; he was a shrewd bugger who would do well for himself in life. A few years later he was playing his football in Singapore and, I understand, buying prime real estate to quickly make himself a wealthy man.

George Jacks, a midfield player, asked for a transfer, maintaining he was worth more than I had offered him in salary. The local press ran the story and a few days later, out of the blue, a wizened old man arrived at my office door and asked to see me. He looked as if he hadn't two pennies to rub together, but he was an avid fan and a great admirer of Jacks. I sat him down and he spilled out how he felt about the possibility of his favourite player leaving the club. It was plain this would be a devastating occurrence for this old feller. I never guessed what he was really driving at until he produced out of an old haversack a wadge of notes large enough to choke a horse. He intimated that it was for George Jacks if he would stay at the club. A phone call was made and thirty minutes later Jacks arrived to meet his 'Sugar Daddy'. The old man handed the satchel over to the astonished player, who was now off the transfer list.

Incredible, and fairly random, things seemed to keep happening. One Sunday afternoon in 1975 I took a team to Buckingham Palace to play the palace staff in a game arranged by a Gillingham fan in the Queen's service. It was a fantastic experience and a wonderful day out, although we entered the Palace by the back door, rather than the grand front gates.

On the pitch three famous celebrities visited the Priestfield Stadium with their teams in 1974/75 and all went away with their tails between their legs. Bobby Charlton's aborted effort at management ended shortly after his Preston North End team were beaten 2-1 on a November evening. Then over Christmas Malcolm Allison departed with his Crystal Palace team after a 3-1 drubbing. Terry Venables was Palace's player-coach at the time and on this day I may have played a small part in guiding his career into coaching as he asked my advice as to whether he should retire from playing and concentrate on coaching and management. His performance that day and my experience at Hartlepool gave him his cue. He would shortly embark upon a career which saw him take charge of Palace, Tottenham, Barcelona and England amongst others. Finally Elton John and his successful Watford manager Graham Taylor were also sent packing after losing 2-1 in the March. Huge gates watched those three matches, which were great box office and fantastic theatre.

But I was never happy. So when, one evening in October 1975, I received a phone call from 'Mr Fix It' Len Shackleton to tell me that he had opened a door for me at Sheffield Wednesday after they had sacked Steve Burtenshaw, who had led them into the bottom four of Division Three after the first ten games or so, I was delighted. I had a clandestine meeting in a private house in Sheffield, accepted the job and headed south to tell Valerie that we were on the move again back to the north of England. Fifteen months after joining Gillingham I was departing, leaving the club in seventh position in the old Third Division.

Valerie was delighted at the news. She had found out where Gillingham was and never wished to return again.

YOU GENERALLY only get a 'big' football club opportunity once in your managerial career. I was fortunate and managed two. Sheffield Wednesday was my first, however the very first letter I opened as manager of this famous club was a personal writ from Gillingham Football Club for walking out on my contract. It was handed to me by a courier as I entered through those wooden oak doors at Hillsborough on the 15 October 1975.

If that wasn't enough the task ahead of me at Sheffield Wednesday was both formidable and onerous. The club had slid into degradation, although I had a fine chairman in Bert McGee. He was not a wealthy man and funds were limited. The club was overstaffed and lacking in quality. Sixty professional footballers and a dozen or so apprentices crowded the dressing rooms. In fact there were more players at this club than my previous two put together. There are always players and staff to move on when joining a new club, the dressing room is always a mix of those who think they can play and those who can't. The problems often come with those who can't play and believe they can. Hopefully you have that nucleus of young players and solid performers that you can build your team around.

Perhaps inevitably given what had happened one of the early fixtures was a home game against Gillingham and the 1-0 victory was sweet as Gerry Summers their new manager had instructed all his players they must not speak to me on pain of disciplinary action. I had given a number of those players their debut and signed others for the club. Summers' attitude was particularly regrettable for those lads.

The return game at Gillingham in February 1976 was drawn 0-0. I was made to feel particularly unwelcome. Summers instructed the groundsman to place my bench on the far side of the field away from the main stand and in front of the bank of home supporters, who were all baying for my blood for walking out on them four months previously. It was futile trying to convey instructions to my players as the home fans took it in turns to shout me down and generally abuse me. The whole episode let a sour taste in the mouth. I could never understand Summers' attitude to me as my departure was no doubt his gain. I had after all left him very good players and a tidy ship.

Just three months after our arrival at the club and following a 0-2 home defeat by Swindon Town had left us third from bottom, two points from safety, and with huge problems mounting on and off the pitch, Tony Toms suggested to me that we should take the players for one of his 'bonding sessions' up on the Yorkshire Moors. Remembering the success of his excursion up at Hartlepool, I agreed to the suggestion, although I thought it was madness as winter was entrenched.

Feeling under the weather, on this occasion I gave the trip a miss. So Tomsie made all the arrangements and set the ground rules. I wasn't aware of where they went or how they arrived there, all I do know it was bloody freezing and the local and national press thought we had gone round the bend. Everyone survived – just – and we went on to beat Chester 2-0 on the Saturday to move out of the relegation zone and into 19th position, so once again Tomsie had come up trumps.

Bernard Shaw, my right-back, was one of the players who was most vociferous in his opinion against the trip and rather pointedly emphasised his objection by doing his warm up before the game in a survival suit, in the process adding a touch of humour to the whole business. The *Sheffield Star* newspaper spawned a cartoon that has gone down in local folklore.

"I've been roughing it on these moors for years and I'm STILL no good at football!"

By Whitworth

We were still in the heat of a relegation scrap, however, and two weeks later, on a cold dark winter's night at Port Vale, we had a goal chalked off for a petty foul which would have given us a precious point. In anger I kicked the bucket of water over which had a wet sponge sitting in it. It was minutes to the end of the game and the water splashed from the bucket and flew up in to the air in a vapour blanket spraying anyone who was within five yards, which included me and a policeman on duty at the end of the players' tunnel. After the game was over and I was chastising my team in the dressing room for a sloppy 0-1 defeat, in burst two police officers and beckoned me outside. I took Tomsie with me for moral support and accepted the dressing down that the senior officer gave me. I had no choice, he was obviously oblivious to the pressures of soccer management and saw the incident as a near public order offence.

Stressed out and at a low ebb, I found myself on my sick bed with pneumonia for the following two weeks. I was so bad that hospitalisation was suggested by our excellent club doctor Dr Purcell, but I declined. Valerie, God bless her, nursed me back to health in our own home. I cannot recollect one director of the football club who came to see me, that should have told me a story! In my absence Tomsie went four games without defeat in caretaker-charge. When I returned my team delivered four successive defeats, at the end of which we were second bottom of the Third Division. Welcome back to the fold, boss!

Huge pressure built up as the season wore on as we won four and drew two of the next nine games. Now our survival as a Third Division club eventually depended on a win in the final game of the season against Southend United. That Sheffield Wednesday, a proud club which had won the Football League title four times and the FA Cup on three occasions should be one game away from relegation to Division Four spoke volumes as to the mire the club was in.

Fortunately for us our fate was in our own hands as Aldershot had completed their league campaign and were only one point ahead of us, so we knew a win would make us safe. A sizeable Hillsborough gate watched a less than classic game as we ground out a 2-1 victory to survive.

The close season of 1976 gave me the opportunity to put my stamp on the team. Having dispensed with numerous players during the season I had now decided to shed around a dozen on free transfers as I whittled the army of professionals I found when walking through the door seven months previously down to manageable proportions. I then added to the staff with some of the players that would eventually turn the club around. Richard Walden from Aldershot, David Rushbury from West Bromwich Albion, Jeff Johnson of Crystal Palace and David Leman from Manchester City. In addition young striker Tommy Tynan, experienced head Bobby Hope, a fine Scottish international ball player and Neil O'Donnell were also recruited from Liverpool, West Brom and Gillingham respectively.

The most important decision I made was to give a debut in goal on the opening day of the 1976/77 season to Chris Turner, who replaced Peter Fox, himself no slouch between the sticks and who carved out a useful career at Stoke City and still holds the record for appearances for a goalkeeper at the Potters. Congratulations Peter as you had done no wrong!

Chris, a local Sheffield lad, became an outstanding professional and during his career was close to being capped for England. He has since moved into management having a spell in charge at Hillsborough and as I write has taken Hartlepool United into the fourth round of the FA Cup by defeating Premier League Stoke City. Little did I know at the time that I would once again work with him as a goalkeeper at Sunderland nearly a decade down the line. Chris was one of the many unobtrusive apprentices at the club when I arrived and was on the rota for bringing the tea in to the staff room on a morning before training. The first memory I have of him was putting the tea tray down, never uttering a word and departing the room. To me this was unacceptable, especially as he was a goalkeeper who should be the most vocal member of the side. I threatened him with death if he continued to be mute. The next morning it was "Here's your tea, gaffer," along with an expletive learnt from the dressing room. He blossomed from that day onwards and never looked back.

One of the most interesting signatures I obtained was Paul Bradshaw from Burnley. The deal was done in the directors' room at Turf Moor with that guru of the Football League Burnley chairman Bob Lord. A ruthless businessman, Lord tortured me this way and that as I tried to have the fee reduced from the £25,000 asking price. It was a humbling encounter. After nearly an hour and a lesson in protocol and negotiation from Bob Lord, my perseverance was rewarded as we negotiated some appearance and sell on clauses which reduced the fee to £19,444, the strangest of numbers. As we stood up and shook hands on the deal, I stared at this ruddy, weathered face of a Lancashire sage whose volatility had shaken many a Football League meeting. He told me to remember what I had learned from his grilling and put the experience to good use in the future.

"I believe you will be in the game a long time, so good luck," was his parting comment as I turned and walked out of the door to meet my new player. I felt elated at his comment and the fact that I had managed to have the up front fee reduced. Bradshaw became a regular and popular member of the team.

Another clever signing to tuck away for the future of the club was a teenager from Canterbury City by the name of Bob Bolder. Bob was a strapping young goalkeeper, who Alf Bentley, a contact I had developed whilst at Gillingham, had recommended. I marched both of them up to the top of the north stand at Hillsborough, a massive grandstand capable of holding 22,0000 spectators and told them I would not leave this highest seat in the ground and allow them down until I received a handshake on a deal of a lifetime. For just £2,000 I obtained the signature of a young keeper who had a great attitude to work and was to serve Sheffield Wednesday and numerous other clubs until his career came to an end close to his 40th birthday.

This famous north stand which thousands of people could stand on to watch their heroes, hid behind its terracing a huge indoor hall which was used for indoor training and recreational purposes. Badminton was a game I fancied my chances at and I discovered that Tomsie had been a county champion at the game – was there anything he wasn't good at? We regularly played each other to relax and release the pressures of the job. They were never matches played under normal circumstances. Tomsie was so much better than me that he took to playing left-handed to give me a chance to beat him. Even that was never to be, so he donned knee pads and played me scuttling around on his knees. It was with great difficulty that I took a week's money as Tomsie read the game so well and his placement of the shuttlecock was superb. I think he was taking the piss.

1976/77 started very well for Sheffield Wednesday and after a good run of five consecutive victories, by 4 December we were 6th, just two points behind Brighton in the third promotion position. We maintained our form throughout the season and with five games remaining, after defeating Preston 1-0 at home on 16 April to register our fourth successive win, we were just three points off a promotion spot, still in 6th position. Could we put together a late spurt to nick the third place which Brighton had occupied almost the whole season?

Our next game was against Crystal Palace, with whom we were level on points. Terry Venables was in his first season in charge and his side ran riot as they thrashed us 4-0. The result effectively put paid to our chances and despite defeating Peterborough United by the same scoreline in our next home game, by the time we reached the dressing room after that result we learned that we could no longer reach the top three. A 2-3 defeat at promoted Brighton the following Tuesday told me that we weren't quite good enough that season. It had been tight, but I felt just a few tweaks were needed for us to be in with a good chance of promotion the following campaign.

I will always maintain that one of my key signings for Sheffield Wednesday was Ian Porterfield, the young lad who had made his Sunderland debut in front of me as a left-sided midfielder. Of course his name is etched into football folklore as the scorer of the winning goal in the 1973 FA Cup final – who will ever forget that famous moment when commentator David Coleman shook the watching football world with his voice proclaiming 'PORTERFIELD!' But now, in 1977, Ian was recovering from an horrific car crash and was finding it difficult to attain the high standard of play he had set for himself over the years. A change of club was suggested by Sunderland manager Jimmy Adamson and Ian agreed to make the move from the north east to join me at Hillsborough on a free transfer at the start of the 1977/78 season.

A number of prominent league clubs had looked at Ian since his return to football following a car accident and had shied away. A pre-accident and fully fit Ian Porterfield would have attracted a near six figure fee. But there was a problem. Ian demanded a signing on fee and my chairman initially said no. From somewhere a brown envelope appeared and Ian put pen to paper. Ian was a player who needed loving to get the best out of him, but I was never able to see those qualities as I departed the club before he reached his best, with Jack Charlton reaping the benefit as Ian went on to be an integral part of Jack's promotion winning team of 1980.

As a professional and as a person Ian was a man of principle and integrity. Our football paths often crossed in later years. Whilst I was working with the FA Premier League its brand carried huge clout, enabling me to help some of my former colleagues to open doors. One day on my way to London along the M4 motorway I received a call on my mobile from Ian, who was out of work at the time. I agreed to meet him at a hotel near his home in Ascot. It was obvious he was distressed and this was not the first time he had called a favour from me. He had been shortlisted for a job with the national team of Trinidad and Tobago and asked me to make a call on his behalf to nudge the decision his way. The job carried with it a paltry salary of $3,000 per month, but Ian was delighted to accept. I told him he was right to do so as once in situ you can then look for your next appointment from a position of strength, instead of from the dole queue. Ian made a useful fist of his work in the Caribbean and through my contact Alf Darcy who ran a sports agency from his home in Hertfordshire, soon moved on to become coach with the South Korean side Busan on a six figure salary. Ian offered me the chance to join him as his assistant, however by that time I felt I had done my stint abroad. After two seasons he then took the post as coach to the national team of Armenia, an outpost in the old Eastern block, and took them to their highest ever position in the FIFA rankings. Sadly cancer then took hold and the outcome was his quick and sad demise.

I last heard from him via email shortly before his death in September 2007 at the age of 61.

From: Ian Porterfield
Sent: 29 July 2007 02:45
To: Len Ashurst
Subject: Re: From Len
Hello Len

I heard from Mandy you were asking for me. Bit hard to make calls from hospital bed side. Private room expensive and no calls. Big rules but must be followed as health is all that really matters just now. As I explained we needed to come home for the radiation treatment and other things turned up, so battling on. Not easy but I will win this battle once again unless God decides its my time to leave – God has always made me fight for anything I get. Treatment looks to be going OK but never much said. Getting too many visitors and the Royal Marsden had to stop things for a bit.

Hope to get home soon then decide what's next to do. Now just too weak.

Hello to all in Sunderland love all the people there. Some of Roy's signings look dodgy to me. We will see how they do. Good luck to him. He'll need all the Irish.

See you
Ian

Season 1977/78 did not start well. We failed to win any of our first seven league games and successive 0-1 home defeats by Shrewsbury Town and Peterborough United gave plenty of fodder to my growing number of critics. With gates dipping below 10,000 at this once proud club, I knew I was in trouble. My cause was not helped when a house brick was tossed through the boardroom window after a home defeat. The decision to sack me was taken by the board on Tuesday 4 October 1977 on the team bus as it returned from Preston after a 1-2 defeat, a result which saw us slump to the foot of the Third Division table.

I thought it strange that as we arrived at Hillsborough around midnight the travelling directors all took the trouble to say "good night" to me for a change. Then one of them, with a slip of his tongue, said "good luck". I knew I was a gonner and the next morning I got up from the breakfast table to make an appointment with Sheffield Wednesday's history.

The Preston result wasn't the straw that broke this particular camel's back. My fate was probably sealed after an evening home game against Plymouth the previous week when Argyle broke away and equalised in injury time. As the ball was being picked out of the net by Chris Turner a huge banner, 20 yards long, unfolded in the sparsely-populated North Stand opposite the directors box for all to see. It was certainly big enough to have the name of Eddie McCreadie, the then Chelsea manager emblazoned across it, pronouncing 'ASHURST OUT – McCREADIE IN.' Holding one end of the banner was the chairman of the Wednesday supporters club, who had been agitating for me to be sacked for months. I recalled as I looked at the banner how I had asked him to leave the team coach at Brighton after that vital 2-3 defeat at the end of the previous season.

Even then, at the end of a decent season, he had taken every opportunity to jump into my seat in the directors' box at Hillsborough, when I vacated it to go down to the pitch side, to catch the ear of chairman Bert McGee. A week later he had his wish and six months of provocation had eventually paid off.

I was told years later by McGee that I had laid the foundations of the club's success in later seasons. That was scant consolation to me, though, as, at 11am on 5 October 1977, he walked into my office and told me I was finished. I think McGee was right in that my stewardship of the club would prove to be for the benefit of Jack Charlton, who succeeded me, as eight of my team formed the nucleus of his promotion squad a couple of years later. Perhaps my biggest legacy was that I recommended Jack, rather than McCreadie, to the chairman as my replacement.

As a postscript to my time at Sheffield Wednesday I should add that twelve years after my departure, in April 1989, I had a bird's eye view of an event which would change for ever the way football is watched in this country. Along with my son Roger and a friend of mine Peter Pollitt, a lifelong Sheffield Wednesday supporter, I watched the Hillsborough tragedy unfold in front of my eyes. We reached our seats in the main stand, but towards the Leppings Lane end of the ground, in heady anticipation of the FA Cup semi-final clash between the two best teams in the country that season, Liverpool and Nottingham Forest, 45 minutes before kick-off. Even then it was obvious that there was a problem in the area behind the goal in the lower Leppings Lane stand as thousands of people were crammed in to one enclosure. Without wishing to dredge up the circumstances which culminated in the catastrophe it was plain to see that a major tragedy was developing. I do not feel that any of the authorities dealt with it at all well. How the game was allowed to start will always remain a mystery to me and I will never be able to remove from my memory the images of the hundreds of supporters who where dragged from the terrace over and through the wire fencing – 96 of them never to return home again. People talk about 'disasters' and 'crises' in football all too often. In my book such phrases should be reserved for real and human tragedies such as this.

After being sacked at Sheffield Wednesday I had time on my hands. I'd been working for six years without a break, learning my trade at three lower league clubs. I was now well-versed in what football management was all about. Moving house three times in eighteen months with very little help from either Gillingham or Sheffield Wednesday had been taxing and my body told me it needed to take a rest. I was going to enjoy the enforced short break from the game. Frankly I thought I would only be spending a few weeks sitting down for a cup of tea with Valerie after dropping my children off at the school gates and tending the garden before I would be back to the managerial merry-go-round.

However it didn't turn out like that. As the weeks turned in to months, each day became a new challenge as the pitiful three months' worth of salary I had been given on my departure from the club ran out. The dole was not an option for me as it was considered by the authorities that I had taken a payment on my exit from the club.

I kept my fitness levels up with regular road runs around the lanes of Ecclesall to the south west of Sheffield, where we had made our home. I would return each day, my mind racing, hoping to discover that the phone had rung with an offer of work from a football club in need. But, as my previous experience with Len Shackleton had shown me, it does not happen like that. Jobs are generally set up for you through journalist contacts or a managerial colleague who is moving on to a new club. It would be these contacts who would open a door for me to step through and sell myself to a football club chairman, who probably had a losing team, inherent money problems and a home crowd who were baying for his manager's head – as well as his own if he did not make a change.

As each successive managerial vacancy appeared my optimistic application letter and CV was posted off. None brought any response at all. It was disheartening at first and then downright worrying. Christmas, that most common time for the disposal of a manager's services, came and went without my luck turning. By now every time the telephone rang I rushed to its insistent bell hoping it would be a club secretary calling me for interview. All through this most difficult of times the question kept nudging away in my mind, 'was this the end?'

14 **Adventures in Europe**

M Y AGONISING wait for that phone call lasted until June 1978 – a full and heart-rending nine months without work. You'll understand, then, when I tell you that when Colin Addison's voice came crackling down the telephone at my Sheffield home asking me if I wanted his job at Fourth Division Newport County because he was moving to First Division West Bromwich Albion to become assistant manager to Ron Atkinson it was the sweetest sound I have ever heard. Beggars can't be choosers, particularly after nearly a year on the managerial sidelines and so I was off to South Wales immediately for a formality of an interview. Colin had already convinced the chairman Richard Ford, a local motor dealer, that I was the man to succeed him. I have always remained grateful and good friends for Colin's leg up just when it was needed. In those nine months since my sacking by Sheffield Wednesday the money had run out and, as the months went by, personal confidence had gradually ebbed away. I had asked myself over and over again if I could ever get back into the only industry that I knew. The answer was now an emphatic 'Yes' and, yes, predictably it had been a colleague in the game who was moving on to better things that put work my way.

I walked in to Somerton Park, Newport and was immediately transported back in time. Flashbacks to Hartlepool and all the travails of football poverty whisked through my mind as I glanced about me at the neglected ground and facilities. I was back to square one after six years of graft in football management, starting all over again at the bottom of the football ladder. I was joining a club that had habitually been applying for re-election and in joining them I was taking a giant step backwards. But most importantly I was back in employment, earning a wage and rejoining once more those exclusive ninety-two Football League managers. At least this time I had the benefit of those six years' experience behind me.

Expectations at this soccer outpost were non-existent when I arrived. In fact it's fair to say that survival was the prime motivator. They had finished 16th the previous campaign, which wasn't so bad, although they hadn't won any of their last 12 games of the season. One big plus for me was that in the dressing room there were a number of young talented players. There was also the usual mix of has beens and hangers on, as well as the odd Jack the Lad, but I realised early on that I had inherited a few little gems which if nurtured properly and polished up could become shining stars both locally and nationally.

I located a house in the countryside near Monmouth, which was what our children wished for, and soon Valerie and I had settled down to a new life challenge. We found the people of south Wales delightful, warm and friendly – much more like those we were used to in the north east. Perhaps it was just the south east corner of the country which we didn't like!

Pretty soon it became obvious that turning Newport County FC into even a semi-decent team was a huge challenge. We opened the new season with six defeats and one victory, a 3-2 win at Wigan Athletic, in the first seven games. By Tuesday 12 September, following a 1-3 home defeat by early title contenders Wimbledon, I was at the bottom of the pile once again.

At this time Valerie's mother Sarah Jane died of cancer. It was a bleak period in the Ashurst household. Every family experiences these sad times and you just want to get through them and onto an even emotional keel as quickly as you can. The last thing I wanted was local sports reporter Peter Walker of BBC Wales pushing a microphone under my nose after that Wimbledon game and asking the question, "You have had six league defeats in the first seven games, are you worried about getting the sack?" That must be some kind of record – seven matches into my reign and my position was being questioned!

We had our breakthrough in the next game as we won 3-1 at Bradford City and it was an upward graph from then on. We picked up our first home point against York the following weekend and followed that up by recording our first home victory of the season, a 2-1 win over Huddersfield Town. Just two defeats in 23 games followed and we climbed the table to finish a respectable eighth. The highlight of that first season was knocking Second Division West Ham United out of the FA Cup in the third round 2-1 at Somerton Park. Their team read like a who's who of the football world at that time: Lampard, Curbishley, Bonds, Day, 'Pop' Robson and, of course, Trevor Brooking. I don't think he fancied it on this wet, muddy pitch on a cold January night! Looking back, the feat was all the more remarkable when you consider that the following season West Ham won the Cup, defeating Arsenal at Wembley.

Included in my team that night was a player called Richard Walden, who made football history when he became the first player to have his fee fixed by an independent tribunal. With our offer on the table of £3,000 this fine right-back threatened at the hearing to walk out on the game if his wish to move from Jack Charlton's Sheffield Wednesday was not granted. This was the position put forward by us and, as Big Jack did not attend the hearing, the Chairman of the tribunal Professor Wood came down on our side, so allowing Walden to rejoin me. I had previously signed him for Wednesday from Aldershot two years earlier.

Another signing for a second time around was Liverpool-born centre-forward Tommy Tynan, a gem of a player with a fiery temperament. I can see his bottom lip quivering even now when he couldn't get his own way. In addition to the transfer fee I had to pay a huge taxi bill to Lincoln City, which Tynan had inadvertently run up when travelling from Sheffield to Lincoln. An accounting error at the club caused this to run to four figures.

Tommy Tynan was an unlucky pawn in the professional soccer machine and he did not quite achieve the heights his goalscoring talent deserved. I had first signed him from Liverpool whilst I was managing Sheffield Wednesday. I remember Bob Paisley informed me after a reserve game when sitting in that famous boot room that Tynan lacked pace. I have to say he had everything else in his game to enable him to score goals. I seem to remember that master of Anfield Kenny Dalglish was not the quickest either. That is the greatest compliment I could pay Tommy Tynan.

The sharp manoeuvres you had to get up to when signing players were countless. I decided to take a look at Keith Oakes, a solid centre-half, and so stood behind the goal he was defending during a reserve game at Peterborough to get a close up view of his ability and character. I wasn't disappointed. In addition I used my position behind the goal over the course of the game to sound out his goalkeeper, the veteran Jim Barron, as to what sort of player I would be acquiring, so making sure that I wasn't being sold a £14,000 pup by my friend and Posh's manager John Barnwell. Jim let in three goals that night, perhaps not exactly helped by the conversation I was having with him from behind the goal. Keith signed and proved to be a pivotal player for me.

In the spring of 1979 I signed John Aldridge from South Liverpool FC for £2,500, but in order to snare him I had to disguise myself to watch him play so none of the other scouts and managers in attendance would recognise me. Then, after the match, as the supporters and the clutch of Football League managers no doubt weighing up whether to put a bid in for him departed the ground, I took off my dark glasses, unzipped the hood that had been wrapped around my head as I stood on the terracing, rather than accept official club hospitality in the boardroom as would have been normal practice, and bowled in to the dressing room area of the club. It was sparsely lit and there were signs of a leaking roof. In fact the whole of the dressing room area and the building generally was in a decrepit state. The first person I encountered happened to be the Chairman and as I looked beyond him to the dressing room I asked if he could bring the manager out as I wanted to speak to them both together. I needed to play one off against the other.

I had been alerted to Aldridge, who was then a part-time footballer, by my brother Robin, who was working alongside Aldo at Ford Merseyside. My opening shot after introducing myself to manager Russell Perkins and his chairman was, "I want to sign your player John Aldridge. I'll give you fifteen hundred pounds?"

The chairman's eyes and face lit up, but then he regained his composure and asked for £2,500. His manager was visibly crestfallen at the prospect of losing Aldridge. My response was instant. "£1,500 down payment and a further £1,000 in 12 months time." I proffered my hand to the chairman and then to the manager and agreement was reached.

Aldridge emerged from the dressing room not surprised at my presence as Robin had alerted him that I would be watching him in one of his forthcoming matches. I did not allow John to linger too long at home on Merseyside for fear that word would spread around the local football community with the possibility of a counter bid scuppering my arrangement. He was whisked off down to Newport and early the next morning he was a Newport County player. His first professional contract earned him a basic wage of £78 per week, £4 less than he had been earning at Ford. John to this day firmly believes that Robin had told me his salary and I had pitched it lower knowing he would not refuse the opportunity.

It had taken me fifteen minutes of that game to decide I wanted Aldridge. In that time he had shown me all I wanted to see in and around the penalty box. At £2,500 he was an absolute bargain and he went on to prove my judgment correct in a wonderful career which took him to Oxford United, Liverpool, Tranmere Rovers and two World Cup finals with the Republic of Ireland.

Six months later, in a night game at Portsmouth which we won 2-0 in front of 20,000 fans, Aldridge's elation contrasted sharply with his strike partner Howard Goddard, who broke a leg following a dubious tackle from a home player. Goddard, another of those likable Jack the Lads you come across in football, was another prolific goalscoring centre-forward and would have gone on to a career akin to Aldo's had fate not intervened. Goddard was never aware, even to this day, that David Pleat, then Luton Town manager, had provisionally agreed to buy him and in essence this was to be Goddard's last game for Newport. As he was carried off Pleat departed the directors' box, tapping me on the shoulder and said three words, "I'm sorry, Len."

I was never more remorseful towards a player after an injury as I was for this man; he needed the intoxication of the game to keep his life in order. A few years later Valerie and I attended his wedding in the Pill area of Newport and once again he was struck another blow as the organist failed to appear and we sang the hymns unaccompanied. The marriage never survived.

It was early spring 1980 when I received a call from my brother that father's health was failing after having had an operation to remove a lung tumour. Needing my own space I left my office at Newport County and drove to a quiet spot near our training ground, which at that time was rented from British Steel at Llanwern. There were pockets of the area which were overgrown with shrubbery and blackberry bushes and I picked some fruit for therapy as I wanted time for quiet reflection. I wondered whether Dad would pull through and if not would I be regretting for the rest of my life that I had not been able to say goodbye and tell him that I loved him. Loved him for everything he had worked so hard for, loved him for his presence whenever my brothers and I needed him for his quiet words of encouragement or the necessary put down, for being there at a regular time throughout the year like a routine that you could set the clock to, as long as he arrived home that was all we wished for. Dad was the fulcrum of the household when he sat in that favourite armchair after his evening meal, which was always on the table for him at ten minutes to eight every weekday and one o'clock on the weekend.

Our next game was away at Darlington on 19 April and success at their Feethams ground would give us a record equal to the great Tottenham Hotspur's in achieving their eleven straight wins in the Football League in the season of 1960/61. The run of results had taken us up to third in the table, in with a serious chance of promotion. We had just five games left, with at least one game in hand on all the clubs around us, so I was feeling very confident of achieving the most unlikely promotion given the side's recent history.

I travelled north by car via Liverpool and took in a visit to Fazakerley Hospital, joining Mum and two of my brothers who were keeping a bedside vigil. Robin was working in Canada at the time. Dad momentarily opened his eyes as Albert quietly whispered close to his ear, telling him I was at his bedside, which was enough for me to know we had connected. We made our farewells, albeit for a fleeting moment. I said what I wanted to say to him, knowing that he was not going to recover. I did hope that he would be well enough to be put in front of a television screen the next day, as at midday the BBC's *Grandstand*, introduced by Frank Bough, would be featuring little Newport County as we attempted to stand alongside those giants of the football world from north London by equalling their record. It would have made Dad the proudest man in the world. The attendant nurse must have known it was a futile request. Dad was not a well man.

We drew the game 1-1 and so failed to equal Spurs' record and, after losing one and winning one of the following two league games we were now in a straight dogfight with Bradford and Portsmouth for the last two promotion places behind already promoted Walsall and Huddersfield Town.

Father died in hospital on the evening we lost the penultimate game of our season away to bottom of the league Rochdale, Tuesday 29 April 1980. I was informed after the final whistle by their club secretary of the call which had come through during the game. My grief was all enveloping. How I hated professional football at this moment for the way in which it ate in to your life. I also hated my own fastidious attitude to my work which had kept me away from his bedside in the weeks before. I had put everyone else who I was involved with at the football club before father, a regret that I have lived with ever since. Delegation was a word I never learnt early enough in my managerial career. At least I had spent that one afternoon with him eleven days before.

I walked hastily away from the messenger of bad news for a private moment with my thoughts, allowing the significance of father's death to sink in. I found myself in the middle of the football pitch at Spotland, the home of Rochdale Football Club, with not a human being in sight. The death of a loved one brings internal reminiscence, grief and recrimination. I said a prayer for father, and mother who was now head of the family. As night was closing in I looked around this soulless theatre in which we had just failed to clinch promotion to the Third Division of the Football League by losing the game 0-2. That result meant we were close to destroying nine months of arduous work over a long football season. We had just one game left. We had to win for so many reasons – promotion, the players, the fans, my family, brothers, Mum and Dad.

Pulling myself together I strode manfully in to the Rochdale boardroom to tell my crestfallen directors to cheer up and reminded them, as I had my team five minutes after the game had finished, that the final outcome was still in our hands. We just needed two points on Saturday at Walsall in our last match of the season. That was easier said than done as Walsall had guaranteed themselves second place. But at least they had nothing left to play for.

We duly delivered in front of five thousand travelling Newport County supporters as a John Aldridge brace secured a 4-2 away win and elevated little Newport County to promotion in a day of fraught tension and elation. Yet for me it was also a day tinged with sorrow and remorse. The players never said anything to me, but I always felt that the team won this one both for me in my personal grief as well as for themselves. Certainly John Aldridge dedicated his goals to Robin, who had travelled back from Canada for the funeral and was in the grandstand watching the game, in thanks for catapulting him off the workshop floor to stardom.

Only nine days later the joy and achievement of promotion was equalled in the success of winning the Welsh Cup for the first time in Newport's history, when over two legs we wiped the floor with Third Division Shrewsbury Town 5-1 on aggregate. In doing so we quite incredibly qualified for the European Cup Winners' Cup for the 1980/81 season.

I took the Welsh Cup to my Monmouth home and stood it on my dining room table and it became the centrepiece for numerous celebrations. The success was tempered throughout that summer by given a domestic chore to toil at. I would often joke to Valerie, "I bet Cloughie doesn't have to do this," or "I bet Big Ron Atkinson won't be mowing the grass today." These were semi-domestic therapies at the heart of family life and away from the media and public spotlight.

At this juncture I felt my decision to turn down the Sunderland job, offered to me at the start of the season as the club sought a replacement for Jimmy Adamson, was fully justified. 1979/80 had been the most professionally fulfilling of my career as those little gems in my dressing room, along with some astute signings along the way, had blossomed and moulded themselves into a special group of players which very rarely comes around in any team sport.

When Albert collected Dad's belongings from hospital, there were just a few personal items which would not fill a plastic bag – a vest which Dad had to wear to keep the precious warmth close to his frail body as the flesh dropped off him, as it does everyone who is afflicted by that abhorrent disease, a collared shirt and tie to bring away. I could never remember father venturing in to the leisure wear department of any shop. To us he would never have been Dad if he had dressed down. He seemed to send a signal of authority when collared up!

Many years later when Mum passed away, there were numerous personal items and a few paper cuttings discovered amongst some sepia-coloured Kodak slides and photographs. There is something tragic about the personal belongings left behind when a loved one passes away. I feel an immediate dislike towards these tokens of their life and have no desire to touch or to keep them as so many do as they represent the passing of a lifetime and the closing of life's door. I prefer to live with my own memories.

As I looked on at both Mum and Dad as they lay on their respective death beds, I felt lamentably inadequate. Their bodies, once vibrant, had been racked by disease. I felt angry and disturbed as transcending my grief was an overwhelming feeling of underlying guilt.

Why was this? You should never question what your parents have provided for you, to bring you in to this world is surely enough. I was asking myself if I had given enough in return for them giving me the gift of life. That was my guilt factor. This may well have been the reason I have strived so hard and long for success and once it was achieved, worked a damn sight harder again to improve and get better, always reaching for their approval in the process of trying to attain greater glory.

So it proved during season 1980/81 when all interest centred on our debut in the European Cup Winners' Cup. Along with all my board members I attended the first round draw in Zurich. Why not? After all we had earned the trip and we thought that there would never be another opportunity of a visit to Switzerland in a professional capacity. As it happened, amongst all those foreign names such as Benfica, Dinamo Tbilisi, Feyenoord and the beaten European Cup finalists of 1979 Malmo, we were drawn against English speaking Crusaders of Northern Ireland. Dates were agreed between the two clubs and we took advantage of the first leg home tie and ran out 4-0 winners. On paper the away leg was a mere formality. It was a cold, damp autumn Belfast day, made grimmer at the sight of gun-toting soldiers and police, as well as British tanks placed at strategic points along the roadside as we drove from the airport. The game was played in an eerie, tense atmosphere and a 0-0 draw was enough to see us through.

The second round draw took us to Norway to play little-known Haugar Haugesund. After overcoming this challenge 6-0 on aggregate, the third round paired us against the crack East German side Carl Zeiss Jena, whose coach Hans Meyer is still in the game, as I write managing Nuremberg in the Bundesliga at 65 years of age.

Roger Malone of the Daily Telegraph

DURING MY sports journalism career spanning forty years, I had cause to be on working terms with successful managers such as Matt Busby and Bill Shankly, Alf Ramsey and Brian Clough, down the divisions to the men who had to seek success with fewer trump cards at their disposal. This brings me to Len Ashurst, who I got to know as a manager of Newport County in the 1980s.

I was able to observe Len displaying his skills as County won the Welsh Cup and so moved into the adventures of the European Cup Winners' Cup in 1980/81. There was the day Len helped me get into Norway without a passport and also the night Len found the answer to a tricky situation in the then Communist country East Germany.

Len's likely-lads including John Aldridge, later to gain goalscoring fame with Liverpool and Tommy Tynan, a deadly striker around the lower divisions over the years, had cruised past Irish club Crusaders in the first round 4-0 on aggregate. The second round draw linked County with Haugursand of Norway, first leg away in the land of the fjords. It was to be my umpteenth football trip abroad, nothing new as I checked the usual travel list including my passport. So, what did I do? Only turn up at the airport without my passport. I sat down for an airport coffee and decided on a certain course of action which would require the help of two people.

The two people would be Len, who I knew well, and our charter flight's pilot. Now, I can think of some managers who would not want to involve themselves in the problems of a journalist – not so Len Ashurst. His personality stretches wider than 4-4-2, the offside trap and the transfer market. He is a warm person who helps people. He helped me, liaising with Chairman Richard Ford and Secretary Philip Dauncey in getting the pilot to agree to take a person without a passport, although he could not guarantee that Norwegian passport control would let me into the country. This brings me to the third man in my plan. The immigration man who scrutinises you and your passport then gestures you into his country.

Len and I planned I would hang back on landing and make sure I was last in line at immigration, so as not to draw attention to my predicament by holding up the queue. Meanwhile Len, his chairman and secretary would explain the problem to the welcoming party of Haugursund Football Club in the airport building, whilst I decided on what I hoped would be my trump card when facing the immigration man. I looked firmly into his blue Nordic eyes and said: "I have forgotten my passport, here is my internationally recognised journalism card. My uncle Jack Thrussell arrived in your county about forty years ago also without a passport. He came down from the skies on a parachute, armed and ready to help liberate Norway from occupying German army. He helped your people then, I am asking you to help me now."

The immigration official paused, pondered and then made a phone call. The outcome was that I could enter. However the Chairman's passport was going to be held at immigration and would be returned when I departed the country. I was able to inform my readers all about Newport's well-planned 0-0 draw in Norway and on departure shook hands with the Immigration man, who told me to say 'Thank You' to my Uncle Jack, who incidentally was awarded the Military Medal for his wartime bravery in action. In the second leg at Newport, Len switched his team's tactics to high-intensity attack on home turf. The result was a 6-0 triumph.

This brought Len's team to a quarter-final draw against Carl Zeiss Jena of East Germany. Having made many football assignments to the other side of that Iron Curtain which stretched across Europe in those days, I knew about the police-state and lower standards of many items of everyday life compared to Western Europe. For the away leg it was a plane and then a long trek in a very uncomfortable bus. We bumped along poorly-maintained country roads before chugging into Jena with very little street lighting whatsoever. I was sensing this was not to be the smoothest working assignment. Cue a complete trans-formation of scene when we arrived at the hotel assigned to team and media.

Dozens of local folk, all dressed up and in full partying mode, thronged the hotel's public rooms, drinking, dancing and cavorting. It was, we discovered, Carnival . . . the big night when the locals celebrated the end of the harsh winter. Some managers I have travelled with would have caused a row and insisted on either the partying being stopped or the team moved elsewhere. Not Len.

In a Communist country that course of action would certainly have been counter productive. Len simply told his men to join the party for a couple of hours, then go to bed at a reasonable time. Typically Len kept cool in a difficult situation. Problem solved, just as it was on the field two nights later as Jena were held 2-2, that artful footballing dodger Tommy Tynan scoring two precious goals.

Unfortunately Newport went out by the only goal in their home leg, Jena being a good enough side to beat Benfica in the semi-final, before missing out 1-2 in the final against the USSR side Dynamo Tblisi.

When I look back to Newport County under Len Ashurst and his astute management, I remember the thorough planning, the happy atmosphere and Len's ability, in Norway and East Germany, to solve tricky problems without fuss or bother. Thanks again, Len

By Roger Malone

Tom Lyons was a sharp, Cardiff-based journalist who accompanied the team to Jena on behalf of the *Daily Mirror*. He asked me to join him as he took a stroll in to the dowdy, half-lit streets of the town on the night before our game, the night of the carnival Roger describes so eloquently in his piece above. Tom, it transpired, was also working on this trip for a London news agency. They had seconded him to write an article on the secret police who would be all around us during the following two days.

As we stepped outside into the night air there was not a soul in sight and not a car in view. This was not too surprising as only government officials had cars. The only noise in the air was coming from within the hotel as the 'Mardi Gras' now being enjoyed by my team, was in full swing. I had told the players to join in the fun and have some drinks so long as they were in their beds at midnight. What would have been the point of changing hotels or sending them to bed listening to the racket from the hotel ballroom. You would simply be inviting them to break a curfew. I was confident not one of my players would break the midnight cut off – and they didn't. None of them would put their place in the game of their lives in jeopardy.

Tom and I walked briskly down the road. He was confident of his bearings and turned numerous corners, crossing a few roads before telling me that he was heading for the huge monster of a church which stood out in front of us against the night sky. He wanted to see if there was freedom of access to this Greek Orthodox Church for the midnight service.

The church was a magnificent building whose walls, I felt, must have been hiding the secrets of a tumultuous and turbulent past. As we entered through the huge wooden oak doors and stopped to look down the aisle and the rows of empty pews towards the ornately decorated alter half a football pitch away, I was struck by the deathly hush that pervaded the air. There was no organ music sounding out from the huge pipes that covered a vast area of one of the walls. There were also no candles lit, where normally there would be dozens flickering away, all representing a soul that had departed or a prayer for a loved one.

Tom made for a pew close to the back of the church. I followed him and knelt down for quiet reflection. Here was I hundreds of miles away from home behind the Iron Curtain, a protestant in a Greek Orthodox Church. A prayer was said for my family. I also asked for strength and guidance for the task that confronted me and my team in less than twenty four hours. Alongside me, Tom had apparently never closed his eyes. He had not asked the good Lord for anything. What he had been doing as he knelt down in apparent prayer was looking backwards underneath his armpits towards the door we had just come through to observe what was happening to those worshippers who entered. As he'd come through the door Tom had noticed two or three men tucked away in the shadows watching and waiting. They wore civilian clothes, but he maintained, as he gave me a running commentary of what he had spotted in a whisper, that they were the Stasi, the feared East German secret police. They would not deny people from entering, but they were there to note who were following their religion and risking that knock on the door in the middle of the night. This communist state did not like a cult following anything other than their red flag. Religion was a major no-no.

Tom pointed out to me that the majority of those who made up the meagre congregation were ageing people, who therefore had little to lose and were prepared to stand up for their beliefs against the oppressive regime. His take on this was that the state would allow the older generation to see out their days with their religion then quietly close this place of worship. It was abundantly clear to Tom that the presence of secret police discouraged younger people to visit the church probably for fear of being spotted. This was the story he wrote for the national newspapers.

However what followed was like something from a Bourne movie. As we arose from our wooden pew Tom calmly made his way straight for one of these men in black and proceeded to open a conversation in German. I was astonished. I stood and watched as within seconds he was surrounded by a number of hostile-looking police who appeared like apparitions from everywhere. Tom had clearly struck a nerve with whatever question he had asked and had put himself in grave danger.

I stepped forward, assuming one of them would understand English. "I am the manager of Newport County football club from Britain. If you arrest him you will have to arrest me and that means we will not play a football match against your team."

A sharp discussion took place between their growing number and, decision made, we were then hustled out and bundled into a windowless jeep along with three armed Stasi officers. We were driven straight back to our hotel where the music and revelry was still in full flow. The locals were now well inebriated and never gave us a glance as we were whisked up to our bedrooms by one of the officers who we knew held a light revolver under his heavy police coat. He told us that if we did not leave the building again the matter would be forgotten.

After he had gone I heaved a sigh of relief and then turned to Tom.

"What on earth did you say to him back there?"

"After telling him I was a British journalist, I asked him why there is a secret police presence in the back of the church. Are you stopping young people attending?"

No wonder we were now confined to our hotel bedroom.

Against a backdrop of poor floodlighting and armed police surrounding the playing area, a 2-2 draw at the home of the East German champions was a feat of great magnitude achieved by my players and staff. Two goals from Tommy Tynan gave us a real chance in the second leg at home, which attracted a full house of 18,000 spectators and plenty of interest from outside our shores. But ultimately it was a huge disappointment as we lost the game by a single goal to bow out 2-3 on aggregate. The shitty free-kick with which Carl Zeiss Jena opened the scoring on 16 minutes which ultimately settled the tie bobbled along the floor and deceived our keeper Gary Plumley.

We totally dominated our opposition that night at Somerton Park and bombarded their goal with shots and headers. The woodwork came to their assistance on numerous occasions. Finally, in injury time, when a goal would have got us level at 1-1 and ahead on away goals, a cross from Karl Elsey arrived perfectly onto Keith Oakes' forehead. The big defender crashed the ball goalwards, but it was brilliantly turned away by the German goalkeeper Grapentine. So near, and yet so far.

Our league campaign went reasonably well in 1980/81 and we finished in 12th position in the higher division. We had a particularly good home record, losing only one game after the turn of the year, and that to eventual champions Rotherham United.

Needing to strengthen my squad for the 1981/82 season ahead, I trialled a Central European player. This turned out to be something I shall never forget as the dealings surrounding this particular fellow opened my eyes to the corruption that has gone on in our game for many years. The player in question was introduced to me, along with his agent, by a prominent Football League manager, who had previously signed two foreign players, presumably through the same agent. I was asked for £50,000 to secure the player's signature. After watching him in a friendly match I lost interest. Although he was a talented player I just could not see him coping at Barnsley or Port Vale on a miserably cold and wet night in the middle of winter. The fee was quickly dropped to £25,000, with half of this amount being offered to me as a personal incentive to take the player. How this incentive might be paid I would never discover, as I flatly refused this huge temptation.

I was not the kind of man who wanted to join the small group of corrupt managers in the game who were allowed to buy and sell players by their boards, handling all aspects of the deals to their conclusion and creaming off money left, right and centre. After experiencing this encounter with temptation I, for a while, viewed with suspicion, possibly uncharitably, the management of any club that had a foreign player or two in their midst.

In the summer of 1981, our European horizons widened by our adventures of the previous campaign, we embarked on what was for us an ambitious pre-season trip to Cork and Limerick. What an eye opener it turned out to be. As soon as we stepped off the ferry it was like stepping back in time. We were taken everywhere in an old, battered bus along highways and byways potholed through lack of maintenance, through as green a rural landscape as you would see anywhere in the world, which was occasionally partitioned by small hamlets, villages and towns where everything seemed to be painted in bright vivid colours.

It was actually a wonderful experience made more colourful when our hotel manager told us that over the weekend there was to be a Romany Wake. The hotel was drunk dry as the mourners ordered dozens of bottles at a time. Their caravans and the animals that pulled them filled the car park, blocking everything in. Training had to be cancelled as the team bus could not be moved for fear of mowing down horses or pissed up Romanys!

What else could we do other than enjoy their grief along with them? It was dynamite! In spite of the alcohol in the blood we beat Cork 3-0 and then Limerick 1-0.

My chairman, Richard Ford, who accompanied us to Ireland, was at the time in training for the full Cardiff marathon, which was a fundraising exercise for Rookwood Hospital. My impetuous promise, made I seem to remember around the time of the wake, that I would join him and consequent total lack of preparation because of the short time frame, saw me, at forty three years of age, a few weeks later clock the sad time of five hours one minute for the 26 miles 385 yards.

Little did I realise that the clock was ticking on my time at Somerton Park. Despite all the success we'd had, finances were about to upset my applecart once again.

15 Black Balled for my own Testimonial Match

I AM PROBABLY the only football club manager in history who has been granted the honour of having a Testimonial match only to see it take place a few weeks after the club has sacked him.

Loyalty brooks no argument where football is concerned. I was sacked by Newport County on 8 February 1982, once again at 11am. I had realised my time was up at Newport a few weeks earlier when I had been given the kind of ultimatum by the board which made me realise that I could not remain at the club.

"Sack your number two or your Testimonial is off" – that was the stark message delivered to me on a Sunday morning in November 1981, a few months before I was to be rewarded for taking a down and out club through the most successful period in their history. In my charge Newport County had reached the quarter-finals of the European Cup Winners' Cup, won promotion from the old Fourth Division and lifted the Welsh Cup for the first time in the club's history. In addition I had turned down the attentions of my former club Sunderland. It wasn't a bad record, I didn't think, and the promised Testimonial was deserved, I also thought. But now the whole thing was being tainted by this ultimatum.

The messenger was my chairman Richard Ford, who told me that with the club leaking money this was one of the cost-cutting exercises the board had decided upon. Having to sack my 'Jack of most Trades' Jimmy Goodfellow, number two, assistant coach, physiotherapist and trainer felt to me a desperate act. I was also now without his greatest asset – tossed without a care to one side – his loyalty to me and the club. But ultimately, with a family to feed and clothe, I was left with no alternative and Jimmy departed.

I remember informing Jimmy that he was fired. His jaw dropped open, aghast at what I had said. However at the same time I also indicated to him that when I acquired another job I would come calling. This was scant consolation to him at that time as he was not aware of what I had up my sleeve. He was not to know that I had a near certainty of a job down the M4 at Cardiff City, who had recently relieved their manager Ritchie Morgan of his post.

It was a good job I had something else lined up because it wasn't long before I was joining Jimmy on the dole. Financial pressure precipitated the decision, although there were also a couple of the directors who were waiting in the long grass for their opportunity to bring back Colin Addison to the club. Sure enough he was appointed a few days after my departure. But still it was humble pie for me less than a year after the nationwide glory of our historic Cup Winners' Cup quarter-final at Somerton Park.

And so it came to pass that I sat in the press box, rather than directors' box, on 2 March 1982 to watch Manchester City provide the opposition for my own Testimonial game. It was truly a surreal experience as the boardroom and dressing room areas were made out of bounds to me. I was at least allowed on to the pitch at half-time to thank those supportive fans who had been so splendid to me. All the members of the board of directors were present, although they had no reason to attend as the honeymoon between us was now well and truly over and there was no love lost. Once again it poured with rain on this my second Testimonial match, badly affecting the attendance. My fortune wasn't made as I banked around £4,000 from the gate receipts.

There was bitterness as I departed. However my conscience was clear as I had left behind a dressing room full of young talent which was worth fortunes. Indeed John Aldridge would be sold to Oxford United for £78,000 before having £750,000 spent on him by Liverpool, who then sold him on to Real Sociedad for £1,000,000.

My two failures in the transfer market at Newport were Alan Waddell, a centre-forward who had scored freely for Liverpool and Swansea, and Welshman Jeff Johnson, who'd been Player of the Year at Sheffield Wednesday and who I had originally signed from Crystal Palace. These two failures however could be offset by the brilliant Tynan and that goal machine Aldridge.

Then there were talented youngsters such as Steve Lowndes and Nigel Vaughan, who could not tackle a paper bag when I arrived, who were all sold on for big money at a later date. Along with Neil Bailey, once these boys heard the crowd respond they never stopped tackling. As far as I was concerned I had written club history and in the process more than balanced the books.

Talking of young players, one who was allowed to slip through the net was future Welsh international striker Dean Saunders, son of Roy Saunders, the former Liverpool wing-half from the 1950s. Roy was a player I had enjoyed watching from The Kop as a youngster and he always put in a good stint on the pitch and was never seen to shirk a tackle. Dean is now Assistant Manager to the Welsh team and was appointed manager of Wrexham in October 2008. He has always been quick to jocularly remind me that as a young schoolboy trialist at Newport I had spurned the opportunity to develop him as a player. Never mind Dean, without me you have still done very well for yourself.

On the Tuesday morning after my sacking I received a phone call at my home from Tony Buckle, the headmaster of the local Hartridge School, who asked me to come in and coach his youngsters. Bizarrely after one session I was again sacked. At 8am the following morning as I was breakfasting with Valerie and family, BBC Wales television news informed me of my second sacking in the space of three days – surely another record? They made a huge issue of the story, which I was unaware of as Buckle had not been able to contact me to inform me of what had gone on. It turned out that the teaching union representatives at the school had protested about a non-member taking football coaching sessions and had threatened to strike. I was history before I knew it – literally. What chance did the youngsters have with this attitude among their school teachers who through their union objected to a professional football man teaching children the basic skills of the game?

A small acknowledgement to my success at Newport came years later when coaching in Qatar in the Middle East when one evening the phone rang in my apartment. It was my daughter Jane on the line and the conversation went like this.

"Dad, I have been asked to find out if you would mind if one of the roads on the new housing estate that is to be built at Somerton Park could carry your name. 'Len Ashurst Way' has been suggested by the local housing association and it is to be put before a sub-committee of the local Newport Council next week."

I did not hesitate and readily agreed to the suggestion and was told by Jane that I would get to know the outcome in a few weeks time. A couple of months later, when home on leave, I enquired as to what the outcome of the meeting was and she informed me rather embarrassingly that the sub-committee had turned it down. It seemed that on that very committee was a long-standing councillor who I had asked to leave the Newport

County board room one Saturday afternoon thirteen plus years before for criticising my team after we had suffered a rare home defeat. I don't know for sure, of course, but it's a pretty safe assumption that he may well have been against this honour, which I would have been proud to accept.

Looking back at my three years at Newport I think this was probably the happiest time of my managerial career. We'd been very successful on the pitch and I especially appreciated being able to enjoy the success with my supportive Valerie along with Jane and Roger as we enjoyed rural life in the Monmouthshire village of Llansoy. None of our success could have been attained without the patronage of Chairman Richard Ford, the excellent club staff and a special group of players who came together at the right time in their careers and responded to each other brilliantly as well as the challenges demanded from them. I want you to know who they were.

Gary Plumley, Richard Walden, John Relish, Keith Oakes, Grant Davies, Dave Bruton, Steve Lowndes, Tommy Tynan, Dave Gwyther, Nigel Vaughan, Karl Elsey, Neil Bailey, Kevin Moore and John Aldridge, not forgetting the unfortunate Howard Goddard.

And yet, a few years later this football club, having purchased the ground from the council at the time of our success, fell under the severest financial pressure. It was not long before they sold the ground back to the same local council at a knockdown price. They have since slid downhill out of the Football League into oblivion. A reconstituted club are now down in feeder league football – a sad situation for this proud little club.

16 **A Capital Job**

FROM NEWPORT COUNTY I joined Cardiff City on 3 March 1982, the day after my Testimonial, with the team languishing close to the bottom of the Second Division, eventually being relegated to the Third Division despite my efforts at the end of the season.

However not only was it a fresh start for me in a higher league and an increased salary, it was also geographically friendly, being only ten extra miles west down the M4, so there was no need for the huge upheaval of moving home. A two year contract was signed in the close season after relegation. It was a contract small in basic but large in bonus. As promised I re-employed Jimmy Goodfellow.

Cardiff is a rugby mad place and, although the football team has always had a decent following there's no doubting where most Welsh hearts lie. However I couldn't see the point in one scheme Cardiff City had come up with to try to augment their income. A year previously Managing Director Ron Jones had pushed through the introduction of a Rugby League team by the name of Cardiff Blue Dragons. Under the stewardship of the likeable David Watkins, a famous and iconic Welsh rugby union player, the team from that other professional code stuttered along and quickly became a loss maker. Surely they must have known that this was a northern game!

I can sympathise with any football club, such as Wycombe or Reading, who have to share facilities with rugby. They not only wreck your pitch, but also make a mess of your dressing room areas and what's more they generally don't give a toss.

My staff had the whole place spotless for them to walk into, but then three hours later thirty strapping rugby players had not only knocked six lumps of shit out of each other, but also the playing surface of my football pitch. When they left the dressing rooms were in a shambles, littered with rubbish with the toilet and bathing area looking like an inner-city wasteland. They were riding roughshod over me and my staff. I simply did not think that soccer and rugby were compatible. With their gates eventually down to just 1,000 spectators it could not last and I made sure it wouldn't as I undermined them at every opportunity.

On joining Cardiff under chairman Bob Grogan, I inherited Ron Jones as Secretary, and he proved to be a man who handled the club's money as if it was his own. He once charged me 80p for two steak pies and refused to give me the 20p change from my £1 note! Ron enjoyed socialising and was good company. Whenever I saw him in an ebullient mood I would tackle him over players' wages and transfers, often without success as he would fob me off until he had cleared his head the following morning and was back to his normal frugal self. He would always tell me that loanees would have to be the way forward as it did not commit the club to permanent contracts for "greedy" players. I think he hated to look at the players, never mind pay them. He had been taught by a ruthless tutor in Jim Gregory, chairman at Queens Park Rangers, where he had held a similar position.

Ron used to drive me mad as he strummed some deep South American rubbish on a huge guitar whilst I was trying to get a team together. As I walked along the corridor to his office I used to hear this crap coming from inside the wooden office door. Instead of knocking I would turn right down the players' tunnel on to the pitch and take a walk or a jog around the track and come back when his session was over.

He was right, though. The loan system had to be used extensively during the 1982/83 season. Limitless loanees were tested out at centre-forward, including Billy Woof and Bob Hatton, who we eventually signed, and no fewer than five goalkeepers were tried. Some of them, such as Eric Steele and Martin Thomas were very successful, but we could not afford their fees, so I gave a debut to Andy Dibble, a young Welsh teenager, who I eventually settled upon to see us through the last few months to promotion. But our scant resources were tested to the limit when Dibble was injured during a match at Bradford City in February, which we eventually lost 2-4. He had to leave the field and we used outfield players Phil Dwyer and Linden Jones to fill the breach. After that match, as Dibble battled to be available for the following game, I was told I would have to play full-back Jones in goal if the youngster did not make it as we did not have another fit goalkeeper. Thankfully Dibble was able to play.

We got through a huge number of loan players. In fact I remember having a slanging match with the then pompous and belligerent Welsh Football Association, who were claiming that I was abusing the loan system. Yet they themselves had approved the rules! Interestingly The

Football League secretary told me at the AGM in London at the end of the campaign that I had used more loan players during that season than any other manager in the Football League.

Sometimes there were other reasons for players being in and out of the team. I loaned out my veteran centre-half Phil Dwyer to Torquay United for a month-long pre-season trial. Phil saw this as a personal insult to a club stalwart who had notched up nearly five hundred games in a Cardiff City jersey. I wanted to rattle this player and set him thinking as he was sloppy and at times undisciplined. I was also establishing with my new charges that there would be no barrack room lawyers in the dressing room whilst I was manager. For a month Phil saw the other side of life on the sleepy south coast. I know he hated every minute of his stay and in the first match of the 1982/83 season against Wrexham I substituted him during the game just to ram my point home. As I arose from my seat in the grandstand, this woman, who must have been staring at the back of my head over the full ninety minutes of the game, gave me a poke in the chest and verbally confronted me – it was Phil Dwyer's wife, a diminutive tiger of a woman who was rightly fighting the corner for her husband. I admired her spunk! I had made my point and I felt Phil, who was as brave as a lion, became a reformed character, so I returned him to the team at Walsall after missing four games. Not only did he shore the defence up alongside Jimmy Mullen, but he also scored the winner in a 2-1 victory. Phil became an integral part of the promotion team and a great strength in the dressing room.

After over a decade as a manager I wasn't into football clichés being verbally bandied around. I was a cross between my father's gentle persuasion with an inbuilt censor to know when to kick backsides or put an arm around a shoulder. I was never into tipping a dressing room table over or throwing tea cups. I put huge emphasis on making sure that I knew more about the game and my players than the players themselves and in doing so I feel I earned their respect. I could be cutting with my tongue, especially to those who chose to ignore discipline, a trait I have always respected. If I was to be stereotyped by players I have handled they would probably say, 'Keep on the right side of him and he is a good old stick. Cross him and you will pay the price.'

That Cardiff side pulled together superbly as I scrabbled together a mixture of free transfers and loan players. In fact my captain Jimmy Mullen being the only one who had cost a transfer fee, just £10,000 from Rotherham United. Experience was the key factor with only two players in the side under twenty, while luck played its part as the small squad avoided injury throughout the season, ten of them playing over thirty-five games. Each and every one of them was outstanding.

The main planks were the Bennett brothers, centre-back Gary, who later had an illustrious career at Sunderland, and right-winger David, who subsequently won the FA Cup with Coventry City. Striker Jeff Hemmerman, a free transfer from Portsmouth, rattled in 26 goals in all competitions playing alongside that superb professional Bob Hatton, who I had watched in a private practice match at the invitation of Sheffield United's manager Ian Porterfield and then leapt at the chance of signing on a free transfer in early December. Ian was returning the favour for kick-starting his playing career after his car accident when I signed him for Sheffield Wednesday.

Another free transfer, this time from Cambridge United, was Roger Gibbins, who clocked up over fifty games during the season in all competitions and never put a foot wrong in any position that I played him in. Then there was David Tong, a classy midfield player who signed on a free transfer from Shrewsbury Town. There was also a handful of local lads, the experienced Linden Jones and John Lewis, along with youngsters Paul Bodin and Andy Dibble, both of whom I gave debuts to and each of whom went on to become established Welsh internationals.

Somehow that seeming rabble of renegades managed to pull together and win promotion after just one season in the Third Division. In essence they were a wonderful group of players who loved playing for their club. Part of the reason for the squad's togetherness and spirit was undoubtedly my wonderful kit man, the rotund Harry Parsons, a former fruit and vegetable market delivery driver, who fortunately for the sake of team morale could not separate his perpetual clowning from the more serious issues of the dressing room. He would unwittingly burst into a team meeting in the middle of a heated debate and want to know if Gary Bennett wanted a change of jock strap or ask if Vaseline would be required in between the legs of one of the Welsh lads. H, as he was known, was a huge gem of a man who could have made a living on the stage as a stand up comic.

Saturday 7 May 1983 was the day that promotion was finally clinched thanks to a fine 2-0 win over Leyton Orient at Ninian Park. Cardiff City had made an immediate return to the Second Division. The fact that my former club Newport County had finished fourth, one place outside the promotion spots, just made it an even better day.

In fact the day actually got even better that very evening. Early that same morning I had played in a celebrity golf tournament in aid of the Welsh Rugby Union injured players fund at that fine parkland course at

St Pierre, Chepstow, returning a card with 43 Stableford points. On returning with Valerie for the evening dinner and presentation, a friend of mine Brian Lewis was walking across the car park which I had just drove in to, after accepting his congratulations on our promotion two hours before, I asked him,

"What score has won the golf tournament?"

"Some jammy bugger with 43 points."

"That's me, Brian!"

I ran the window up and drove on, a double celebration was in the offing and I was not going to let it pass without enjoying a rare moment in one's life!

Preparation for the 1983/84 season took place in a training camp at RAF St Athan in South Wales. I took along my 15 year-old son Roger to join the players in their billet, believing that it would be an experience that he would never forget. I called upon the expertise and equipment of the RAF's fitness personnel, as well as their daunting assault course.

During the trip we set up Peter Walker, yes that very same reporter from BBC Wales who'd had the temerity to suggest that I should get the sack after only seven games of my tenure at Newport County. As he stood alongside me for an interview at the very bottom of the death slide, Tarkie Micallef, a lad of Cypriot origin, hurtled down the rope towards Walker. Tarkie had huge white front teeth and was baring these in fearsome fashion as he clung on for dear life. The Cypriot looked like a squat guerrilla as he careered towards the unsuspecting reporter, who on hearing the sound of the approaching rope slide managed at the last second to take a leap out of the way only to land in a deep water hole used for squaddie training purposes! Pleasingly this was all captured for posterity by BBC Wales television. It was now my turn to feel a little smug.

We held our own in the Second Division up to March 1984 despite having a much-changed group of players. My team was lying fifteenth in the Second Division when I received the call from the north east of England which would set me off on my football travels once more, this time to Sunderland.

One footnote to my first stay in the Welsh capital: as I departed the Rugby League team went into liquidation, being bought by Clive Millman and Lauri Tattersall who moved the team to Bridgend. The Cardiff Blue Dragons were no more. My perseverance had won out.

DESPITE LEAVING to take what I had always felt was the job I was destined for – managing Sunderland – I could not keep away from Cardiff. Having returned from coaching in Arabia in 1989, I received a call for help from Jimmy Mullen, my former captain whilst at Cardiff for those couple of happy seasons, who with six games to play was struggling at the wrong end of the Third Division in his first managerial post in charge of Blackpool. We won four of those last six to survive, a 2-1 victory at Swansea seeing us sneak to safety and Southend consigned to the drop instead.

Although I started pre-season training with Blackpool in readiness for the 1989/90 campaign, my stay was curtailed when I was lured to my former club nearer my Monmouthshire home by Tony Clemo, the new chairman of Cardiff City. However I soon realised it was a flawed decision made with the heart and not with my head.

Despite the very different picture Tony had painted to me the club was in terminal decline. The players were once again queuing at the office door on a Friday afternoon for a wage cheque unduly delayed until the bank had closed for the day and then it would be Monday before they could draw their salary. Of course I had to motivate them to play a football match on the Saturday in between. Players without money in their pockets, rendering them unable to socialise over the weekend, are never happy bunnies. Our supporters would never have believed the scenario. It was tragic and exacting for everyone at the club!

The following is an extract from one our matchday programmes which really says it all.

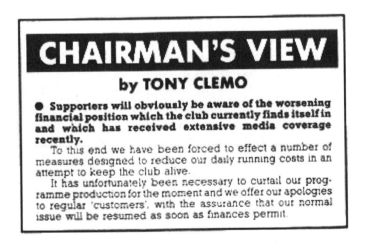

CHAIRMAN'S VIEW
by TONY CLEMO

● Supporters will obviously be aware of the worsening financial position which the club currently finds itself in and which has received extensive media coverage recently.

To this end we have been forced to effect a number of measures designed to reduce our daily running costs in an attempt to keep the club alive.

It has unfortunately been necessary to curtail our programme production for the moment and we offer our apologies to regular 'customers', with the assurance that our normal issue will be resumed as soon as finances permit.

I returned to begging and loaning players and eventually used an incredible 33 in all competitions throughout the season, 13 of those being loanees. It would be a similar scenario the following year.

Being a professional football manager is a tough task. Hundreds of players pass through your keep during a football lifetime, all of varying degrees of ability, skill and courage as well as diversity of personality. A dreadful flaw in my make up is that I tend to blot out from my football memory bank anyone who has not done me any good on the football field. They are immediately history and conversely I fondly remember the winners I have worked with. One of the myriad of loan players that season was David Kevan, who arrived from Notts County. However his loan period was never completed as I sent him back to his parent club because we were in a relegation dogfight at this time and I did not feel he was an influential player in that scenario. He was immediately consigned to the dustbin of my memory.

The next time I met David was by chance, fifteen years later at a Premier League Academy football festival. "You don't know who I am, do you?" was his opening line as he put his hand out to greet me.

I am ashamed to say in response I said, "As a matter of fact, no I don't. I only remember those players who did me some good."

It was a humiliating, unnecessary and shameful put-down by me, aimed at a genuine, honest lad and a decent footballer. Sometimes my tongue gets the better of me and I was dreadfully sorry at the hurt I must have caused him.

Over the course of that season my staff and I witnessed the most extraordinary routine undertaken by Tony Clemo. Rather than engage Securicor to take the match cash receipts to the bank, Tony would often be seen loading it into the back of his car. He maintained he was saving unnecessary expense by not employing a security firm. It was, in fact, the princely sum of £28 per match! That said, it was his club and he could do what he wanted, but I felt it was a dangerous procedure with a huge chance of him being robbed on the journey between football ground and home and then home to the bank on Monday morning. This was only an issue anyway because the club could not afford to have the alarm repaired.

We had reached the third round of the FA Cup thanks to two 1-0 wins over non-league opposition and the prize was a third round home tie against top flight QPR. I upset their respected manager Don Howe by narrowing the pitch and shortening its length to the absolute minimum, after all we could not have Ray Wilkins spraying passes all over Ninian Park on a full size pitch, they would have murdered us! Before the match Don was livid as he looked at the green emulsion paint, bought at B&Q the day before, obliterating the original lines of the pitch. To help disguise our deviousness, and the pitch was a mudheap anyway, I piled cuttings from the grass verge at the side of the main road that ran past the side of the ground all the way round the original perimeter lines. Even that wasn't as easy as it sounds. The mower ran out of petrol halfway through cutting the roadside grass and our groundsman had to borrow a fiver from a passer-by to refuel and complete the subterfuge.

Against the odds we drew 0-0 and after the game Don just stared at me, as much as to say, "Wait till we get you to our place." They duly beat us 2-0 in the replay. As the final whistle sounded at Loftus Road I shook hands with Don and wished him and his team good luck in the next round, saying, "Don, you would have done the same yourself if you had have been in my position." He smiled and nodded his head.

My team had travelled to London for the replay under yet another a financial cloud, although this time it was a slightly unusual reason because South Wales police were looking for the thieves who had busted the safe at Ninian Park on the previous Saturday night, making off with the £38,000 in hard cash of match receipts from a healthy 13,000 gate for that original tie. An inside job was suspected simply because the safe key was easily accessible and had obviously been spotted by the perpetrator, I kid you not!

I remember it so clearly. Basking in the minor glory of earning a replay against a First Division side, and the extra gate money we'd earn because of that, on the Monday lunchtime I was deep in a management meeting with my staff when the door opened and the chairman sheepishly popped his head round the door and asked to be invited in. He was distraught to tell us that £38,000 had been stolen from the safe. He told us he had been relying on the gate money to keep creditors at bay. On asking him why he had not taken it home with him as he had done for most of the season, Clemo's reply was that it was too heavy to go in the boot of his car.

As we all mulled over the consequences of losing the money, with the chairman, close to tears, implying the club could fold there and then, there came a knock on the door. Heads turned as it half opened and with beautiful timing a hand, belonging to Harry Parsons, poked through the gap holding a bulbous bag with 'SWAG' written on it. The place erupted as Tony Clemo made a bee-line for the exit. A magic moment at a club that was out of control!

It transpired the thieves were employed as staff at the club selling pies on match days. They were very quickly identified and the money retrieved, most of it being found at the homes of those involved, with the balance discovered buried on a mountain outside Caerphilly. The detectives on the case must have been highly amused and annoyed at such ineptitude and the farcical safety precautions in place at the club.

Rob Phillips, a local journalist, suggested in an article about the incident that if a chairman of a PLC company had been so negligent he would have been asked to resign his position. For having the temerity to suggest such a thing Clemo banned him from the ground. This did not deter the determined Phillips as he donned a scruffy overcoat, flat cap and dark glasses to watch games from the terraces. One match an eagle-eyed steward recognised him behind this disguise and said to him, "We know it's you Rob, but we can't see you." Magic!

Needless to say with such enormous problems besetting the club at every turn we could not really compete in the Third Division. We spent most of the season in the relegation zone and try as we might could not get our heads above the dotted line on Ceefax. A horrible 1-5 home defeat by Huddersfield in March really put us in the mire and despite three wins and a draw in the last six games we went into the final match of the campaign needing to win to survive. We actually played very well, but a 0-2 defeat at play-off contenders Bury condemned us to the Fourth Division.

Immediately after the last game of the dour and unremarkable following season that was 1990/91, a 0-0 home draw with Maidstone United which confirmed our 13th-placed finish, I was in my office at Ninian Park when I suddenly began to feel quite ill. This was not the match adrenalin subsiding, the heart rate slowing down or the blood pressure abating, it was a nauseous feeling, something I had never experienced ever before. Dr Leslie Hamilton our club doctor checked me out and told Valerie to drive me home insisting, I go away on the holiday that we had already planned for the week ahead and rest. As I did so I realised it was a singular warning of the pressures on a manager of a football club that was fighting against impossible odds. The holiday cleared my head. I decided I did not need this, so two weeks later, on my return, my resignation was tendered.

The wheel had turned full circle, after sixteen years in the Football League my managerial career was over. I had for the good of my clubs begged, borrowed and stolen and many more things besides. Along the way I had made and broken many a player's career. I had started out at the bottom of the football ladder and had found myself back down there once again.

I never gave it a backward glance.

17 **Milking The Wembley Magic**

IN PROFESSIONAL football and every facet of business life you have to be fortunate to make a break through into top management positions. Mine came at a chance meeting with Tom Cowie at the funeral of the former chairman of Cardiff City, the amiable Bob Grogan. It had been held in the north east of England in 1983. Cowie was on the board of Sunderland at the time, under the chairmanship of Keith Collings. Neither the Sunderland manager or members of the Sunderland board were mentioned as we made a conversational journey around all aspects of life as well as the football scene, touching on most issues that were topical at the time. So when the phone rang in my house in Monmouth after the sacking of manager Alan Durban in early March 1984, I listened intently as Tony Hardisty, a journalist with the *Daily Express*, told me that there was an unmissable opportunity to become manager of Sunderland if I could sell myself to Tom Cowie.

The dismissal of Durban on a split board vote had opened the door for me to fulfil an ambition that had fermented in me since I had turned down Collings' offer to manage the club in the close season of 1979. Now I felt the time was right to make a homecoming to the club that I had served with much loyalty over a decade or more and had been so good to me in return.

Thanks to Tony's matchmaking I was unveiled as the new manager of Sunderland on the morning of 5 March 1984.

After a run of eight games without a win the team was close to the bottom of the First Division and, although the Sunderland fans immediately accepted me as one of their own, from the outset it was vital I obtain results to satisfy one of the most fervent and demanding sets of supporters in the country.

My problems were compounded by the feeling, from the outset, that I was facing a thick and somewhat hostile atmosphere in the dressing room. Alan Durban had been a popular figure with most of the senior players. He had allowed a relaxed culture to develop which the established players enjoyed and took advantage of. It was obvious that his approach had been 'keep them happy and you will be popular.' Mine was right at the other end of the spectrum, so I realised I was walking into the lions' den.

When I first spoke to the players I decided to go for it. With a home game in two days time against Queens Park Rangers the players needed to know where they stood, so I told them that the 'Holiday Camp' was over and that hard work and discipline would prevail from now on. My message had been delivered loud and clear.

It was not only in the dressing room that I faced difficulties, but also with numerous local and national journalists, to some of whom my appointment as manager of Sunderland was a huge disappointment. Some made their admiration for Durban clear, while others pined for Brian Clough to be enticed to the club. His champions were obviously not aware that Clough had rejected overtures from that direction in favour of staying with Derby County and then Nottingham Forest on two previous occasions. There was not to be a third approach.

One of the bright shining faces amongst the local scribes was a fine ex-player-turned-journalist called Albert Stubbins. Albert's smile is transfixed in musical history as he famously featured on the cover of the Beatles' *Sgt. Pepper's Lonely Hearts Club Band* – he is the one behind Marlene Dietrich – and apparently was placed there on the instruction of John Lennon, who had idolised Stubbins as Liverpool's post-war striker. Stubbins had also been a hero of mine when I was a lad. His mop of red hair had illuminated many a drab Merseyside winter's day as he fearlessly threw himself amongst the flailing boots to score. I always had a touch more respect for an ex-player who had turned to journalism simply because he had experienced the smell of the liniment and Albert was a real gentleman.

Unbeknown to me to add into this turbulent mix there was also deep unrest amongst the board. My appointment had been forced through by Tom Cowie and was certainly not approved of by all five members of that board, although I never discovered how they were split. The only way I could change the doubters' minds and ease the pressure was to win games.

As I was now in charge I wanted to ascertain who would be available for selection for the home game on the Wednesday night so I immediately set up a meeting with the physiotherapist and the unpretentious 'Pop' Robson, who had taken charge for the draw against Arsenal on the previous Saturday. It was established that all the squad was available to me except the talented Paul Bracewell, who the physiotherapist had ruled out due to a groin injury.

Whilst I was changing into my training kit ready to take my first training session I was confronted by an agitated Bracewell, a player I admired immensely and who insisted that he was fit to play. I asked him to prove his fitness in the training session I was about to take. He wanted to rest until the game and then take his place on the night. I refused on the basis that if he sat this one out he was sure to be available for the run in to the end of the season. This was the first of many altercations with which I was confronted by senior players over the next few months. Clearly I had walked into a rebellious dressing room, intent on having things their way. At the same time some of them were attempting to work their ticket to a new club before the transfer deadline later that month.

I had other ideas, and in fact none of the players moved on as I made it quite clear that no one was going anywhere except to the training ground for morning and, often, afternoon coaching sessions. Those, I was told by staff, had been unheard of under Alan Durban.

Shortly after joining the club the telephone rang in my office. It was John Aldridge's father to say that Oxford United had offered £75,000 to Newport County to sign his son. He informed me that John really wanted to rejoin me at Sunderland, but I had just one hour to get an answer as Robert Maxwell, the redoubtable Oxford chairman, was impatient for the deal to go through.

I was immediately on the phone to Tom Cowie, who was out of town on business. I told him of the situation and, although agreeing to pay the money, he said it would have to be on the proviso that the fee had to be paid in instalments. Not only that, I would have to sell a player before the transfer deadline passed, which was only days away, to offset the cost. The second part of the deal I could probably fulfil, but the insurmountable problem was that a cash deal had been agreed between Oxford and Newport and that was what we would have to agree to. The chairman gave me an emphatic 'No.'

I was crestfallen at missing out on Aldridge, as over the years I had rarely been wrong on plucking a hidden gem from the lower leagues. I knew Aldridge was going to be a superstar having watched him develop from my brother's workmate at Ford into a goalscoring machine. He didn't know it yet, but Tom Cowie had missed out on an opportunity of everlasting popularity on Wearside, which he would have certainly enjoyed.

We won the first game against Queens Park Rangers 1-0. That was a great start, but then we went five games without a win to drop to just three points above the relegation zone with seven games remaining. I was delighted with that QPR result, not least because it came as a direct result of spending numerous hours in training hitting right to left balls to play in Leighton James on the left wing. One of James's crosses lead to our winning goal, which was very pleasing. James, a self-publicity maniac, was a nightmare to work with; he knew it all and used to drive me mad. He was in the twilight of his career when I arrived and was eventually dropped for the last game of the season at Leicester City. Sunderland's First Division survival was on a knife edge that day. Incredibly going into the last match of the campaign six clubs could still fill the final relegation spot alongside Notts County and Wolves. Only a win would guarantee safety for us, although I knew half an ear would be listening for news of results from elsewhere.

With the situation as it was you would have thought that everyone at the club would be pulling together to ensure survival and First Division status. Far from it. I'd become aware that Everton, who at the time were a top First Division club and won the FA Cup that season, had set their sights on some of my better players. The situation had been simmering for a couple of weeks and came to a head on the Friday morning before that vital last game of the season when Paul Bracewell and Lee Chapman came to see me. They both wanted a transfer and intimated they were not fussed about playing at Leicester the following day, despite the fact that I had named them in my starting line up. Both intimated that they did not want to be at the club the following season. With the team bus leaving within the hour I had to respond quickly.

What was paramount was Sunderland's First Division survival; next season could look after itself. Thinking on my feet I gave them an ultimatum, "win at Leicester tomorrow and you will be at another club for the start of next season."

Both were magnificent the next day with Bracewell the Man of the Match, along with captain Ian Atkins, another player who wanted to depart. All three had their wish within a few weeks and sure enough it was Everton who took two of them – Bracewell and Atkins – to Goodison Park. Chapman joined Sheffield Wednesday. However I found it incredible that two footballers had acted in such a way the day before a crucial relegation match. Instead of Leighton James that day at Filbert Street I played Pop Robson, now aged 38, tucked in behind Colin West and Lee Chapman. Pop scored one of the goals as we won 2-0 to confirm our First Division status, Birmingham City somehow ending up being relegated despite drawing 0-0 at Southampton.

James seemed to carry a chip on his shoulder from the minute I walked into the club, I don't know why as he'd had a wonderful career. In fact he told club director Ted Evans that "I should have had the job and not Len Ashurst." I gave him a free transfer at the end of the season.

In fact I undertook a major clearout of players in the summer, along with some of my staff. The most heart-rending decision was to dismiss Pop Robson. This was particularly upsetting for me and more so for Bryan as he had done no wrong and had helped the team survive, but I wanted my own man alongside me, so Frank Burrows was brought in from Southampton. Ideally Pop would have stayed on in some capacity, but the budget did not stretch to another member of staff. Bryan and his family never forgave me, although I still see him on the football and golfing circuit. We exchange pleasantries and as time has passed I feel the wound has been healed.

I was still making my pilgrimage to Lilleshall for the annual Managers and Coaches Course run by the Football Association, only this time it was with a difference as I had been privileged to join the staff for the summer course of 1984 alongside some of my original tutors, Malcolm Allison and Don Howe included. The week flew by and I put on some good coaching sessions for those up and coming managers and coaches from both at home and abroad.

On the final night of the course, the Thursday evening, it was traditional and expected by the locals that most of the football people attending would congregate at the Working Men's Club to unwind after their intensive week on the playing fields. Football talk and stories abounded and the locals were never disappointed with the congenial atmosphere. On this particular evening Malcolm Allison set up a game called the Oxford and Cambridge boat race. For those who are uninitiated this is two 'crews' of alternate men and women sitting on the floor with legs astride of each other. They become the 'boats' and row themselves from one end of the room to the other. However with all of the participants worse for wear with drink, no one ever makes the finishing line. You can use your imagination as to what chaos prevailed. It was hilarious.

The following morning after breakfast I was driving away from the Great Hall at Lilleshall when I spotted Allison standing at the door of his private lodge at the top of the drive in his nightwear. He was smoking his habitual Havana cigar and waving to me as I passed. I drove back home to Monmouth with that image of one of the greatest characters to grace our game in the past fifty years in my mind. I was privileged to have worked with him.

Many successful businessmen have come in to the game as football club chairmen. Tom Cowie fell into this category. He was hugely successful as a businessman and Cowie's Limited eventually became Arriva, the UK's biggest car and transport business. He had a genuine desire to help his hometown club back on to the big time football map. Unfortunately for me, as the John Aldridge episode proved, during my time at Sunderland Tom Cowie never approached the transfer market with a cavalier attitude.

The signing in the close season of two black players Gary Bennett and Howard Gayle was a seminal moment. Although they were not the first to join the club, racism and bigotry was prevalent in the game at that time. I was determined it would not rear its ugly head during my time on Wearside.

Bennett was signed from Cardiff City in July 1984 for £65,000, with the fee being set at a tribunal held in Sheffield. Gary tells the story that I had insisted that he travelled back to Sunderland and joined the team in pre-season training. He had no clothes with him, so Frank Burrows, who wore gear as close to a fifties Teddy Boy as you could get, told Gary that he could borrow some of his clothes. Benno nearly died as he weighed up what Frank was wearing at the tribunal. I was elated at the signing as I knew he would be a huge hit on Wearside. At that fee he was a snip and for the next ten years no one was disappointed. John Aldridge would have had the same, or even bigger, impact.

I signed striker David Hodgson from Liverpool. I had travelled to Israel to watch him play for them against the national team. I was impressed at his quality. He turned out to be a player who had a propensity for shooting himself in the foot and who had an interestingly cavalier approach to the game. Roger Wylde was signed from the Belenenses club in Portugal. Another long journey was made to check he was the same player who had been in my keep at Sheffield Wednesday. He arrived on a free transfer and, although staying at the club for only a short time because of family reasons, he was nevertheless a popular team member and proved his worth. Clive Walker was another class signing from Chelsea. The left-winger had pace, skill and a goal touch. One of my cleverest achievements was persuading Clive to join Sunderland away from his comfort zone in London. He repaid my efforts and support with many fine displays – with the exception of the one that really mattered on the big stage.

We kicked off the new season with a much-changed team and with everyone in the club signed on a contract except me. When leaving my family in Monmouth, I had happily joined the club without Tom Cowie making me a contract offer as I just wanted the opportunity to manage Sunderland. We started the campaign well with progress in the Milk Cup running alongside decent league form and when we beat Manchester United 3-2 at Roker Park in early November we rose to seventh in the table. The following day, a Sunday, Tom Cowie asked me to his home in the Durham Valley. It had been nine months since my arrival at the club and he was pleased with the progress made by the team, but not with the headline of the day that a couple of Sunday sports pages carried implying that I was unhappy at not being offered a contract after my probation period had long gone. The chairman was livid that the press were putting pressure on him to have me tied down on a contract. As it happened he had already drawn up a two-year contract for me on a salary of £30,000. I think he was most angry that the papers had blown the news that he was about to break to me.

I was not unhappy at the length of the contract on offer; however it did not entice me to uproot Valerie from our family home in Gwent. I continued to live out of my suitcase on Wearside.

The third round draw for the Milk Cup, which was to come to dominate our season, handed us an away tie at Brian Clough's Nottingham Forest. I was thrilled to know that I had the opportunity to pit my tactical football wits against Brian's tried and tested ways. We managed a 1-1 draw. After the game I made sure that I called in to Brian's office for a post-match drink. I was plied with as many as I wanted and he was the perfect host. I had told Frank Burrows to follow me in when our dressing room was clear of the players and he announced his appearance with a request for a soft drink. Cloughie blew his top and told him he could have a whisky or nothing at all. Frank turned on his heels and departed the room telling Brian to stick his whisky back in the bottle. I downed my beer and quickly followed suite. Why oh why did my contact with Cloughie always end up in acrimony?

The replay a week later at Roker Park went into extra time after a goalless draw, with Forest down to ten men for the second period of extra time I moved Mark Proctor to a position tucked in behind the front two giving him licence to pull the strings. It was a masterstroke of the kind usually pulled off by the gentleman sitting in the opposite dug out. A Howard Gayle rocket took us into the fourth round with a 1-0 victory.

As the final whistle blew I dug Frank Burrows in the ribs with my elbow as a well done gesture towards my coach. I was calmness personified as I stepped out of the ground level dug out. Turning towards the opposition dug out, Cloughie was already walking towards me, amidst the deafening roar of a home victory. He shook my hand and in his trademark green top and baggy grey track suit bottoms strode off down the tunnel, turned right at the end and disappeared into the away dressing room. That was the last time I saw him alive in person. A glass of wine with him after the game would have been appropriate, but it was not to be.

Tottenham Hotspur were beaten 2-1 in a pulsating fourth round replay at White Hart Lane. That game saw a magnificent goalkeeping perform-ance by Chris Turner, who I had given his debut at Sheffield Wednesday ten years before. He saved a penalty and performed heroics to help us through to the next round. Tactics worked out on the training ground was my contribution to the success on the night. I played Gary Bennett, usually a centre-half, in midfield to mark Glenn Hoddle. His orders were to tightly mark the midfield general and stop him hitting those trademark defence-splitting passes. Then, when we gained possession, he could break forward to support our forwards as I felt Hoddle would not track back. Hoddle was nullified and Bennett caused havoc with his raking runs from midfield, with Glenn trailing behind him.

In spite of having six injured players for the trip to Watford in the fifth round we came away with another extraordinary performance in winning 1-0. Some said we were lucky. I prefer to believe that luck is what happens when preparation meets opportunity.

A two-legged semi-final against Chelsea was the reward for our fine cup run. We entertained the Londoners on a frost bound pitch in the first leg and this was not to our visitors' liking. Two Colin West penalties (one of which he netted on the rebound) gave us a valuable lead to take with us to Stamford Bridge.

The away game was compelling, one of the most violent of my managerial career both on and off the pitch. It bristled with hatred just below the surface and was lit up with tension and animosity which crackled in the night air. The mercurial but unpredictable David Speedie caused the onfield mayhem and in doing so had my captain Shaun Elliott booked. Devastatingly this caution denied Shaun a place in the Wembley final. We ran out 3-2 winners on the night for a 5-2 aggregate win. Clive Walker, on his return to London, tucked two goals away with Colin West heading our third at the same time as a white police horse chased Chelsea supporters off the pitch from around the goal area in which he scored, an extraordinary scene.

The violent and ugly atmosphere spilled over in the second half as hundreds of Chelsea fans attempted to gain access to the enclosure housing the Sunderland fans. Hatred also emanated from the grandstand as seats were ripped from their hinges and thrown onto the pitch. Valerie had made the journey along the M4 to watch the team play and was petrified at what she found herself amongst, finally finding solace in one of the ladies rooms inside the ground.

As the final whistle approached I was warned by the police to get the players off the pitch and make for the dressing rooms as quickly as possible. Under no circumstances should the players go across to our supporters to acknowledge them for fear of danger to life and limb.

At the end of the game I walked straight down the player's tunnel and waited at the Chelsea dressing room door to shake manager John Neal's hand. As both teams followed me down the tunnel David Speedie was trying to pick a fight with anyone in a red and white shirt. Gary Bennett was one of the players he was getting stuck in to. That was a huge mistake. I can remember Gary picking Speedie up off the floor by the collar of his football shirt, his legs treading thin air like a spoilt child. It seems that Speedie tried to get his own back on Gary at Roker Park a few years later and ended up in the clock stand paddock. It all continued in the players lounge afterwards with the massive Chelsea centre-half Micky Droy eventually hauling his excitable team-mate out of the room.

As you can imagine the Sunderland dressing room after the final whistle was electric as we all enjoyed the moment, none more so than Barry Batey, a director of the club, who, as chairman Tom Cowie was on holiday in Barbados, was the most senior board member at the game. Batey rushed in to congratulate the team and in the euphoria of the moment told them that there would be £10,000 for the players' pool for reaching Wembley.

As you can imagine this instantaneous gesture went down well with the players, who in appreciation showered him with champagne. However Batey's promise would eventually cause me no end of problems in the run up to the Milk Cup final.

The Chelsea win was a just reward in so much as no other manager could have worked so hard and put so much time in as I did, both during the cup run and for this particular two-leg tie. The game of football is not always indulgent towards those who work hard. However on this occasion my team and I had given blood, sweat and tears and between us we had earned our reward.

Success in any walk of life brings its own problems, jealousy, resentment and greed. Success as a manager is no different. From my previous experiences I knew this victory against Chelsea was certain to have its dark side. As we started to plan for a day out at Wembley in three weeks time, it took but a few short hours for scroungers and long lost acquaintances to arrive on the scene for a slice of the glory and a ticket for the big game.

Tom Cowie called a board meeting as soon as he arrived home from his Caribbean holiday a week after the Chelsea game. High on my agenda were all the issues that would enable me to have my players mentally prepared on the big day. Hotel accommodation, a training camp during the week before the final, ticket allocation for the players' family and friends, club suits and tracksuits for all the staff among a dozen other issues. Most of the agenda discussed was approved, with the exception of the ticket allocation as the board dug their heels in as to how many tickets each player would be allowed to purchase. It became obvious that they were not going to budge, so I let the meeting head to a close before asking, "Oh, by the way chairman what about the £10,000 that was promised to the players in the dressing room after the Chelsea game?"

"What money is this?" enquired Cowie.

"The money that Mr. Batey promised to the players' pool after the win at Chelsea." I could see Batey sinking in to his seat.

"Is this correct, Barry?" enquired Cowie. "If it is, you will have to find it yourself, as if it's not in their contracts they will not be receiving anything from the club." Board meeting closed.

This and the ticket issue became huge problems during the run up to Wembley. That became obvious when Shaun Elliott and Barry Venison knocked on my office door telling me that the dressing room was distinctly unhappy at the money not being paid in to the players' pool. Actually they did not have to tell me, I had read it myself etched onto their faces on the training ground, draining their enthusiasm. It was made worse by them discovering through former colleague Gary Rowell, who was now a Norwich City player, that the Canaries squad had been allocated any amount of tickets to purchase, whereas my team had been offered the statutory ten.

I had a major problem to deal with and spent hours of my time and energy talking to all parties trying to resolve it. This twin impasse was poisoning my dressing room before the biggest game of my career.

I asked Tom Cowie how Barry Batey, a local man who wore his Sunderland heart on his sleeve had become a board member. It would appear it was because he had been causing so much aggravation as a shareholder at the annual general meetings that on the recommendation of a fellow director, Batey with his considerable shareholding, was elected to the board. Cowie's thought apparently was 'better to have him on your side than against you.' I am sure that Tom regretted that move later in time.

It was a week before the big game that an agreement was finally reached and the money was paid over to the players. Where it came from I never knew and did not want to know. In addition they were given the opportunity to purchase a batch of tickets. But it was all far too late as the malignant damage had already been done to both the morale of the team and the trust between management and players.

Perhaps not surprisingly given all that had gone on in the run up to the game the Milk Cup Final on Sunday 24 March 1985 was an abject experience for me.

The wonderfully exhilarating journey to reach the Twin Towers had felt like that never-ending dash for the winning post in the Grand National at Aintree. It was the most exciting cup run that Sunderland supporters had been taken on since the magnificent FA Cup final win over Leeds United twelve years earlier. It pains me greatly that as a club we conspired to fail to give them a day to remember in any way, shape or form.

The problems just seemed to keep on coming.

I decided I would only announce the team to play Norwich before we departed the hotel for the ride to Wembley. However this did not suit certain journalists who wanted the scoop of having the Sunderland team the day before the game. Fairly obviously this not only would have suited the press, but also Norwich City who would be able to plan their tactics. Some journalists were unhappy at the late announcement and the antipathy towards me was summed up when a phone call from Bob Cass, a national journalist, was cut short by me. He responded to my decision not to give him the team with the comment, "You had better watch out as I will be waiting in the long grass for you." A few days later he was as he and other journalists made hay over my management and my team's display.

Then, whilst out walking the Wembley turf before the game along with George Herd, my head scout, and youth team coach Ian Hughes, I saw Frank Burrows walking briskly towards me. I could tell by his demeanour that there was something amiss.

"Len, we have a problem," he said. "You need to come to the dressing room; Barry Venison is going to wear Adidas boots to play in."

As we had a two-year deal with Nike for all our kit and equipment what Venison was no doubt innocently attempting to do was akin to treachery towards the club who were paying his wages. It transpired later that in the run up to Wembley a number of other players had individual sponsorship deals outside the auspices of the club. Unbeknown to me Puma footwear was also being worn by some of the team. It transpired that all the dressing room knew except me.

It was now forty minutes before the kick-off. Venison was replacing the suspended Shaun Elliott as my captain for the day. I had given him the honour of leading out his team at twenty years of age to become the youngest captain ever in a major cup final at Wembley. In his youthful ignorance Barry had put himself in the position of almost letting down the club before a ball had been kicked. I simply couldn't allow it, so came to the point swiftly.

"Barry, if you intend wearing your Adidas boots you don't play at all. I will give you five minutes to make your mind up." It was now him or me!

I then walked out of the dressing room and stood in the Wembley tunnel chewing over my ultimatum. Here I was shortly before the kick-off of this massive game standing alone with another potentially huge problem on my mind. I was thinking of the television close up of the two captains tossing the coin and the possibility of Venison lifting the cup with the wrong make of boots on. Nike would have withdrawn their sponsorship of the club for breaking a contract if our captain was seen wearing Adidas boots at such key moments. It was a bleak couple of minutes.

Frank Burrows came out of the dressing room and stood along side me. "What if I blacked out the three Adidas stripes with black paint?" he said.

"Do it, Frank."

It was a good enough compromise. Venison, Frank and the dressing room had found a solution, I had to accept it. I felt that a brittle parity was restored and with only thirty minutes to kick off we could now get on with the job in hand. 35,000 Sunderland supporters were never aware of the negative drama that had unfolded in their team's dressing room.

I didn't give the players' footwear another glance as I mentally prepared them for the match. It was pouring with rain outside and although it stopped as the game got underway it was obvious to me that the surface water would wash off the black emulsion paint so making a mockery of the compromise I had agreed to.

The issues didn't stop there. As Ken Brown, the Norwich manager, and I led our teams in to the middle of the lush Wembley pitch, I turned to him and asked him above the noise of 85,000 supporters.

"Ken, who are you waving to in the Royal Box?"

"My wife and family," he replied,

I had been waving to my family and friends before we had reached the goal line markings, as they were in the wing stand along with the players' ticket allocation in some of the cheaper seats. This was another grudge to be born by the team – another pin prick along with the dozens of others in the pin cushion that was me!

Incidentally I had lined up a red and white umbrella to protect myself from the heavy rain that was falling a few minutes before Ken and I lead our teams out. Thank goodness it stopped before we came out of the tunnel as I would have looked a right clown. I could have been pilloried as much as Steve McClaren on his last match at Wembley as he stood forlornly under his brolly watching Croatia destroy his England side's chances of qualifying for the European Championships.

After the introduction of both teams to Sir Stanley Rous, I made my way up to my seat in the grandstand above the halfway line. I had always watched the first fifteen minutes of every match from the stands. It gave me a picture of the game and the opposition. But when I got up there I found sitting in my seat a Sunderland Council member. I spent three minutes traipsing around Wembley looking for somewhere to sit feeling like a right prat. What more could be sent to try me?

The game itself was woeful and deserves little comment. Norwich City's deflected goal was avoidable, a defensive error by young defender David Corner who played because of Elliott's suspension. David should have kicked the ball out of play when he had the chance to. That misfortune was followed by a penalty miss by Clive Walker which would have given us an equaliser. It was the first penalty Clive had missed in his professional career.

At the end of the game a number of the players were reluctant to climb the famous Wembley steps to receive their losers' medals as apparently they were disgusted at the way they had played. At least some of them had a conscience!

Others less so. Whilst Gary Rowell in the opposite dressing room was drinking champagne, some of my players were storing up their vitriol ready to be thrown in all sorts of directions except at themselves.

The evening reception at our London Hotel was a real damp squib as Chairman and directors as well as management put on a brave face. There were still twelve league games to play and we had a relegation battle on our hands. I needed the players on my side, so when a somewhat the worse for drink Clive Walker defied the family only rule for the reception and threatened me with some of his 'Heavies from the Smoke,' I for once admired his 'spunk' for bluffing me out. With two huge minders looking on he let fly at me with both barrels and verbally slaughtered me over everything he could think of from team selection to hotel accommodation, allocation of final tickets and anything else which the players had a grouse about. Clive was an important and popular member of the team, so I listened patiently then shrugged my shoulders and walked away from a potential flash point.

Walker was not the only player who brought their cronies to the party. Howard Gayle, a man of very few words and to me a powder keg ready to explode at any time, had an entourage of friends in tow. If ever I thought a player would be in trouble in later life he was the one, however I understand he is now doing excellent work amongst the youngsters of the Toxteth district in the City of Liverpool. Well done, Howard.

What should have been one of the most satisfying achievements of my career became an exercise in fire fighting at every corner I turned. As the troublesome storm clouds gathered above my head, I had made few friends along the way.

As a complete contrast to this devastating outcome of the most high profile game of my career, watched by millions of people around the globe, one of my most satisfying soccer experiences came whilst I was Director of Football at Weston-super-Mare FC in the preliminary round of the FA Cup away at Cirencester in Gloucestershire. There was the proverbial one man and his dog to witness what was for me a one-off opportunity to indulge my football brain without conscience or concern over a negative outcome. Only nine of my team had turned up for the game, so weighing up the limited options I had I decided to play a 2-4-2 formation. The two lads at the back were experienced ex-professionals who used their football know-how to play an offside trap throughout and we managed to sneak a 1-0 victory against all the odds. I will always feel that was a remarkable achievement.

Little did I foresee the seismic proportions of supporter backlash over my team selection for that Milk Cup final. Hundreds of supporters have asked me the question, "Why didn't you play Colin West at Wembley?" I often have to remind them that Colin West was not dropped for the game as he had not been in the team the week before when we had beaten Norwich 3-1 away at Carrow Road. Indeed Ian Wallace, his replacement, scored one of the goals that day. My decision not to play West at Wembley was made without reference to any of the players in the team or for that matter media pressure. We had reached Wembley without dressing room opinion and without the influence of the press or our supporters, so I was not going to change my approach for the final and ask all and sundry. Only Frank Burrows would be consulted.

There is no earth-shattering revelation as to why Colin West was not chosen. It was simple. He could muster only three league goals from the previous 19 games, so I had decided two weeks before the final that change was needed. During the week leading up to the final, I watched carefully for a reaction in training from those fringe players who should have been killing themselves to force me to play them at Wembley. West was one of the players I was particularly looking for a reaction from. It never came.

After Wembley, West gave the impression of being a disappointed and disillusioned footballer and I sold him to Watford just before transfer deadline day in March 1985.

An amusing footnote to this story was that many years later when I had occasion to call Sheffield Wednesday on Premier League business, their manager Chris Turner picked the phone up and, after finishing our business conversation, he told me that he was in the midst of a management meeting with the staff, indicating that his assistant manager Colin West was also in the room.

"Chris, can you get him to the phone?" I asked.

On taking the telephone Colin pulled no punches in expressing his disappointment towards me, but he was now in management himself and appreciated that difficult decisions had to be taken at times, indicating some sympathy with the predicament that I had been in all those years before.

At that moment I had a conscience prick.

"Colin, I'll tell you what I would like to do for you seeing as you didn't make a Wembley appearance," I said.

Colin asked what it was.

"I would like to give you my runners up medal from Wembley."

"That's very kind of you Len but no thank you. I'll tell you what I would like you to do with your medal . . ."

"What's that I said?" with an open mind as to what he might say.

"You can stick it up your arsehole!"

We both had a good laugh and as I put the phone down both of us I am sure felt better for the conversation.

That Wembley final still haunts David Corner, who is now a Detective Constable in the police force. To his embarrassment David is constantly reminded of his mistake in the lead up to the goal. A full ten years after the game he was chasing a burglar over some back gardens and as he grappled the man down to the floor and was putting the cuffs on him, the guy looked up and said "I've not been arrested by David Corner, have I? Not the David Corner who cocked up at Wembley!"

Plenty of vitriol came my way in the aftermath of defeat. Weeks after the Cup final when standing waiting to cross the road towards my parked car in the city centre, an old Ford Cortina pulled up with four lads inside. One of them ran the window down and I thought to myself, 'here it comes.' Sure enough the lad let rip, "Ashurst, you're an arsehole." Before I could respond they had gone. For me that moment just about summed up the whole Twin Towers experience.

Had I cocked up at Wembley? If after 24 years I now said I would do the same again, I would be verbally slaughtered and quite rightly be accused of being stubborn and self-centred. Yes I would have done a few things differently going right back to that definitive negative moment in 1984, when I was refused permission to sign John Aldridge. I should have pressed Tom Cowie to the limit. I should not have accepted 'No' as his final answer.

The run to the Milk Cup final generated enough funds to put the Sunderland balance sheet into the black. However it was also a disaster in another way as the team plummeted down the league table into the relegation zone winning only one game from the final twelve matches. The loss on New Year's Day of astute midfielder Mark Proctor through a groin injury which kept him on the sidelines for the rest of the season was a huge blow and our eventual demise only confirmed what I already knew, and that was Proctor's value to the team was immense and a number of the other players were not good enough. Ultimately that was my responsibility. Others were totally self-centred and had allowed personal differences over discipline, tickets, finance and team selection to come between them and what they were being well paid to do – perform on the pitch. That cost Sunderland Football Club dearly.

We were relegated, losing the last game of the season 1-2 at Roker Park against Ipswich Town. We had been 18th in the table when we lost at Wembley but earned just six more points. Relegation hit me like a hammer to the stomach.

As I turned to walk down the players' tunnel after the final whistle condemned us to Division Two I was showered with season tickets thrown at me by angry supporters, I could understand their fury.

This was the first time that they had vented any acrimony towards me since my debut in 1958. I had believed and will always believe that Sunderland's fans are the best in the land. Their loyalty to their colours through every generation knows no bounds. Culpability stops with the manager, a defeat at Wembley taken in isolation would not have cost me my job, but bring it together with relegation from the First Division and my fate was sealed. I knew I would be dismissed.

Driving home after the Ipswich Town defeat the ignominy of relegation weighed heavily. But that and my impending personal demise was all put in stark perspective as the full horror of the fire at Bradford City's Valley Parade unfolded as I listened to my car radio. What was supposed to have been a family day out in glorious sunshine in South Yorkshire ended up with 56 men, women and children perishing with another 400 people fighting for their lives.

So what was relegation? A mere trough in the history of a famous club who would in time recover, that's all. It paled to insignificance when compared alongside those souls who would never recover their normal lives and those who had gone for ever.

11am on Monday 24 May 1985 was the exact time and date that Tom Cowie sacked me. 11am again! Tom had probably sacked hundreds of people in his time, however I got the distinct impression that in my case he found it an extremely difficult exercise. There were certainly no skeletons in the cupboard as far as I was concerned. There had been a professional respect between us, so I was not surprised when Cowie telephoned me at my home to ask me make the journey to his Millfield office the following day as he wanted to discuss immediate club business before he departed on a family holiday. I knew what that covert comment meant! My journey took five hours and what Tom Cowie had to say took two minutes. No sooner had I walked in to his office than I was walking out to make the long journey home without a job.

I could not call this brief meeting amicable, however it was financially productive as to their credit the board paid up a fair proportion of my recently-signed contract. I asked myself at the time why he forced me to trawl ten hours there and back just to sack me. I now understand as I have had to do the same thing myself on numerous occasions. If it has to be done you face it up and get on with it. There is never a good dismissal.

I have always had the approach to life that when one chapter abruptly closes another one opens, as long as you are prepared to work to make it happen. The short chapters are not necessarily the unfulfilled ones. On the contrary, my short experience at managing clubs was often very fruitful. Managing Sunderland was an example of this, a wonderful experience, certainly eventful and never drab or mundane.

Tom Cowie found his chairmanship of Sunderland draining. He had a handle on his own business and knew it inside out, but football clubs are more often driven by passion rather than sensible business management. He was a bottom line man and 'Heart over Head' was never his style. He admitted to me that his inability to head up a successful Sunderland Football Club was the one failure in his business life.

Later in life Cowie was honoured with a knighthood for his brilliant entrepreneurial ability, as well as his own charitable trust and his work as chairman of the Conservative party in the Sunderland area. His generosity and commitment to the City of Sunderland University placed him thirteenth in the Sunday Times list of philanthropists in Britain. However Sunderland fans will only remember him for his failure to arouse their passions through providing them with a successful football team. This will be of little concern to Sir Tom, who, I am sure, would consider it a minor blip on a hugely successful business and social life.

18 **Middle and Far East Escapades**

Kuwait 1985/86

No sooner had the Sunderland Football club door closed, than I was taking on the challenges of dealing with a new culture in the Arab world by accepting a post with the Kuwait Sporting Club.

John Cartwright was vacating the job at this high profile Kuwaiti club to join Arsenal as first-team coach. He had finished second in the league and painted a vivid picture to me of the demands required to please the local Sheik and his twelve man committee. It was plain as a pikestaff – "Win the league, Len, or you are on the plane back home."

It was just a few months on from that ill-fated Wembley appearance as I stepped off a jumbo jet at the airport in the city of Kuwait and was flabbergasted at the wall of heat that hit me at 9pm local time. I thought it was the heat from the huge engines of the plane that had just brought me from London, but this 35 degree furnace was the norm for the next few months until autumn and winter came along.

It was made clear to me from the outset by the twelve man committee that I had to finish above Dave Mackay's team Al Arabi, who had swept all before them over the previous two seasons. Dave Mackay was a complete professional – hard as rocks in competitive football and contrastingly a very personable guy off the pitch. We became good friends socially as we fast-walked the Cornice every morning to clear the head for handling the Kuwait players at evening training sessions.

Kuwait being a 'Dry State' further helped Dave and I to keep ourselves in good shape. Along with Malcolm Allison, who was at that time the Kuwait national team coach, I was in good football company. In addition I was delighted to have George Herd join me at the club to run my youth team. It was my payback for having sacked this quality man many years ago when managing Hartlepool. George stayed for five further years after I had departed.

Kuwait was ostensively a police state. The eyes of officialdom were everywhere with the government very sensitive to outside scrutiny. British newspapers were available, but generally censored and had articles on Israel blacked out. An example of their sensitivity was an occasion when Valerie arrived on a flight from London along with Jane and Roger. I wanted to record their arrival at the airport for a month's holiday over Christmas, but as I focussed up I was manhandled by airport police, who opened up the camera and destroyed the film.

Welcome to the country, family!

The season kicked off splendidly with success in the final of the Kuwait pre-season National Cup, beating Dave's Al Arabi club in the final 3-2. He walked up to me after the final whistle and shook hands, but his only words to me were poignant. "This means bugger all, Len. You have to beat us in the National League."

How true those words rang nine months later as distressingly Dave's club pipped us for the league title by just one point. They would be playing in the prestigious Pan Asian tournament instead of my team as I was taking the plane back home to Britain, my contract not renewed for the following season.

After eleven months in the desert and the acrid climate of Kuwait it was heaven to see the green of England and the spring flowers bursting through, any of you who have experienced that same desire for home will appreciate what I am referring to.

Qatar and Wakrah Sports Club 1986-89

He was a greying Arab who had been a player at the Wakrah club for several years, but he wasn't the most enthusiastic about training. He walked in and out of the club when he wanted and in addition he seemed to pick up an injury easily and often.

"Coach, play him as he is influential and puts money into the club."

That was the dictum given to me when I arrived at this provincial Arab town football club for my first of two stints as their coach. I had a choice – compromise your reputation and your principles or go along with this ludicrous unprofessional request. As always I went with my principles and suffered for a long time afterwards as the player clearly resented my attitude to team selection. This was nothing new as my Kuwait experience had taught me how to cope, I was often one step ahead with my man on the inside working on my behalf.

It was imperative that you had to have your plant within a club like this. My man in the camp was Fahad-Al-Kater, a genial and intelligent businessman who took a shine to me and the work I was putting in on the club's behalf. He kept me briefed on the attitudes and plans of the committee, so I was able to play the balancing act without compromising myself. I revamped this ageing team and put the young players in at the deep end alongside three or four of the stalwarts who still had an ambition with something to offer. None of them let me down as we spent hours on the training ground bedding in a team pattern to suit some less talented individual players. Absence and unpunctuality by the players was heavily punished and sloppiness never tolerated. Show a weakness to any one of your players and you would be a dead man as the others would ride roughshod over you. My work paid off with a top four finish and a win in one of the minor cup competitions. The club's first ever silverware was won with me at the helm. I was a hero for the time being.

Leisure time was spent at the Umm Said Golf Club, an eighteen hole course cut into the desert. It served a purpose both socially and as a sporting outlet away from work. The fairways were rolled sand and oil with the firm elevated 'greens' (in reality browns) made of lightly-brushed sand. Alan Dicks, the former stalwart manager over thirteen years at Bristol City, was coaching the Rhyan Club in Doha and we became a regular two-ball on most mornings of the week. In addition once a month ex-patriots could purchase under licence a certain amount of alcohol for their own personal use at a police-guarded bonded warehouse. Caution had to be shown as late night police checks invariably caught out unwary and careless ex-pats drinking and driving. Jail or immediate expulsion from the country was the penalty for being caught.

During a month-long international break for the Asian tournament held in Far East in 1988, Valerie, who had stayed in the UK to look after the family, made arrangements for us to visit friends in Australia. But two days before our departure from the UK my mother died in Walton Hospital, Liverpool. This was now a family dilemma. I had visited mum to say my farewells days before. I consulted my brothers and without hesitation they told me that I must take the plane as mum would have approved. Consequently I missed her funeral. My conscience weighed heavily during our trip down under and tainted my view of that wonderful country.

I lasted three full seasons at this soccer backwater and we created a team that eventually no one wanted to play against in a stadium packed with 15,000 people. In my first season you could count the spectators at any one match when my team were playing. We eventually made it a fortress and swept everything before us with the exception of the league title, this eluded me and after three seasons I returned to the UK and back to sanity.

Malaysia 1992-93

Having had a belly full of scrimping and scraping to keep Cardiff City alive I walked out on them for the second time in the summer of 1991. I had tasted the sour survival end of football management once too often and was glad to put this latest chapter behind me, vowing never to be tempted again.

Well rested after a rare sabbatical and having spent a soccer-free Christmas and New Year with my family, my agent contacted me and put in front of me an attractive package to coach in the far East in the state of Pahang on the east coast of Malaysia. I departed the UK in mid-January 1992 arriving at the small provincial airport of Kuanton, the capital of Pahang.

Tengku, the young local royal prince in his late twenties with a touch of acidity to his tongue, was head of the Pahang FA. He was the man to whom I answered. He telephoned me a week into my tenure instructing me to wait outside my apartment, within minutes the sound of sirens grew louder as his cavalcade of motorcycle outriders flanking two huge limousines, one for Tengku and one as a decoy car, approached. They slowed down in front of me and I got in. We then swept through the town with lights flashing, while his highnesses personal bodyguards cleared safe passage through the choking traffic. As we left the city I found myself amongst stunning views above the town five hundred feet below.

We arrived at the site on which a completely new royal palace was near completion. We both alighted from the car and wandered around the construction. It was astonishing, with only the finest quality materials from around the world being used in this sumptuous build. It reminded me so much of the riches of the Arab world that I had observed in previous years. Strangely not a workman was to be seen. Apparently they had been instructed to down tools and make themselves scarce as royalty was to view the building site. Noise, dust and sweaty workmen I was used to, for the prince it would not have been appropriate.

Having had a royal as a tour guide, which was in itself a surreal experience, I was now sitting alongside the boss in the rear of the royal car. What followed was for me another first considering we had not yet kicked a ball in preparation for the new football season. His opening shot was, "Coach, what do you expect me to do if you don't win matches from the start of the season?"

Aware of the instant culture in the Middle and Far East, I replied, "Sack me, I presume."

It was the response he had wanted. With us both in no doubt as to what our targets were he summoned his chauffeur and we headed back from whence we came. I felt I would be the winner in this one.

Three weeks before training started for the coming season I sat down and spent many hours viewing videos of the previous season's matches, so acquainting myself with the strengths and weaknesses of the team and the players. It appeared that I had inherited some good footballers, so at this stage I was very relaxed about the whole new experience ahead of me. I had pointedly been told by my assistants that there was a betting ring in operation within the country amongst the Chinese population, with players from various clubs heavily involved. I was told, "If you see a reliable player under par or not trying then he could be or probably is involved in a betting scan."

Heaven help me there were enough problems for me to solve without having to second guess whether a player was throwing a match!

My two local assistant coaches were excellent people, young former players wanting to learn from this English coach. They took it in turns to treat me to the local cuisine which was always doused with hot peppery chillies. That as it turned out a few months later would prove to be the cause of my deteriorating health.

Tengku was keen to ascertain the progress of the pre-season training before we departed for a three match tournament in Thailand. He had watched many of the training sessions and was very upbeat about our prospects for the season ahead. His visits to the training ground were no means clandestine as he arrived in style in a growing cacophony of sound, two or sometimes three limousines sweeping through the town and onto the playing area of the training ground. My players needed no motivation when he was arriving, they were always nervous in his presence and probably tried too hard to please as he sat watching from the back seat of his luxury vehicle.

I was invited to be his guest at the royal palace for tea. I was astonished at the opulence of his home. It was breathtaking. The most exquisite Italian marble walls were splashed with the brilliant colours of Italian renaissance paintings. Fantastic Austrian cut glass chandeliers hung in clusters from the art deco ceilings, while the best Iranian carpets were dotted here and there to break up the wide expanse of marble floor.

I took a seat on one of the luxurious settees that could have seated all my football team and Tengku proceeded to tell me that he was delighted with my work and was confident that we would win the championship for the first time in many years. Once again he was applying the mental pressure, even more so when he opened a briefcase he had by his side and spilled the contents onto the table between us. Thousands of American dollars were now spread in front of me. And he wasn't finished as he then opened a side pouch in the briefcase and placed a solid gold ingot in the middle of the table.

"Coach, if you win the league the gold ingot is yours, and if you win the cup you can have the money."

With that he swept up the hoard and placed it all back into the briefcase and instructed his bodyguard to take it away. That was the last time I saw the briefcase and the prince's ransom.

We had tea and then he invited me to view his collection of vintage British cars which were lined up in individual opened garages at the rear of his palace. There was one for every month of the year and not a speck of dust upon them as a small army of cleaners were employed keeping everything spotless.

The colonial influence was never more obvious than in Malaysia. Over the period of a millennium and a half or more, the inhabitants of the British Isles had chiselled out a concept of a modern state, developing an independent judiciary, an impartial armed service and a navy that patrolled the oceans of the world to maintain peace. Most importantly, however, Britain oversaw a succession of constitutional monarchs who gave the seal of approval to a parliament and prime minister duly elected by the people of the land. This was certainly the case in Malaysia.

Pre-season results were exceptional. We won the tournament in Thailand, then in front of a full house of 25,000 we handsomely defeated the previous season's League Champions Johor Bharu 2-1 in monsoon conditions. We opened up the new season with three more victories, however this promising start was personally tarnished as I was losing weight at a rate of knots, not able to keep any food on my stomach. Under the supervision of a consultant surgeon medical tests proved negative. I could not complain at the treatment I was receiving, but I was desperate for a conclusive medical opinion. It eventually came five games in to the new season.

Having won three of the opening four games we then played Sabah on one of the many islands in the South China Sea. It was early afternoon on the day of the game and I was feeling low in spirit and devoid of energy because of the undiagnosed illness that had caused me to shed 10 kilos over four months from my already tired body. My sumptuous hotel room was on the water's edge facing across to a peninsula jutting out into the South China Sea. I was 7,000 miles from the comforts of home and feeling depressed. My mood was not helped by the slight drizzle in the air, rather like a cloudy day in Grange-over-Sands, the difference being it was humid to the extreme. From my window I saw a smart white boat travelling swiftly towards the small hotel jetty, it was flying numerous brightly coloured flags proudly stiffened by the strong breeze. As it sped across the water towards me I fantasized as to who could be inside the sleek lined cabin. Maybe they have brought Valerie to me, secreted away on an unannounced visit, there was a hope! Or could it be a mythical Sultan of Brunei's messenger who was trying to bribe me by supplying me with a local fair lady of the night. That would not have worked anyway as I never had that sort of inclination and anyhow my body strength was close to zero. None of these fantasies materialised as it transpired this was a welcoming party from the Brunei Football Association hierarchy who were to be entertained to a pre-match banquet by our club's committee. Amongst them were the match officials who were to officiate the game that evening.

Protocol would normally determine that the football coach would be sitting amongst the top brass of this tiny Football Association, but this was hardly a normal situation. I recoiled at the prospect of not only having to make small talk, but even more so at the possibility of having to sit next to the offspring of a former local terrorist who had colluded with the Japanese during the war to help trap and murder thousands of allied troops (my uncle included) in the jungles of Malaysia. I was determined to skip this meal and to stay in my bedroom to rest before the big match. The pre-match nerves causing my shrunken stomach to churn with anxiety were adding further stress to a body already wracked with 'Western Tummy'. My decision was correct in view of my personal condition, but the wrong one from the point of protocol and goodwill, as I was to find out later.

The Sabah game was won in spite of the referee sending off myself and two of my players as well as awarding two spot-kicks against us, both of which were missed by the opposition. A last minute breakaway goal gave us an unlikely 1-0 victory, and we hung on in spite of over ten minutes of injury time. I wondered whether this win against all odds pleased or upset the betting syndicates back on the mainland!

My sending off was vindictive. Needing to use the toilet rather frequently I had stood at the tunnel, which was against the rules and so was sent to the dressing room which brought me closer to the toilet but away from the action. I sneaked to the back of the stand and watched the game unfold. I was told later that my absence from the banqueting table implied a snub and the sending off was a reprisal for not attending the pre-match function. I also missed out on the gold watch presented to my two coaches at the afternoon banquet. It meant little to me as I fought with myself at the prospect of an untreatable disease.

A couple of days later, in the middle of May, I was summoned to the hospital fearing the worst. Thankfully the extensive tests had indicated nothing that I had reason to worry about. Dr Weng the consultant surgeon suggested I should take the team for the following game then resign as coach and make the journey home to England. He was convinced that I had 'Western Tummy', having over indulged in the local cuisine, and that the red-hot chillies had burnt the lining off my stomach.

Although finishing on a high note with a 3-0 win over Singapore which took the club to the top of the league, without fuss, ceremony or a last goodbye I climbed aboard the overnight flight to London. In the words of Valerie as she and Roger met me off the plane, "I looked like a cancer patient". Within a couple of months of eating Valerie's homemade food I was back to full health as Dr Weng predicted.

Tengku had not paid me a bonus for our Charity Shield success, so arrangements were made to meet him in London in the middle of July. He had no obligation to pay me as there had been no such clause in my contract and after all I was not now on his payroll. However he was charm personified and after having presented my case instructions were given that on my way out one of his bodyguards, who was built like the proverbial, would pay me a belated bonus of £1,000. As the team had gone on to become champions I was half expecting the full briefcase of American dollars for bringing his club national glory, but it was not to be and what I received was better than nothing. I also never learned whether my successor Mick Brown, now Sunderland's chief scout, ever received the gold ingot. Or if we had upset the Chinese betting ring with our 1-0 victory against the odds in Sabah.

1993-95 Back to the desert at Wakrah

I received a call from Qatar asking me to return as my former inside man Fahad had been elected chairman of the Wakrah Club after it had fallen on hard times. A two-year contract was agreed upon and I was once more making my acquaintance with my former players and that secretive committee. Fahad was now the poacher-turned-gamekeeper and I had now to find a new ally inside the camp.

On rejoining the club in the summer of 1993, I spent ten days in Jordan in burning hot sunshine on a three match pre-season tour and was able to explore the old City of Jarash and its ancient Roman amphitheatre, as well as having the unique experience of floating in the Dead Sea. My Arab players, lacking cultural history, preferred to go shopping. I elected to visit the Dead Sea. I had our team bus to myself and my Muslim driver tore downhill on the twisting narrow roads as if he wanted to join Allah. My heart was in my mouth as I was shouting 'Shway Shway', meaning to slow down. I was imprisoned in this runaway death trap with neither of us able to communicate as he surged on down the single track road. My soak in the waters of the Dead Sea brought me both sanity and my heartbeat down to normal! The return journey uphill was much more sedate and I was able to take in the historic biblical scenery.

In the Arab states Thursday night was the end of their working week as Friday is their rest day. It was a dangerous time to be out and about especially if you strayed from the main streets of the town. You ventured into the back lanes or side streets at your peril as the locals let their hair down and sped around these areas in their four wheel drives at mad speeds and with reckless abandon.

Another local pastime was 'Sand Duning'. No ride at Alton Towers could match this local craze for thrills and spills played out in the pitch dark of night. Using headlights only they first geared up the side of monstrous forty to fifty foot dunes and then on reaching the peak hurtled down the other side at breakneck speed, their wheels hardly touching the downward slope of the sand dune. Fatalities occurred and yet many continued to ignore the dangers and opted time and time again to try to defy gravity.

But that was a piece of cake compared to the danger I managed to get myself into when, in August 1994 the government invited my team to undertake a goodwill trip to Baghdad and the Gaza Strip. With both places being amongst the most dangerous on the planet this was going to be a dice with death – with no danger money forthcoming!

19 Baghdad to Gaza in One Piece - Just!

In August 1994 I kept an 18-day diary of my club's pre-season tour to Iraq and the Gaza strip. I naively presumed it would be safe, especially after seeking advice from the British Embassy in Qatar. How wrong I was ...

Tuesday 23 August 1994

Dear Valerie,

Departed at 7am from Doha airport, arriving in Jordan mid-morning. The pilot made a heavy landing, which convinced me this trip will be a traumatic experience. There is an embargo on flights into Iraq, so we will continue our journey to Baghdad by coach. At this early juncture doubts are creeping into my mind over my decision to make the journey.

The Wakrah Sports Club team bus was late in arriving, what is new when it comes to time keeping in the Arab world? When it finally arrived, trepidation engulfed me. It was a throwback to the 1950s – no toilet or washing facilities with springs sticking through the seats, which eventually at times forced me to take a standing position during the course of a nineteen hour journey. In addition to our team bus, there was a lorry never far behind us carrying some large wooden crates which had been brought from Doha. I am not yet aware of the contents.

No sooner had the journey commenced than the Arab players started their infernal chanting and singing, so I buried my head in a book, put the earplugs in from my Walkman and made myself as comfortable as possible for an arduous journey across poorly-constructed roads and desert terrain.

Stopping for food on the journey was an eye opener as the Qataris devoured the sheep's meat which we had brought along with us from Amman, decent food being scarce inside Iraq. The captain of the team had the honour of cutting the sheep's carcass and kept its eyes as his privileged delicacy! I kept to bread and bottled water, not wanting to take any chances on the food being served up. My fears were justified, as four hours later numerous players needed the toilet.

We eventually reached the Iraqi border and dozens of gun-toting soldiers and border guards surrounded the bus. What came instantly to mind was the part played by Western forces in driving the Iraqis out of Kuwait in 1990. I wondered what would be their attitude towards me, a British citizen coaching an Arab team?

The border police boarded our team bus and checked our passports, paying particular attention to Flamarion, my Brazilian coach, and myself. All was well until they saw that I had a Kuwaiti passport stamp, from when I had been coaching there in 1985/86. I was taken off the bus into a small interrogation room. I made sure that I was accompanied by one of the Iraqi players and a number of my committee. There must have been a dozen Arabs in the room, my officials questioning why I should be held and the Iraqis making their point in return. I couldn't understand them but I was aware that they were discussing my fate.

After what seemed an eternity my English-speaking chairman, Fahad Al Khater, explained to me the authorities were going to photograph me and impound my British passport, leaving me with a copy of the original for the journey ahead. When we exit Iraq they will then return it to me.

With the inquisition complete, we continued our journey. Whilst all this was going on our bus was decked out with the national flags of Iraq and Qatar, apparently for safety reasons – they were there for us to be seen! Bloody Hell it was the middle of the night, so I wasn't sure who'd be able to see them, but the question that crossed my mind was without the flags could we be blown off the road?

The border police had informed the security police ringing the city of Baghdad that we had been cleared a few hours before, so with the formalities complete we arrived, relieved, at our destination at 3am on Wednesday morning.

Wednesday 24 August

I awoke mid-morning, pulling the curtains back to reveal a massive sun beating down from a cloudless sky. Our hotel was sitting on the banks of the river Tigris which splits the city east and west and there was a poignant reminder of the recent past – a gun emplacement alongside each of the numerous bridges presumably in readiness for future use.

I made my way down to breakfast, obviously not expecting an English fry up, but what hit me was alarming. There was very little available, no tea, coffee or sugar. For your cereal, which was a roughage of sorts, milk was a puree made from goats' milk. There was plenty of 'mam' bread, which would become my stock food, along with bottled water. I have never appreciated water so much as I did at this time!

Just as alarming were the armed Iraqi police that were situated at most vantage points in and outside of the hotel. It transpired that these were top army marksmen put in place for maximum protection for us during our stay. Can you imagine the political fallout if anything happens to any of the Qataris, one of whom has royal blood? We are supposed to be on a visit of reconciliation on behalf of a Qatari government and the royal family.

A health check was carried out amongst the players and we found four of them unavailable for light training at 6pm. Even at that hour it was close to 30 degrees as the sun set. Training was routine and then it was back to the hotel for a shower and dinner.

Thursday 25 August

No training this morning as the players needed the extra rest. I had recovered my sea legs and it gave me a chance to explore the hotel and its grounds, not withstanding the uncomfortable company of the army marksmen. The place is very run down but in its heyday it must have been the social playground for royalty, diplomats and millionaires, with its magnificent marble floors and walls, formal gardens, pagodas and a swimming pool which is still functional.

Our three Iraqi international players joined the team for training this evening. These are the privileged ones playing soccer abroad in Qatar and earning sufficient American dollars to be able to send some back home to their families.

Friday 26 August

Arrived down for breakfast and walked into the first of many problems I am anticipating. The previous night a wedding with celebratory alcohol available had taken place in the hotel and some of my players and the two Qatari managers had joined the celebrations. The Sheik, who is also President of the club, had walked in from an evening out and found them all still awake in the early hours. Footballers, at least some of them, wherever they are, don't change their spots! We gave a stern warning to all who stepped out of line, so that will be the end of the nonsense.

Training at the Iraqi national stadium went well tonight in spite of the indiscipline of last night. The grass was long and will remain so as the mowing machine has broken down and spare parts are only to be had on the Black Market.

The stadium dressing rooms are near to primitive. The toilets are simply a hole in the floor and you have to hang on to the handles battened to the side walls of the cubicle with the obligatory tap to wash your backside! I know what goes down, heaven knows what must come up! We shall now be using the hotel facilities after every game. How the Iraqis get the place past FIFA I will never know. Neglect is all around us.

Lukewarm beef and potatoes for supper. The team ate every morsel. They must have stomachs made of leather.

Saturday 27 August

Had breakfast then browsed around the hotel lobby, which is massive. There was an exhibition of oils by local artists. All the time I was browsing I felt police eyes upon me. Tonight we play our first match against the Arabi club, who are the League Champions. We shall be hard pressed to get a result with four of my best players away on international duty in Malaysia, however we shall see.

The match was a rare experience with nearly 50,000 people packed into the stadium to welcome home the three Iraqi nationals in my team. We departed the hotel with a Warrior tank heading up the cavalcade of Mercedes limousines and outriders leading our coach to the ground. The police were ruthless as they sent dozens of people crashing to the floor, wielding their three metre long whips to clear the way. The passion was bordering on hysteria! The local population have been starved of major sporting events for a long time and the significance of our trip to Baghdad is now evident. This is clearly a political exercise to mend bridges.

It was rumoured that the dictator himself, Saddam Hussein, would be attending the game. I wondered if my inference a day or two ago during my interview with Iraqi national television that I would be pleased to meet the man might be realised. But it was not to be. The dignitary was Tariq Aziz, the Christian, bespectacled deputy Prime Minister, a man of around my height who did not proffer his hand as he glanced at me from behind his black-rimmed, darkened glasses before quickly moving on to shake hands with the three Iraqi born players.

We lost the game 0-1 to the team who won the Iraqi National League last season by a handsome margin. It was really just a case of getting 90 minutes under the belt. We defended well and showed a good attitude in a hostile environment.

Sunday 28 August

I asked for the players to be down at the swimming pool by 10am for recovery from the game. At 10am prompt there I was at the side of the pool with not an Arab footballer in sight. They were all still in bed the manager told me. "Keep your cool coach – Enshala" that Arab word, which means something along the lines of 'it is God's will', that explains all for them! I had a swim and waited for the players to arrive in their dribs and drabs. Unpunctuality is a terrible trait which the Arabs have in abundance.

Never rushing and certainly never apologising they all eventually showed up. Afterwards I disappeared to my room for coffee, which one of the managers has managed to barter in exchange for the contents of the crates that travelled with us – shrewd bastards. Bartering with the locals for the little luxuries of life is one of the things Arabs do best.

I gave the team a free day and arranged for one of the Iraqi players to show me Baghdad. At 6pm I went to church, visiting St Augustine's a Christian place of worship with a high service near to a Catholic mass. There are, I am told, many Christian people in a mixed population living along side the Sunni and Shiite Arabs, Turks and East Europeans and the congregation was made up of all creeds and colours. It was very comforting to hear the name Jesus spoken by the Irish minister in a church in the Middle East.

Monday 29 August

One of the players with royal connections decided to have a lie-in this morning. The rest of the team are livid, but to suggest a fine is ludicrous as the player, being so well connected, would scoff at the reprimand. His family own oil fields! He will be dealt with by the committee when we return to Doha.

We visited the Al Rasheed Hotel, the domain of our Sheik. I was told there was a trade delegation from Turkey, no doubt smoothing relations with the Saddam Hussein-led Iraqi council in readiness for when the trade embargo is lifted. I spoke to an antique shop owner who told me that the locals are selling anything to survive. Iraqi citizens are starving as the local police and the army personnel grow fatter by the day. Can they eat rice?

Tuesday 30 August

Another game over, losing 1-2 to the Army National team last night. There was not the hysteria of the first game, but nevertheless it was bedlam getting to and from the ground. I was delighted at the way we played and our committee are surprised at the commitment of the team.

I allowed my three Iraqi players to have a couple of days off to visit their families in the city. They have earned it. All three have been brilliant in their attitude in the matches to date. They are very much like European footballers. They are hungrier and want it more than Qataris. Having witnessed the poverty in this country with my own eyes, I can understand why their approach is so focused. They have mouths to feed at home. I do worry about them getting into trouble, as all three are Sunni and this is mainly a Shia area. Religion in this country equates to hatred at times.

Wednesday 31 August

Took my first stroll with an Arab headdress on my head around the locality today, but was advised to stay on the main streets in case I was being targeted. I was taking no chances, so I made sure I took with me a couple of the senior players and an armed guard as security. Not the best way to see the sights, but under the circumstances the safest. I was not prepared for what I saw as locals laid out for sale on the pavement all their worldly goods. I found myself literally stepping in and out of all sorts of household items – the kind of things that would be left over from a church jumble sale back home. It was sheer desperation by hungry people to put food on the table.

Thursday 1 September

Trained at 6am with the temperature at 25 degrees. Tomorrow is Friday, the Muslim holy day. We have a match against the national Under 21 team. The three Iraqi players I allowed home returned on time to rejoined the squad. They seemed to have a story to tell, there was plenty of laughter, typical footballers wherever you are.

Friday 2 September

Holy day for the locals, so I went for a short walk at sunrise to see what I could see. Around the corner a couple of streets along I found a wonderful church called St. George's tucked away up a side street. Its steeple broke the pattern of a skyline containing various shaped domes of mosques. No one was around at this early hour.

The church was derelict and had been ransacked for anything that was valuable. The lead had been stripped from the ceiling and roof. The organ was missing, leaving an alcove in the wall where it had obviously been ripped out, although some pipes were still in place high above where it had stood. Amazingly the glorious stained glass windows had survived and on their surface were printed the names of military regiments who had served in this part of the world. It was a beautiful sight as the early morning sunshine alighted upon them.

The floor was littered with hundreds of hymn and prayer books. I tucked some into my pockets. I also found the church register from just after the Second World War containing the names of visiting ambassadors from as far afield as America, New Zealand and Australia along with royalty from Jordan and Europe. They had all signed the visitors book for posterity. This was a rare prize I was not going to leave behind.

Saturday 3 September

In another hostile environment, we were beaten 2-4 last night by the Iraqi Under 21s. The novelty of Iraq is wearing thin for the players and during the match they looked disinterested. The sooner we get back to Jordan the better.

This evening the whole team was invited to the Al Rasheed Hotel to take a meal with our Sheik, hosted by the Qatar Ambassador to Iraq, in celebration of Qatar National Day. It was sumptuous. Life is never fair and here was a good example of the rich and the privileged feasting off the fat, whilst outside their door the people starved.

Most of the Arab states were represented by their ambassadors, with Asia and Far East dignitaries also in attendance. Few women accompanied the men, which is normal here. I managed to take some photos of the spread of food, which was large enough to feed a nation. I also caught on camera some of the hierarchy being piped in at the grand entrance. It was grandeur on the grandest of scales.

Sunday 4 September

Took a walk this morning accompanied by the armed guard who keeps his firearm tucked out of sight, then occasionally conspicuously displays it as a deterrent to possible opportunists. He is certainly a comfort to me when I am out and about. I counted dozens of broken down old cars at the side of the road, the redeemable ones were being pushed along the road by a handful of locals in 35 degrees of heat, poor buggers! Vehicles with doors, bonnets and windows missing still use the roads, headlights and reflectors torn from their mountings are commonplace. The air pollution is tangible.

Monday 5 September

In preparation for a match and a two-day stay in Palestine, then a day in Jerusalem before returning to Jordan, tonight we trained for the final time in Iraq's humid hot conditions. It was an effort to coax my players to work and I have to say I found it difficult to motivate myself, I had to as hundreds watched us work out for the last time. They are fanatical about football in this country and I was flying the flag of the English coach.

Tuesday 6 September

This morning we went on an official guided tour around the city to view some of the mosques, monuments and huge pictures of Saddam Hussein that are dotted around in abundance. Surprisingly, when I asked to see a bombed out underground bunker that had been targeted by American missiles and had made headlines all over the world, our guides agreed to take me and Flamarion. It was a gory, eye-opening experience. The building, a solid concrete bunker with the roof hardly above ground, had been turned into a gruesome museum. The allied missiles had been so precise that they had gone through the door and into the bunker. Intelligence had suggested that it was an Iraqi military bunker. It had turned out that around 500 ordinary civilians were taking refuge there on that fateful night when the missiles struck.

No one escaped the inferno and I was not going to argue as I viewed with a certain sadness the blackened, twisted metal and the charred wood fittings indicated the extent of the horror. In case we had any misgivings about the extent of the grisly sight our guide, with a certain amount of vitriol in his voice, showed us the human hair and skin that had been seared to the walls as the victims melted like butter in a frying pan. I managed some photographs of the twisted metal, the hole in the roof and the crater in the floor where the missiles had hit. They make unpalatable viewing. We then climbed the steps towards the daylight, something which 500 local people never did.

We lost our fourth game 1-2 tonight, getting off lightly as it could have been a real hammering as the Combined Services XI tore us apart. The contents of one of the crates that had accompanied us on this journey was distributed to the spectators before the game. The deep cherry red kit of the Qatar National Team was spread out in front of them on the pitch. This was a generous and clever Qatari government public relations exercise. I allowed my three Iraqi Nationals to spend the night with their families and instructed them to report back shortly before departure tomorrow.

Wednesday 7 September

Over lunch Flamarion told me of a harrowing experience he'd had whilst taking a photograph of a mosque that morning. The police had swept him into a van and he was taken away and grilled as to his identity and what he was doing photographing Iraqi buildings. He was fortunate that he'd had his passport in his possession. After confiscating his camera and destroying the film he was released and driven back to the hotel. Poor bugger – in the space of 24 hours he had got the shits, been arrested, had his camera and film from the previous night's match confiscated and we have lost our fourth game in a row on this trip. With bad luck like that, why did I employ him?! Then he told me his previous photo shoot was ruined as he had left the cap on the camera!

This evening I was informed of very disturbing news. My Iraqi player called Radi, the handsome Sunni Muslim who is a huge name in Middle East football, did not make it home after last night's match. They believe he was kidnapped in the Shia area of the city. I feel terribly guilty as I had given all three of my Iraqi players the night off to visit home. The other two local players have rejoined the squad for the journey to Gaza.

Thursday 8 September

We travelled from Baghdad to the Gaza Strip, a journey which took 27 hours in all. However I have some news for you. Let me assure you right away that I am feeling fine and in one piece!

We started the journey around 11pm on the Wednesday night. I took the front seat of the bus with the driver and his co-driver alongside each other, sitting directly in front of me. This was a near fatal decision as, when we had been on the road just five minutes, a large boulder crashed through the front window of the bus smashing the head of the co-driver. I did not know it at the time, but he died instantly,

The piece of granite then hit me a glancing blow to my cheek. I initially thought I had been shot. Apparently blood was pouring everywhere from both me and the co-driver. The bus skidded to a halt and a panic-stricken tumult prevailed as players and officials scrambled off the bus to assess the damage to personnel and our transport. I thought my jaw had been broken, but I could open and shut my mouth. I was OK aside from the cut. I was starting to feel delirious from the shock and the loss of blood as I lay on the grass verge at the side of the road. A towel of sorts was pressed against the wound and I started to drift in and out of consciousness.

For some reason a flashback came to me as I lay on the floor. It was the last time I was in any kind of danger in a football-related incident. A vivid picture emerged in my mind of many years ago when I was on the groundstaff at Anfield as a fifteen year-old boy when Don Welsh the Liverpool manager was practising his golf standing on the halfway line, crashing golf balls into the Kop where we apprentices had to retrieve them as they ricocheted around the terracing. Strange tricks the mind will play!

As the flow of blood was stemmed I cleared my mind and was able to stand and walk to a police car that was travelling with us through the city to the open road. Accompanied by an armed guard and two of our officials I was whisked to the nearest hospital. What could I expect to find? Would it be clean, would they be able to help me, would I have to stay in the hospital? These were the questions I was asking myself and, more importantly, would there be any permanent damage or disfigurement to my face?

A sympathetic Lebanese doctor assured me all was well and explained to me what he would like to do but couldn't as he had very little medical equipment. Instead the wound would be sutured to pull the gash together with a long needle and cat gut as thick as a violin string. "Oh, and also there is no anaesthetic," he said.

I was grateful for whatever treatment I received, although it seemed to last an age. I gripped the bare metal table as I was stitched, and eventually the excruciating pain diminished as the wound was dressed with a huge swatch of linen. I also had my eyes cleaned out at as particles of powdered glass had been blown in to them when the windscreen caved in. The doctor turned my eye-lids inside out with a clever finger flip; he had obviously done this a thousand times before.

As my club officials, our bodyguard and I made our way along crumbling hospital corridors towards the exit, I thought of my Dad's Confirmation Book which I had as a travelling comfort. I thanked God for my life, prayed for those left behind and also that I would not be lying in a hospital bed overnight. I was grateful for the personal attention given to me by these very professional people.

It was now early morning and we returned to the scene of the incident and the team bus, I was informed of the death of the second driver, which apparently had been instant. The windscreen had been patched up as the driver's side had remained intact. The police and the Qatar Embassy officials who had arrived at the scene whilst I was away where very animated over the incident and its consequences. Apparently a pedestrian bridge that ran above the road at that point had provided the opportunity for the attack. There was still a high level of tension around, however we soon restarted our journey with me sitting halfway down the bus in a more central, safe seat.

I was fussed around a lot, but eventually left to reflect on who might have been the culprits. We would never learn the truth, but to me it was retribution – a British national was on board a Qatar football team bus. Their country had been the base for allied planes as they pushed the Iraqi troops out of Kuwait not so long ago.

Having retrieved my British Passport at the border, we arrived at the Qatar Embassy in Amman on Thursday around noon, thirteen hours after we started the journey from the centre of Baghdad. My wound was throbbing. Fortunately I could now have the dressing changed and my physiotherapist applied his skills to the stitches which in his own words "looked like a dirty arse on fire".

After a quick freshen up and a meal of sorts we boarded a more modern bus for the next stage of our journey, into the Gaza Strip. We are scheduled to play one match against the self-styled Palestinian national team, a country not recognised by FIFA. First of all we had to make it through the Israeli border past soldiers renowned for their toughness. This group of Arabs were not relishing the prospect.

We reached the Israeli-controlled Qarni border crossing only two miles from Gaza City just before sun set on a hot and dry afternoon. It would be five hours before we would be clear of the checkpoint and allowed to travel onwards. I had never seen a sight like this – young men and women, Israeli soldiers, with live armoury draped around their bodies as they ordered the occupants of cars, lorries and our bus to disembark to be body searched. They also searched through the vehicles with a fine toothcomb.

As I stood and watched I saw Palestinian nationals wishing to cross the border being herded into a cavernous interrogation room, their luggage searched and then tossed aside for its owner to identify and claim.

As a British citizen there was a certain respect shown towards me, a brief glance at my passport and I was through within minutes. The same could not be said for my players and committee. They were verbally grilled, half-stripped and scrupulously searched. What humiliation for our Sheik and the player with royal blood.

My physiotherapist had to reassemble and repack all his medical kit as every single item, including tubes of medical creams, had been opened and checked. Once we had all cleared customs we met up with our Palestinian hosts who had waited patiently for us. We reached our hotel close to the sea front just past midnight.

I was beckoned to a meeting which was the last thing I wanted in the early hours of the morning, especially as my head was still throbbing. We discussed the protocol and procedure for the match the following day. I was told that the guest of honour for the game was to be Yasser Arafat, leader of the Palestinian nation. This was very big news indeed.

Friday 9 September

An official welcoming party on the cliff top close to our hotel provided us with lunch in an open Bedouin tent, the sides of which were left flapping in the breeze to allow the sea air to sweep through as the temperature soared to the mid-thirties. On entering I noticed there was a large number of armed police guards dotted around the perimeter of the site. The spread of food was magnificent. There were a dozen waiters serving us, all in Palestinian dress. There was meat in abundance still on the carcass, sheep's eyes, liver and heart were piled high on the plates amongst the vegetables and fresh fruit. I made for the succulent fresh fish which tasted as if it had been swimming around in the sea less than twenty four hours ago. Wine was on offer, but I avoided the temptation as meeting Arafat with hazy eyes and a pungent breath would not have been appropriate. I have never seen my committee so happy. It was obvious they were unwinding amongst their own after the traumas of the previous twenty four hours when confronted by their bitter enemies the Jews. They ate and drank, and then it was time to board the bus for a match of momentous significance for locals and Qataris alike. This was a visit to build relationships with our hosts.

The stadium was an ugly concrete structure in the heart of the city with a capacity of approximately 4,000 spectators. As we drew up alongside the makeshift portakabin dressing rooms, the main dressing rooms having been hit by a mortar bomb from across the border, I could see a high wire fence surrounding the edge of the playing area. The ground was packed to the rafters with people who were hungry for a glimpse of the first Arab football club to visit the area in a long time.

The pitch was shocking. It was just rolled sand and red gravel and as you walked across the surface a thin red dust arose from the floor. My players where aghast at the prospect of playing on such a surface and a number approached me to have the game cancelled. With the ground already full it was too far late for that and after a brief meeting with the Sheik their overtures were rejected. He was obviously clear-headed enough after his lunch to assert his authority with those who wanted to bottle out. Not playing this match would have meant blood on the floor and my Sheik knew it. Shortly afterwards we were lining up for the national anthems, sung robustly by the home crowd.

Now came the highlight of the afternoon for my team and our officials, the meeting with Yasser Arafat. He made his way along our line up of officials and players, and I wondered if he could speak English. If so, what would he say to me and how would I respond? As he got closer to me, surrounded by his armed minders, I was surprised at how small he was. His trademark black and white kutra on his head wafted in the light breeze that was blowing across the ground. With his gnarled face unmoved, he was upon me. I put out my hand but found it ignored as he gave me a cursory glance and moved onwards with his entourage of minders to take his place amongst the other dignitaries to watch the game. The moment had passed, but would never be forgotten. With those piercing olive eyes set amidst an ugly face of wizened skin caused by years of sunshine and mental torture and a huge red encrusted spot at the side of his forehead just below the line of his kutra, he was not the prettiest sight you will ever see!

It was no surprise to lose the game 1-4 as my players avoided going to ground for fear of having skin burns. As the players swapped jerseys at the end of the game the sun set and the call to prayer went up from a myriad of mosques surrounding the ground. What followed was an extraordinarily wholesome experience, as the police opened the gates in the high wire fence close to the pitch side, masses of spectators flooded onto the playing surface spreading their prayer mats on the gravel surface wherever they could find a space. They duly prayed to Allah alongside the players of both teams and the Palestinian officials, Yasser Arafat included.

I was the only person amongst those thousands of Muslims to remain on my feet, a Christian Brit alienated by religion. I thought quickly and not to look conspicuous I strolled to the dressing room as I realised that as I was stood there erect I was presenting a sitting target for any trigger happy gunman!

After prayers a human tunnel opened up on the playing area as Arafat and his entourage made their way to their cars, applauded all the way by his loyal supporters, who by the looks of them had only their Muslim religion to hang on to for their belief in the future. Minutes later we had departed that massed cauldron of humanity whose lives had been lifted by our visit, albeit for a short while in what must be for them a tenuous existence.

Saturday 10 September

We departed for Jerusalem around 8.30am and were on the outskirts of the Holy City a couple of hours later. This time we passed quickly through the border checkpoint and found ourselves driving along smart new dual carriageways into another world entirely. We passed impressive smart houses and apartments, tree-lined carriageways with all the traffic lights working, green fields of fruit and vegetables with healthy-looking cattle grazing on emerald green grass. There was no shortage of water here. It all contrasted greatly to Gaza City just a few miles down the road.

We were soon in the heart of the Holy City and off went the majority of the players and staff for a visit to the Golden Mosque, while I made my way along with Flamarion to the old part of Jerusalem. It was the Jewish Sabbath and the streets were quiet until we reached the Old City. There tourists were thick on the ground admiring the historic spires and domes, and I heard an English accent for the first time in weeks.

Sunday 11 September

I am now over the border into the comparative safety of Amman in Jordan within the confines of the Hotel Jerusalem. Reflecting on the past two weeks, I can only think that if I was to stay in football for another ten decades I will never endure such a tumultuous period of time. I have presided over an Arab football team whilst prevailing around me was an eventful experience of fear, bewilderment and also enjoyment at the many happenings and the contrasting sights that I have seen.

I have witnessed the greed of a few amongst the poverty of a humbled nation. However, over and above all this, is the knowledge that a small football team from the east coast of Arabia have left behind a lot of goodwill and lifted thousands of people out of their mundane misery of everyday life, if only for a brief moment in time. That team was my team. I am pleased to be part of a fulfilling one off experience.

I have just been told the good news that the abducted player Radi, our Iraqi centre-forward, is safe. He was dropped by his captors on a lonely road outside Baghdad and eventually was picked up and brought back to his family.

On a lighter and more humorous note, the player with the elite connections will get a shock when he arrives home in Qatar. I have been informed that his numerous wives have been taken away from him and sent on a holiday to a so-called 'Unknown Destination'! However this was not disciplinary action for when he lay in bed after the first game in Baghdad. Unbeknown to me and the managers he had also gone absent without leave during the trip, slipping out of the hotel to a secret rendezvous in Baghdad where it is believed he met up with some local businessmen to purchase from them a flashy, pink Mercedes which was now on its way by road under escort to the airport in Amman.

I pondered on how many people had been bribed and how much it will have cost him to allow safe passage for a motor car from the heart of the city of Baghdad, through the border crossing into Jordan for it to then be freighted by air to Doha, Qatar?

Tomorrow we will be following it home.

* * * * * *

I NEVER experienced any ritual killings pre-match in Qatar. Only when on a pre-season training camp in the United Arab Emirates whilst playing a game in Fujairah did I watch in horror as the locals slit the throat of a goat on the centre spot before the kick-off apparently to provide drink for the holy spirits that they believed in. This, however, was not as horrific as what Ian Porterfield experienced in Ghana when managing the national team. He painted a vivid picture to me of how, in the dressing room before each international match, the team sacrificed an animal, dancing in the pool of warm blood on the dressing room floor, then smearing their bodies. Strict FIFA blood rules would nowadays never allow them to have that same ritual and then take to the field of play.

My final season in Arabia was a mixed bag. We finished third in the league, as we had done the previous season, and I decided to depart before they pushed me. I had six seasons with this small town club bringing relative success and laid a foundation for the future which turned out to be a bright one as under a Balkan coach they later accomplished a deserved league title triumph.

I still never quite got to grips with the vagaries of the Arab world. I fear it is something I shall never understand. However I shall always remember them.

20 **The Betrayal Of Grassroots Football**

FORMER LEEDS UNITED manager Howard Wilkinson was Technical Director at the Football Association in the mid-1990s and was given a brief to overhaul the way that English league clubs ran their youth development systems. Through diligent research he took the template for the FA's new Academy structure from the best he had found in Europe. After a year and more of deliberation and many miles travelled he produced a brilliant blueprint for football in his 'Charter for Quality'. It was well intended and radically changed for ever the way that Premier League and Football League clubs ran their youth set-ups. It also had its flaws and some fine tuning has been applied along the way. I believe more is still required as some of the fundamental problems which affect our game on a national scale today are reinforced rather than negated by the system.

The main structure, laid out in Howard's report, was that the clubs could sign boys at eight years of age and bring them into their own academies, then up to eleven years of age they would be playing their football on small-sided pitches with seven-a-side being the optimum number of boys for each team encouraging more touches on the ball. The goalkeeper would be playing in smaller goals and allowed to roll the ball out to one of his team mates without pressure from the opposition, so encouraging skill rather than power. This was a huge step forward from the kick-and-run football that had prevailed for so long at all levels of our game. The majority of the Academy clubs embraced the ethos wholeheartedly and spent millions of pounds on bringing their shabby facilities into the new millennium.

I was employed by the FA Premier League to help oversee the development and implementation of the Academy structure. But even with my appropriate coaching qualifications and my vast experience in the game, my brief would not allow me any input or opinion as to the quality of the coaching at the Academies in which I observed some frankly dreadful sessions occasionally served up to the youngsters by lazy coaches who were not good enough and were not prepared to improve their work with innovation and dedication. That frustration I can only alleviate now by publicly stating my feelings about how this vital area of the game, crucial to the development of top players for our national team, is failing.

Another problem is that it is endemic in the English game that the youth team coach in many clubs is the lowest earner amongst the coaching staff. His status is undervalued here. A few top echelon clubs such as Manchester City, Manchester United, Arsenal, Middlesbrough and Blackburn Rovers set a fine example. But as a consequence of being underpaid and undervalued, as soon as that youth coach has the opportunity to move on, he will.

I also found that poor scouting was prevalent, meaning that youngsters were selected based on their physical attributes and the player's ability at too young an age. That showed little knowledge of the physical development that takes place in a young player. Often a star at 8 or 9 years of age is bypassed by others when they have progressed to 14 or 15. Plus, taking boys into the hothouse conditions of a Premier League club and away from their environment too early, thus making it difficult for them to retain links with their mentors and friends, is also, in my opinion, wrong. Every season hundreds of youngsters are cast aside by Academies within two years of taking that huge step away from their junior team and their friends. There is no system for dealing with the fall out from this.

The selfishness of some coaches within the structure was apparent with numerous clubs merely wanting to beat neighbours down the road. The emphasis remains on winning at all costs as Academy Managers were put under pressure from some chief executives and directors of the clubs. But you cannot do that and also work on skills and technique with young players all of the time.

The principle of playing competitive matches at 8 or 9 years of age I am not totally against, however when on a Sunday morning it entails youngsters travelling vast distances down the motorway for a 'Games Programme' it then becomes a travesty. Those weary youngsters will leave home at 6am and do not arrive back until early evening. I witnessed this scenario week in and week out over many seasons, however my protestations proved futile. For those boys who travel all that distance, but do not even make it onto the field of play because of the win at all costs mentality, there can only be disappointment and disillusionment.

I am strongly of the opinion, along with many Academy Managers, including Manchester United, that a games programme should only start at Under 11 and until that age the precious time should be used with a football for one-on-one coaching and small-sided games such as 3v3 and 4v4 inside the wonderful Academy facilities that exist up and down the country. Those youngsters could then learn to win and lose, develop skills and learn to play together without the enormous pressure of results. That will come in time. When you compare the miniscule amount of time given to technical work at our Academies compared to Europe and Africa you can understand one of the major reasons why they are more technically gifted compared to the British youngsters, who make up 89% of the Academy students.

It fell to me to see that the rules and regulations pertaining to the correct registration procedure for students were applied to all players who took part in the games programme. If a youngster was found not to have been registered then a mandatory fine was supposed to be implemented by the Premier League. But the system was flawed as we who monitored the scheme were not fully supported at all times by the FA Premier League, who proved reluctant to apply financial penalties to their own members.

GREAT AT developing youngsters as they are, Arsenal's decade-long love affair under Arsène Wenger with a preponderance of foreigners is not doing much good for the England cause. Arsenal Football Club provide superb facilities as well as a brilliant, rounded football education for all their youngsters. There is none better anywhere else in the country, possibly even abroad. However when the time comes to blood English youngsters at first team level they are, in my opinion, short on patience.

The admirable Wenger considers that English players are often technically lacking, nevertheless Arsenal's academy manager Irishman Liam Brady is confident that in three to five years they will be producing the best crop of English footballers that they have seen through their academy. If this is the case it will have taken nearly fifteen years for this quality to emerge since the inception of the Academy structure.

Middlesbrough Football Club conversely are a fine example of a Premier League Club showing patience and wisdom where English players are concerned. They blooded eight Academy players over a short period of time in 2006/07 and chairman Steve Gibson has been patient, not demanding instant coffee from Dave Parnaby, his Academy Manager, or his promising young players.

When an Italian blasts the English game for not helping homegrown talent to prosper we should sit up and listen, more importantly think and act. Gianfranco Zola's outburst in June of 2007 before the official opening game at the new Wembley was scathing about our clubs not giving a chance to home grown youngsters. We shall observe keenly his approach at West Ham United now he is manager there. His major signing in the transfer window of January 2009 was German under 21 striker Savio Nsereko. The youngster's fee broke the club record, but showed that even this club, with its proud traditions of producing homegrown talent, and which in the recent past has given us Rio Ferdinand, Michael Carrick, Jermain Defoe, Joe Cole, Frank Lampard and Mark Noble, is struggling to find more when the immediate priority is survival in the Premier League.

Almost a decade ago, when Kevin Keegan was the England team manager, he sat next to Aimé Jacquet, the French coach, at a game between Arsenal and Chelsea at Highbury. This was an English Premier League match of the highest calibre and yet only one English player of international standing was on the field for Keegan to watch, compared to the nine that Jacquet could observe for his French national team – Henry, Vieira, Petit, Lebeouf, Desailly and Deschamps among them. Surely there could not have been any clearer clarification of the dead end road down which we were travelling even then. It has only accelerated ever since. It is nearly too late to make that U-turn and reverse the chances of an England team manager one day taking the country to a prestigious final.

Hugh Jennings, the former Premier League Youth Development Manager, has gone on record as saying, "I lament the way in which the talent here is not given the opportunity."

A concern also to me is the worryingly high contracts being paid to young players well before they have made the grade and really earned the rewards. Too much is given too soon. They have not had the grounding in having to work to give them some semblance of discipline, responsibility and, particularly, values. Take a look at the car park of any Premier League Academy and see the trappings of the young footballer of today, then you will understand what I mean. On salaries of up to £3,000 per week, they can afford the best. I am not complaining that I never had these opportunities when I was their age, simply pointing out that in many cases the comfort levels merely serve to stunt their development, a state of affairs not helped by their attitude.

The overseas scouts employed by English clubs are now infesting the Dutch youth game attempting to poach their best talent. It is wonderful that the cream of the world's players want to come and ply their trade in our country, but think what it will be like in five to ten years time when an England team is chosen . . . we will have a Premier League that is multi-cultural to such an extreme that we may actually struggle to find enough English players. It will only get worse, you have been warned!

The Premier League has recently been dubbed a 'Cultural Melting Pot' that benefits from the presence of numerous world class players from abroad. The author of this opinion was a foreign player (Moritz Volz, who was then a Fulham defender). I would not disagree with him. The best players should and deserve to be in the Premier League. And they deserve to be earning a king's ransom. We adore their quality. However there are also in their midst a whole host of poor-to-average overseas players who simply should not be here. Are we interested in Volz and his opinion? Yes, we should listen, but judge for ourselves what is best for the English game.

This might sound radical, but I propose that we keep the brilliant players and rid ourselves, through a far more thorough, rigorous and discerning selection process, of 50% of overseas players. This would obviously have to be done within the confines of what European Law will allow, but too many players not qualified to play international football for a Home country are taking the squad numbers which should, by rights, be for young British players.

Incidentally I fully believe that supporters will have a greater affinity to homegrown players, which in turn will lead to better merchandising sales and more bums on seats, something which is beginning to worry some clubs who see season ticket sales and attendances falling in difficult financial times in 2009.

Recently Chris Lightbown, a freelance journalist, in collaboration with Gordon Taylor at the PFA, published *Meltdown*, a most informative document revealing disturbing statistics which must send shudders through the game. Here are some:

- 14 English goalkeepers played in the Premier League in its first season, 1991/92. In 2001 there were just five, a number which remained consistent for the following six seasons.

- 88% of all players were English in '92, now that figure has more than halved to 43%. In Italy the figure for their nationals was, in 1992, 80%. Today it is still a healthy 71%. Is it any coincidence that they are the World Champions?

- 363 English players started a Premier League game in that first season. That figure is now down to 191 and worryingly only a paltry eight English Academy-tutored boys made their debut in 2007.

Was this the vision that Howard Wilkinson's blueprint perceived for our game?

Number crunching can sometimes distort the picture, but I firmly believe this publication has got it right. It decisively concludes that ready-made foreign players, many of them poor to average in ability, but long on cheapness and instant gratification, are blocking the path of young English/British players into the Premier League.

Add to this the total lack of leadership which led to the temporary shelving of the Burton project – hopefully now back on track – their timidity when dealing with the all-powerful clubs that form the Premier League, plus the failure to qualify for Euro 2008 and disenchantment at grassroots level then you can see how the FA have been failing our game for too long.

Alongside numerous other initiatives, the FA should now flex their muscles with the Premier League and insist on the involvement of more of our homegrown youngsters in Premier League football. It hardly helps matters that we have the anomaly of Premier League club officials sitting in both camps simultaneously to ensure the status quo is kept and not challenged.

You will probably not be aware of the lengths that a number of our top Premier League clubs have gone to so they can cream off the best of the young talent across the globe, particularly from Africa. In the process of doing so they increase the competition for our ignored young British players, to the detriment of the national teams.

To achieve the signing of as much young talent as possible, feeder clubs have become the vogue. Manchester United have Antwerp, Blackburn Rovers are joined with Cercle Bruges, Arsenal have an interest in Beveren and more recently Fulham and Germinal Beerschot Antwerpen have linked up. It is no coincidence that Belgium is the chosen country as it is out of the way, rarely covered on television and is French-speaking, the natural tongue of so many of those talented young Africans.

We have been accustomed to players from these Premier League clubs occasionally being loaned to their twinned club to gain experience in what is a poor standard European League. That is acceptable. What is not is how Premier League sides are using these clubs to farm the best young players from abroad.

The most obvious benefit is that these players soon become qualified as European nationals through a period of residency, and so can avoid many of the criteria in place to wheedle out the wheat from the chaff when they move to the Premier League.

Fast forward five years from now and I will guarantee that there will be a steady flow of young talented footballers, mainly African, making life even more difficult for our own homegrown players. The British Empire crumbled a while ago. You are now witnessing the erosion and disintegration of English football and in particular the almost certain demise of the national team.

Barclays Bank, the Premier League sponsors, and the Football Foundation are doing sterling work to support and encourage boys and girls through community schemes as well as educating and working with children both able-bodied and disabled. This is a magnificent initiative and already around 140 sites have been opened throughout the country.

Richard Scudamore, the chief executive of the Premier League was quoted in *The Times* in May 2007 as saying that the Premier League clubs do huge amounts of community work with projects on education, health and crime reduction. So they do and that is commendable. However it is imperative that even more direct financial support into grassroots soccer should come from the Premier League and the Football Association.

In 2001 the FA agreed to put £6 million over five years into training Primary School teachers to introduce football to our young children. Has this happened? We don't know.

Kelly Simmons, the FA's Head of Football Development, informs us that the government have invested nearly half a billion pounds in school sports. That's all well and good, but over what period of time, how has it been monitored and which areas has this cash pile been fed in to? Harrogate, for example? Most certainly not.

In 2006/07 whilst former England Head Coach Sven-Göran Eriksson was receiving the best part of £6,500 a day as his pay off, schools up and down the country were struggling to keep a sports curriculum functioning for their children because of lack of funds. Half of what the ex-England manager was receiving in a day was the total budget of Rossett School in Harrogate in North Yorkshire for the school year. Yes £3,300 was expected to fund 1,100 pupils for two hours of physical activity a week. In addition an extra-curricular programme for nine football teams, hockey and netball teams had to be provided from that budget. Mr MD Fenton, the school's Director of Sport was being asked to work miracles.

Recently another body blow at school level was struck as time allocated for sport has been cut down from three hours a week to two. In my opinion we are propagating a nation of young people who live in a comfort zone and, because of their soft way of life, have an approach of take it or leave it. Youngsters seem to get everything on a plate nowadays. I ask the question are they now endowed with a beaten before they play attitude? And will that not manifest itself in pretty much every walk of life over the coming decades?

Other than Dennis Howell, who had sport in his blood and fulfilled his promises and was undoubtedly the best Sports Minister from either side of the house, successive governments have allowed the trend of neglect to continue amongst grassroots sports.

The programme of the sale of school sporting fields under the Thatcher administration did not help – and neither did the fact that it has continued ever since – around 34,000 since 1992 have disappeared under bricks and mortar at the last count.

And it's not just the pitches themselves. A coach of a boys' team in Cambridgeshire, who devoted all his leisure time to running a junior football team, hit the national headlines in 2008 because his team, wherever they have played, had not had an after-match shower for over two years. They should think themselves lucky to have a grass pitch to play on.

Then there is the example of the huge and unfair anomaly in FIFA/UEFA regulations which are a disgrace and cause junior soccer in this country enormous problems. You may not be aware that a junior club in Ireland, Scotland, Wales or from abroad can benefit financially from nurturing a young boy's talent until he is signed by a professional club in England. If that boy progresses within the club and eventually signs his first professional contract the junior club immediately benefits with a substantial financial payment for 'Training and Development' for the time spent on that boy.

All well and good, you might think. That's how it should be. But the anomaly is that an English junior club cannot receive this financial kickback. Incredible isn't it? It should be the simplest of things to sort out, and the Football Association have regularly been asked to try and rectify this disgraceful anomaly in the regulations, yet still they sit on their hands when they should be fighting the corner of junior soccer in this country as guardians of the game. They are instead doing nothing and should be ashamed of themselves.

In the north east of England there are around 15,000 boys and girls registered with The Russell Foster League, a flagship of local junior soccer. Russell Foster is a successful local businessman who has supported financially and spiritually the organisation into its sixteenth year. Although producing numerous youngsters who have progressed to become professional footballers both locally and further afield, there has not been one penny filtered back into any of the local clubs or the league itself for development costs. If Russell Foster and his league had been operating anywhere else other than in England his annual running costs through 'Training and Development fees' would now be covered. That is an anomalous and ridiculous situation which must be changed.

It's not all doom and gloom, though. There are sprigs of green shoots emerging from football's wintry wilderness. The Football Association's *National Game Strategy 2008-12* is a long overdue initiative for grassroots football in England. Its committed intention is to spend millions of pounds to improve standards, facilities and respect by the time of the 2012 Olympics when the eyes of the world will examine in minute detail the sporting fabric of our country. One vital question has not been asked of the FA, however, and that is which outside body has been given the task of regulating this huge cash injection and ensuring the targets set are achieved? Or is this vital function once again to be self-regulated and kept hidden away in house to ensure the avoidance of any awkward questions being asked?

This National Game Strategy and the money to be invested has come too late for the present day pupils of the Harrogate School and the Cambridgeshire devotee and his youngsters, as well as countless millions of youngsters up and down the country. Several decades of opportunity have been lost for ever. All these projects and more are admirable, but you have to ask the question why now and not years ago? The only conclusion can be because in the past our national team could hold its own against the best in the world. But the birth of the FA Premier League has put paid to all that.

Multiply those same problems in Harrogate, Cambridgeshire and the north east to the rest of the country's schools and junior football clubs and it is very easy to see how we are failing the grassroots level of football. And it is not just about producing world class footballers for the national team. Sport is, and should be, for all. The benefits of a co-ordinated and concerted programme to get our youngsters exercising and playing all sports might just help reduce the number who will require medical attention for obesity, diabetes and other associated illnesses because of their inactivity.

If we do not overcome this challenge, we will have millions of physically illiterate children who will have been morally ignored by government and cash-rich sporting bodies.

A while ago I was privileged to be in the company of Sir Bobby Robson, a man revered by the nation for what he has achieved in his lifetime. I can tell you, along with me, he frets at the corroding state of our national sport and like me he fears that millions of youngsters will never have the opportunity that we had in our youth to play sport. Like me he also maintains it was vital in building our characters and honing our bodies for the rigours of life – and in the process we made many life long friends along the way.

Like Sir Bobby I have enjoyed fifty years in my chosen profession and I now make this plea to the authorities. Please build a platform for the future of our children's health and happiness.

This chapter paints a sad picture of where I believe we have sunk to. Try as I might I have not been able to make the difference. Someone has to break down the barriers of red tape. We thought this would be tackled after Trevor Brooking's appointment as Director of Football Development, but in my opinion he has turned out to be a great ambassador and a fine figurehead, but an undynamic operator, afraid to ruffle the FA's feathers. I have waited for some time now for Trevor to truly assert himself, but to no avail. Oh for the far more belligerent approach of the previous incumbent Howard Wilkinson.

I feel driven to ask: Trevor do you know what is going on around the country? There are places where full size pitches are being used for junior games, where metal goals are not safely weighted down and may fall on youngsters, where seemingly deranged parents shout abuse from the touchline, which has not been roped or coned off, and where there is either loose or no monitoring at all of the managers' and coaches' qualifications to run junior teams. Has everyone who is involved in junior football acquired their Child Welfare Certification? Such a monitoring scheme was put in place for the Premier League Academy programme when I was in situ and still operates to this day. This model should be applied at the more important level of grassroots football. It can and should be done.

In the summer of 2004 I wrote to Trevor Brooking offering my experience of fifty years in the game, with six of those years having been dealing directly with youngsters at the Premier League Academies. I had decided I wanted to help grassroots football as I had relocated back to the north east of England in July of 2004. Brooking's reply was jaw dropping. Simply put there has not been one. I am still awaiting a response.

My stark warning is this, if children and adolescents do not have their energies channelled into outdoor pursuits or sport of some form, then we will be breeding a generation of obese video game-obsessed youngsters, primed to slip into the seedy world of cheap teenage sex, drugs and violence, with the inevitable personal and social consequences. Lack of opportunity will see too many youngsters slip into social oblivion.

The revenue of the Premier League was set to exceed £1.75 billion in 2008/09 as my book went to print. Would a substantial tranche of that vast sum be directed where it is truly needed, to the grassroots of football to build a future for the game I love and the young people of this country? I will not be holding my breath.

21 **Giants and Footballers**

OTHER NATIONALITIES, especially the Australians, regard one victory in sport as just the bottom rung of the ladder. It is programmed into them to think, 'we must win again!' The more they sniff blood the harder they work.

In this country we seem to take victory as an excuse for an almighty booze-up. Cricket's popular and talented Freddie Flintoff, along with his England colleagues, indulged himself on a three-day bender after the 2005 Ashes victory. Oh, and what a mess he made of himself in the Caribbean twelve months or so later over the drink-related 'Fredalo' incident. Not withstanding injuries, Flintoff has never hit consistent form with bat or ball since. Is that a coincidence?

Why do they do it? Probably because we are a nation with a built-in drinking culture. Booze permeates our society like a plague and leaves no age group untouched. We have been and probably still are a sports-mad country, but we are not now a nation that is particularly good at sport. Depressingly we are becoming watchers rather than participants, although the outstanding results of many of the team at the Olympics in Beijing and the forthcoming excitement of the London Games could change all that.

Over the years we have produced some outstanding winners in sailing and rowing – Sir Matthew Pinsent and Sir Steven Redgrave being obvious examples, but for me Sir Robin Knox-Johnston, who at 68 years of age sailed 30,000 miles around the globe, is a particular hero. Then there is Dame Ellen MacArthur MBE, who thrilled us with her exploits on the high seas, and who can forget the late Jane Tomlinson MBE, that most resilient of ladies who, although riddled with cancer, swept everything before her as she took on and conquered many tough challenges? All these people's achievements go way beyond those of our cosseted, so-called superstars.

Personally I believe that comparing our footballers to these giants is nonsense. Fame should be based on the criteria of achievement alone. Sadly, though, we have become a celebrity-obsessed nation. It is all around us, on most pages we turn to in our newspapers and magazines, on our television screens, on the internet and it is endemic in soccer. It has got close to the stage at which nearly everything surrounding our once great game is more important than football itself – just think about how the public has remained obsessed with David Beckham, his wife and their sons despite the fact that it is over five years since he was at his peak. Celebrity and column inches has been too easily confused with ability. It is screwing our game.

The problem is if you try to change it you will have the traumatised people of a celebrity-obsessed nation down on your head. But for the good of the future of the nation and the game this must change. We must encourage our youngsters to go and work out on the playing fields, indoor sports halls and swimming pools.

When I grew up players were just footballers – and there were some very good ones, as well as a fair number of brilliant individuals such as Tom Finney, George Best, Bobby Charlton, Jimmy Greaves and latterly Kenny Dalglish, Ian Rush, Glenn Hoddle and Roy Keane. These fine players had a philosophy which is simply summed up as play with freedom, play to win and enjoy it. Couple that with the fact that they badly wanted success and they earned it and this was, for me, the Golden Age of Football, which died with the foundation of the Premier League in 1992.

This age of the devalued celebrity contrasts sharply with that era and it may well be that the path to our current malaise began 48 years ago on that January day in 1961 when Judge Wilberforce scrapped the maximum wage, so opening up the financial floodgates to all.

During the last decade and a half football's very foundations have been gradually eroded away by the greed perpetuated by Sky money. Selfish and self-centred Premier League clubs have been allowed to build themselves into seemingly impenetrable fortresses and many incorrigible agents who, until recently, have pervaded our game more or less unchecked have taken millions of pounds out of the game. Above all a weak Football Association have, in my opinion, persistently reneged on their duties to grassroots football.

As time moves on I engross myself in my charity work and I walk the cliff tops near our Whitburn home in my adopted north east, the same cliff tops that I jogged along many years ago as a professional footballer of Sunderland Football Club, the same cliff tops that later our children Jane and Roger ran along and now our grandchildren scamper over and down to the beach below. I feel I have achieved everything I could have wished for since departing my Fazakerley family home in 1957 as a young, adventurous footballer. I have been fortunate, a man blessed during his lifetime.

I may never have played at Wembley, but I managed Sunderland to a Milk Cup final there. I never won a full international cap or scored a run for Lancashire schoolboys, but I have also never been chosen for jury service and I've never hit a hole in one at golf, although Valerie reminds me there is still time for both these last two occurences!

However the things I did achieve in the game I am proud of. In a competitive, narrow profession those modest achievements will have evaded many a contemporary along the way.

What I have established is that my unknown, misty future is now behind me, the hurdles have been jumped and the mountains climbed. Throughout I have lived my life by walking the straight line in the years that God has given me. I have a clear conscience, having lived by my principles and values. They have worked well for me as I have survived the marathon journey and been more fortunate than most during my time. I am grateful and humbled for that. The majority of that time has been spent living the life in the glorious game amongst friends, foes and enemies alike, all of us chasing that elusive goal – victory.

I have had many peaks and troughs during the journey. Success and failure in equal amounts – enough to have realised that without failures you never learn, improve or grow stronger. Risks have been taken and outcomes enjoyed and accepted. There have been crises, triumphs, victories and defeats . . . however the bright sparkling dawns have always outshone the fading sunsets and rainy days. I know I have achieved a great deal spiritually, enjoyed it as it happened and for that I have to be and I am deeply grateful for those opportunities.

Underpinning it all was the strength of a family unit, initially with mother and father, then my wife Valerie, daughter Jane and our son Roger and now our grandchildren. Always there have been my three incredible brothers and my trusted friends. Thank you all.

Career Statistics

Honours
Promotion from Second to First Division with Sunderland 1963/64
Promotion from Fourth to Third Division with Newport County 1979/80
Welsh Cup Winner with Newport County 1980
Promotion from Third to Second Division with Cardiff City 1982/83

As Player

Season	Club	League	FA Cup	Lge Cup	Other	Goals
58/59	Sunderland	33	1	0	0	0
59/60	Sunderland	32	2	0	0	0
60/61	Sunderland	40	5	1	0	1
61/62	Sunderland	42	4	5	0	0
62/63	Sunderland	40	4	7	0	0
63/64	Sunderland	42	6	1	0	1
64/65	Sunderland	39	2	3	0	2
65/66	Sunderland	37	1	2	0	0
66/67	Sunderland	28	0	2	0	0
67/68	Sunderland	22+2	0	1	0	0
68/69	Sunderland	17+3	0	0	0	0
69/70	Sunderland	31+1	1	1	0	0
Total	**Sunderland**	**403+6**	**26**	**23**	**0**	**4**
Overall	**Sunderland**	**452+6**				
70/71	Hartlepool United	13	0	0	0	0
71/72	Hartlepool United	23+3	2	2	0	2
72/73	Hartlepool United	6+1	2	1	0	0
Total	**Hartlepool United**	**42+4**	**4**	**3**	**0**	**2**
Overall	**Hartlepool United**	**47+4**				
Overall Totals		**499+10**	**30**	**26**	**0**	**6**

As Manager

Hartlepool United
(7 March 1971 - 1 June 1974)

Season			W	D	League L	F	A	Pts	FA Cup	Lge Cup	FL Trophy
70/71	Div 4	23rd	3	3	8	10	24	9	N/A	N/A	N/A
71/72	Div 4	18th	17	6	23	58	69	40	1st round	2nd round	N/A
72/73	Div 4	12th	12	17	17	70	34	49	2nd round	1st round	N/A
73/74	Div 4	11th	16	12	18	48	47	44	1st round	1st round	N/A
Totals			**P155**		**W48**		**D38**		**L69**		

Gillingham
(1 June 1974 - 15 October 1975)

Season			W	D	League L	F	A	Pts	FA Cup	Lge Cup	FL Trophy
74/75	Div 3	10th	17	14	15	65	60	48	1st round	1st round	N/A
75/76	Div 3	5th	4	4	2	13	10	12	N/A	2nd round	N/A
(when resigned)											
Totals			**P57**		**W21**		**D18**		**L18**		

Sheffield Wednesday
(15 October 1975 - 5 October 1977)

Season			W	D	League L	F	A	Pts	FA Cup	Lge Cup	FL Trophy
75/76	Div 3	20th	12	16	18	48	59	40	3rd round	N/A	N/A
76/77	Div 3	8th	22	9	15	65	55	53	2nd round	4th round	N/A
77/78	Div 3	24th	0	5	5	6	13	5	N/A	4th round	N/A
(when dismissed)											
Totals			**P92**		**W31**		**D27**		**L34**		

Newport County
(10 June 1978 - 8 February 1982)

Season			W	D	L	F	A	Pts	FA Cup	Lge Cup	Welsh Cup
						League					
78/79	Div 4	8th	21	10	15	48	66	55	4th round	1st round	N/A
79/80	Div 4	3rd	27	7	12	83	50	61	1st round	1st round	Winners
80/81	Div 3	12th	15	13	18	64	61	43	2nd round	1st round	N/A
81/82	Div 3	17th	7	8	10	30	31	29	1st round	2nd round	N/A
(when dismissed)											

Totals   P182   W76   D43   L63

Cardiff City
(3 March 1982 - 1 March 1984)

Season			W	D	L	F	A	Pts	FA Cup	Lge Cup	FL Trophy
						League					
81/82	Div 2	20th	5	4	7	21	23	19	N/A	N/A	N/A
82/83	Div 3	2nd	25	11	10	76	50	86	2nd round	2nd round	N/A
83/84	Div 2	13th	11	2	15	36	45	35	3rd round	2nd round	N/A

Totals   P92   W41   D17   L34

Sunderland
(4 March 1984 - 23 May 1985)

Season			W	D	L	F	A	Pts	FA Cup	Lge Cup	FL Trophy
						League					
83/84	Div 1	13th	5	3	5	12	12	18	N/A	N/A	N/A
84/85	Div 1	21st	10	10	22	40	62	40	3rd round	Finalists	N/A

Totals   P66   W21   D16   L29

Cardiff City
(31 August 1989 - 1 May 1991)

Season			W	D	L	F	A	Pts	FA Cup	Lge Cup	FL Trophy
						League					
89/90	Div 3	21st	12	14	20	51	70	50	3rd round	1st round	1st round
90/91	Div 4	13th	15	15	16	43	54	60	1st round	2nd round	1st round

Totals   P98   W30   D32   L36

TOTALS: P742   W268   D191   L283